SHAQ UNCUT

SHAQ UNCUT

MY STORY

SHAQUILLE O'NEAL

with JACKIE MACMULLAN

GRAND CENTRAL
PUBLISHING

NEW YORK   BOSTON

B O'NEAL

Grand Central Publishing
Hachette Book Group
237 Park Avenue
New York, NY 10017

www.HachetteBookGroup.com

Printed in the United States of America

RRD-C

First Edition: November 2011
10 9 8 7 6 5 4 3 2

Grand Central Publishing is a division of Hachette Book Group, Inc.
The Grand Central Publishing name and logo is a trademark of
Hachette Book Group, Inc.

The Hachette Speakers Bureau provides a wide range of authors for
speaking events. To find out more, go to www.hachettespeakersbureau.com
or call (866) 376-6591.

The publisher is not responsible for websites (or their content) that are not
owned by the publisher.

Photos edited by Kate Giel.

Library of Congress Cataloging-in-Publication Data
O'Neal, Shaquille.
Shaq uncut : my story / Shaquille O'Neal with Jackie MacMullan.—1st ed.
p. cm.
Includes bibliographical references and index.
ISBN 978-1-4555-0441-1 (regular edition : alk. paper)—ISBN 978-1-4555-
0725-2 (large print edition : alk. paper)   1. O'Neal, Shaquille.
2. Basketball players—United States—Biography.
I. MacMullan, Jackie. II. Title.
GV884.O54A3 2011
796.323092—dc23
[B]
2011029520

This book is dedicated to Philip Harrison and Lucille O'Neal, creators of my game and my character.

Shaq

To my late sister Karen, who loved life almost as much as Shaquille.

Jackie

ACKNOWLEDGMENTS

To Taahirah, Amirah, Me'arah, Shaqir, Shareef, and Myles, you are the reason I get up every morning and start my day with a smile. Grandmother Odessa, Grandmother Irma, and Grandpa Harrison, may you read this in heaven as you continue to watch over me. To the entire O'Neal and Harrison family. To Dale Brown, Mike Parris, Jerome Crawford, Perry Rogers, Colin Smeeton, Cynthia Atterberry, Joe Cavallero, Danny Garcia, Anthony Hall, Mark Stevens, Amy Martin, Derek Mallet, Will Harden, Tommy Johnson Jr., Evelyn "Poonie" Huval, Dane Huval, Caprice Huval, Ken Bailey, Alex Conant, Dewayne Davis, Michael Mallet, and Nicole Alexander, thanks for looking out for me. To Chief Ronald J. Boyd of the Los Angeles Port Police, to Chief Don DeLucca and Chief Carlos Noriega of the Miami Beach Police, and Chief Tom Ryff of the Tempe, Arizona, Police, thanks for training me and trusting me to be part of your law enforcement units. Thanks, also, to Jackie MacMullan for doing a great job in helping me tell my story, and to Rick Wolff of Grand Central Publishing for turning out a cool book.

Shaq

Thanks to Rick Wolff of Grand Central Publishing for his superb guidance, and thanks to the Grand Central team, most notably Linda

Duggins, Meredith Haggerty, David Palmer, Bob Castillo, Flamur Tonuzi, and their great sales team. Thanks to Jay Mandel for making this book happen. Many thanks to Joe Cavallero, Danny Garcia, Michael Parris, Jerome Crawford, Cynthia Atterberry, Colin Smeeton, Perry Rogers, Nicole Alexander, and Alex Conant for letting me in. Lucille O'Neal was gracious, helpful, and passionate in discussing her oldest son. Thanks to the more than one hundred coaches, teammates, general managers, and team officials who provided valuable insight, especially Dale Brown, Phil Jackson, Brian Shaw, Gary Payton, Danny Ainge, Doc Rivers, Kevin Garnett, Jerry West, Stanley Roberts, Wayne Sims, Dennis Tracey, Herb More, Alonzo Mourning, Dennis Scott, Mike D'Antoni, James Posey, Pat Williams, and Zydrunas Ilgauskas. Thanks to Ian Thomsen, who is both an amazing sounding board and a wonderful friend. Thanks to the Ya Ya's—Janice McKeown, Jane Cavanaugh Smith, Elizabeth Derwin, Elaine Keefe, Val Russell, Arlene St. Onge, Gretch Hoffman, and Patty Filbin—who never cease to amaze me with their kindness and generosity. Thanks also to Eileen Barrett, Monet Ewing, Liz Douglas, and Stephanie Baird for their support and encouragement. Many thanks to all the Boyles, far and near. I'm blessed with two great parents, Fred and Margarethe MacMullan, and my sister Sue Titone and her wonderful family—Vinny, Julia, and Christopher. Cheers to the Good Things basketball crew; may we always have each other's back. Much love to my husband, Michael, and children, Alyson and Douglas, who were so sweet and understanding whenever this book pulled Mom away. Finally, thanks to Shaquille O'Neal, the most generous athlete I've ever met and the most fascinating superstar of his time.

Jackie

AUTHOR'S NOTE

When I was a little kid, I used to dribble my basketball around the Boys and Girls Club in Newark, New Jersey, dreaming about being Dr. J or Magic Johnson.

Then I went home and dreamed about being a famous DJ, spinning records and hanging out with the most successful rappers in the business.

At night, when I was watching television with my friends, I'd fantasize about being a movie star or a famous actor, the one who always landed the most beautiful girl to set up the perfect fairy-tale ending.

How many people can say almost all of their dreams came true? I'm pretty sure I'm one of the lucky few. I got to be an NBA superstar, a rapper with platinum and gold records, an actor who starred in movies, got to be on *Saturday Night Live*, and had my own reality show.

When most NBA players retire, the best part of their lives is over. I feel like mine is just beginning. Although I love the game of basketball, I've never wanted that to be the only thing that defines me.

I've always had dreams. Big dreams. Yet there were days I thought they would never come true. Days when I was teased because of my height, because I stuttered, because I was clumsy. Days when I hung out with the wrong crowd and made the wrong decisions. When I got cut as a freshman from my high school team, I lay in my room, devastated, wondering if I'd ever get another chance to prove myself.

My life hasn't been nearly as smooth as you might think. You see a seven-foot-one giant with an easy smile and figure, "He's got it made."

Well, sometimes I did. Sometimes I didn't. I had my own doubts, my own fears, my own disappointments. At times, the expectations of others nearly suffocated me. At times, the weight of my own expectations threatened to crush me.

For more than twenty-five years, people have been scrutinizing me. They have painted their own picture of who I am and what I stand for. Some of it has been positive, and some of it has been hurtful.

It's time for you to hear from *me* what makes Shaquille O'Neal tick. I'm ready to let you inside so you can understand where my journey has taken me and how it has shaped me as a man, not just as a basketball player.

Hopefully some of it will make you laugh. Some of it might even make you cry.

People always say I'm bigger than life.

Let me tell my own story this time, so you can decide for yourself.

Shaquille O'Neal
Summer 2011

SHAQ UNCUT

JUNE 4, 2000

Los Angeles, California

Game 7, Western Conference Finals

The Portland Trail Blazers strode to their bench with a 71–58 lead over Los Angeles after three quarters of the winner-take-all Game 7 in the Western Conference Finals. The boasts of the Lakers, who vowed to steamroll the competition on their way to the NBA title, suddenly rang hollow.

Lakers coach Phil Jackson gathered his assistants on the court for a conference while Shaquille O'Neal and his teammates plopped onto the bench and waited.

Jackson prepared his team long ago for this moment. His instructions were succinct: "When all hell is breaking loose, go to your 'safe place,' a personal image or memory that will exude serenity, happiness, and peace of mind."

"Shaquille," Jackson asked shortly after he accepted the Lakers job. "Where is your safe place?"

"In my grandmother Odessa's lap, while she's sitting in her rocking chair," the big man answered.

"And how did that come to be your safe place?"

"She would find me after I messed up when I was a kid," Shaquille said. "After I did something really stupid and my father gave me a beating.

"When he was done hitting me, she'd sneak into my room and slip me a piece of pound cake and rock me and tell me, 'It's okay, baby. Everything is gonna be fine.'"

As Shaq fidgeted in frustration on the bench on the night of June 4, absorbing the catcalls and boos from LA's angry and shocked fans, his first thought was if the Lakers choked away this series, he knew who would get the blame.

It would be him, just as it had been in Orlando, when they failed to win it all.

Not again. O'Neal closed his eyes. He conjured up an image of Grandmother Odessa, just as Phil Jackson had instructed him to do. He focused on her soft voice, her gentle smile, her soothing words.

The Lakers broke from their huddle, but not before veteran Rick Fox challenged his teammates, "Is this how we're going out? Is this how it's gonna end?"

No, the big man told them. Not again.

Portland pushed the lead to 15 points with 10:28 left in the game. It was then that Shaquille O'Neal, double- and triple-teamed for most of the night, broke free and dunked on their heads. His basket ignited 15 consecutive Laker points, a stunning comeback punctuated by another O'Neal slam, this one expertly delivered by Kobe Bryant in the form of a slow-motion, looping lob.

Usually Shaq cooly turned after such demonstrations of

dominance and jogged up the floor, expressionless, as if to say, *Been here. Done this.* Not this time. He exuberantly thrust his fingers aloft as he sprinted down the floor, his mouth agape and his wide eyes shining.

Grandmother Odessa was right. Everything was gonna be fine.

My GRANDMOTHER CALLED ME SHAUN—NOT SHAQ, NOT Diesel, The Big Aristotle, Shaqtus, or The Big Shamrock. Back then, I was just a little boy running around the projects in Newark, New Jersey, who needed someone to look out for me.

I may have looked big, but I was just a kid. I was surrounded mostly by women, and if my grandmother or my aunt Viv or my mother saw the drug dealers slinking around our apartment they came out and told them to keep moving along. They warned them they better not mess with their Shaun. Once, when one of those shady guys started talking to me, my aunt Viv came flying out the door and started throwing punches.

"You leave him alone!!" she said, pounding her fists on the dude's back. "That boy is going to be a ballplayer!!!"

I was going to be someone special. That's what my mommy always told me.

I was going to be Superman.

My full name is Shaquille Rashaun O'Neal. My mom, Lucille O'Neal, was on her own when she had me. She was seventeen years old when she got pregnant. I never knew why my mother gave me a Muslim name. I guess it might have been because she felt like an outcast, or thought nobody loved her. *Shaquille* meant "little one" and *Rashaun* meant "warrior." I was her little warrior. It was going to be me and my mom against the world.

My grandmother Odessa Chambliss was a Christian woman, so she insisted on calling me Shaun. My grandma was the one who always told me, "Believe in yourself." Odessa always talked in a low voice, kind of like I do now, and she was always smiling.

Grandma Odessa looked like the perfect church woman. She

wore a dress all the time. She never cursed, never raised her voice, always had a Bible nearby. I never really saw her hair because she wore these curly wigs all the time.

Grandma was a dreamer, and she let me know it was okay for me to dream, too. I always felt safe when I was with my grandmother. Of course, she used to sneak up on me and give me cod liver oil. I hated that stuff, but she swore by it. She was sure it would cure everything. I'd be filling up a big bowl of Trix cereal in the morning and just about to dig in when she'd slip that teaspoon of cod liver oil under my nose. A perfectly good breakfast ruined.

For the longest time I didn't understand why my last name was different from everyone else in the family. My mom and dad were Lucille and Philip Harrison, but I was O'Neal. So how does that work? Turns out that O'Neal was my mother's maiden name. When my mother married Philip, she took her husband's last name, but she kept me as O'Neal. I really didn't care too much, I guess, but one day in school one of my teachers asked me, "Shaquille O'Neal? How come your name is different from your daddy?" I went to my mom for some answers.

She decided I should go meet my biological father. His name was Joseph Toney. I think I was about seven years old. I remember he was tall, a nice-looking guy, but he didn't have a whole lot to say to me. They told me he had a scholarship lined up at Seton Hall to play basketball but he got into drugs and blew his chance.

The day I went to meet him he was nice enough. He said, "What's up? Hey kid, how are you doing? I'm your daddy." I wasn't really sure what to think. I had this other guy at home who sure acted like my daddy. Philip Harrison had given me a place to live, some toys, and even though I got in trouble a lot, I was cool with my life. When you are a kid, all you know is what you've got. After I met my "real" daddy, I went home with my mom to Philip, who as far as I was concerned was the only father I was going to pay any attention to.

The area of Newark that we lived in was poor, with mostly black people on every corner. It was dangerous, there was lots of crime, and it was the greatest place on earth if you were a drug dealer. Business was always booming for those cats.

I was born five years after the Newark riots, which was one of those memories that all the grown-ups talked about in real serious tones.

The riots apparently started after this guy named John Smith—like the English guy who loved Pocahontas, only this cat was a black taxi driver—passed two cops driving on Fifteenth Avenue. The two cops are white, and they arrest John Smith because he passed them on a double line, so they drag him down to the precinct, which is right across the street from the Hayes Home housing project. Everyone in the projects is watching the police beat this guy as they haul him in, and they're convinced those white cops are about to kill a black man for a traffic violation.

The place explodes.

For the next six days Newark is a war zone. There's rioting, shooting, and looting. People are throwing rocks through windows and tipping over cars. Too much poverty, anger, drugs, and inequality.

My parents were in the middle of it. They couldn't leave their house because it was too dangerous. They had relatives who were killed during the riots and some uncles and cousins who were arrested and thrown in jail for no good reason at all. But even so, they never talked about racism too much with me. I didn't grow up in a home where white people were the enemy. My parents didn't feel that way, and they didn't teach me to hate anyone, even after what they had seen with their own eyes.

Besides, do you think when I am eight years old that I care about the Newark riots? All I want to know is how do I get myself a skateboard.

I didn't know I was poor. I guess I should have. We moved all the time because we couldn't make the rent. My mom tried to feed a young family of six on Chicken a la King out of a can. We ate a lot of franks and beans and noodles. Lots of noodles. I was hungry all the time, but I figured that was just because I was so damn big. Every morning that I woke up it seemed like I had grown another couple of inches.

That was a problem for two reasons: shoes and clothes. I kept growing out of everything. I had to wear the same stuff to school over and over again because we couldn't afford to keep buying me new threads all the time. I heard about it. Kids would say, "Hey dawg, didn't you have that shirt on yesterday?"

Nobody was shocked that I turned out to be a big guy. My natural father was tall and my mom is six foot two. Lucille O'Neal is my best friend. My mom has always, always, been there for me. She learned to be tough at a very young age. Life wasn't always very kind to her, so she did her best to protect me from all the bad things that could happen to a wise-ass kid like me.

She knew how difficult it was to be taller than everyone else, because she had to deal with the same thing when she was growing up.

For example, my mom had to bring my birth certificate everywhere with her. They didn't believe I was only nine. The bus driver, the subway conductor, the guy behind the counter at McDonald's. Can't a kid get a Happy Meal without all this hassle?

I got teased a lot for my size starting when I was around five or six. I remember walking down the street one day and this kid called me Big Foot. I looked down and he was right: my sneakers were huge.

As I got older, the names got nastier: Sasquatch, Freak-quille. Sha-quilla Gorilla. I didn't like that last one at all. I figured out I had a couple of choices. I could learn to be funny to get kids to be on my side . . . or I could just plain beat them up.

I did both.

When I started growing bigger I realized I had to master the little things. I had to be able to do all the things regular people did so they'd stop concentrating on my size. That's why I started break-dancing. I just loved to dance. I had good feet, so I could really move. We used to have contests and I became a really fabulous dancer. I could twirl around, spin on my head, all the stuff you see those little black kids do on television. I was so good all the kids forgot I was tall and goofy, and they started calling me Shaqa-D cuz I could move.

I was dancing all the time. Everyone loved it. I loved it. But one day when I was dancing I hurt my knee. It was really bothering me so I went to the doctor, and he told me I had Osgood-Schlatter disease, which is something kids get when they start growing way too fast for their bodies.

When I got home, I told my father I had Osgood-Schlatter disease. He punched me and said, "You ain't got Osgood nothing! You're out there break-dancing and that's why you're wrecking your knees!" So I got a good ass whupping for that.

The truth is, my dad spent a lot of time beating me. If I did something wrong, he'd smack me and say, "Be a leader, not a follower." I was really scared of my father. He beat me all the time, but I would never call any of those whuppings unjustifiable. I deserved it. He did it to keep me in line. I swear, if he hadn't, I'd probably be in jail right now—or worse. Without my father staying on me, I never would have become Shaq or The Diesel or any of those other crazy names I've invented for myself.

Philip Harrison was a military man all the way. His friends called him Butchy, but all my friends called him Sarge. He was very, very big on discipline. Things had to be done his way, or else.

Ironically, that kind of tough-love approach hurt him in his military career. At one time he was a drill sergeant, but he spent so much time challenging people and cussing them out he was demoted. They put him in charge of running the gym on the base, but his temper got him into trouble there, too. They got tired of him cursing at people, so they made him a supply sergeant.

Nobody messed with Sarge, especially me. His family was Jamaican and when he did something wrong as a kid, he got a beating. He just did what he was taught.

And it's true—I did a lot of stupid stuff when I was a kid because I wanted to be cool. I'd carry chains in my book bag. I'd go to the store and steal stuff. I'd break into cars, just because I could. I'd break into people's houses and take little things, nothing big, then brag about it after I was sure I wouldn't get caught.

That kind of stuff drove my dad crazy. He wanted me to make something out of myself. He made mistakes when he was a kid and his father beat him within an inch of his life. So that was what he was going to do with me. He'd get me with his fists, his belt, a broom, whatever was around. It was his version of corporal punishment. Whenever I did something stupid he'd beat me so hard I'd have to think twice about doing it again.

Sometimes fear really is the best weapon.

Because my dad was in the military we moved a lot, so every time I went to a new school I would find out who the toughest guy was and I'd measure him up. I'd test him out first by being funny, then I'd beat him up. That way I'd be the New Guy in the school, instead of being the "new guy" in the school. Big difference.

When I was really small we lived on Oak Street in Jersey City. We were living with my grandmother Odessa, and she lived across the street from a park. She was a nurse and my mother was right there, with the TV in the window, so they were watching me all the time. It was safer in Jersey City than in Newark; there were only a few juvenile delinquents in the neighborhood instead of one on every corner.

There was this guy Pee Wee who lived right near the park, and I was scared of him because he had this big dog, a German shepherd named Sam. Every day like clockwork around 4:15 p.m., we'd be in the park and Sam would come charging out of the house and chase all the kids. Pee Wee and his brothers were drug dealers. I hated that dog. I was scared to death of it.

Now, my father came home from work one night and he brought me a present. They were Chuck Taylor sneakers, brand-new, the original white canvas ones. I couldn't believe it. I never had shoes like that. I knew we couldn't really afford them. So my dad tells me, "Hey, you've got to wear these shoes to school, to play ball. You've got to wear them in the summer. They've got to last. Don't mess them up, you hear me?"

I go outside in my new Chuck Taylors and I'm strutting around and I'm feeling good. I am *The Man*. But at 4:15 the screen door opens and that damn dog Sam starts coming right for me. I start running and I try to jump the fence, but I'm so big I'm having trouble scrambling up there. My feet are dangling and I'm trying to hoist myself over, but the dog gets the back of my shoe and rips it. So I go home and tell my dad and he says, "I don't want to hear that crap!" and he punches me.

The next day I get myself a stick, and when Pee Wee's dog comes out I try to break his neck. I'm so mad about the Chuck Taylors I'm trying to kill that dog Sam. The dog runs back in the house and Pee Wee comes out acting real tough and I hit him with the stick, too. Next thing you know his three brothers come out and they beat the stuffing out of me. I am so messed up my father doesn't even bother to whip me again.

I was on punishment a lot. I used to be sent to my room, and to keep myself from going crazy I'd close my eyes and create all these dreams. In one dream I was the Incredible Hulk, so I'd close my eyes and start growling, "Aaaaaahhhhh." In my next dream I was Superman, so I'd close my eyes and flex my muscles and then I was flying. Next time, I was a hero in *Star Wars*.

Once in a while, I'd close my eyes and I'd dream I was one of those drug dealers on the corner. They always had money. The wads of bills would be sticking out of their pockets so we could see how well they were doing. I'd think about what it would be like to be them for a second, but I was always on punishment so I couldn't even get out of the house to do something stupid like that. See, Pops? Your "tough love" worked.

Grandmother Odessa hated it when I was on punishment. Funny thing was, I was on punishment in her house, because we couldn't afford our own place. After I screwed up and my dad beat me, she'd wait until he left and that's when she'd sneak in with a glass of milk and a slice of Entenmann's pound cake and tell me in that low voice, "Here, have this. Stop crying now. It's going to be all right. You're my baby. Don't worry."

I used to tell my grandma, "When I get rich, I'm going to buy you a house." She'd smile and tell me, "Baby, I don't need a new house. This one is just fine."

We lived with my grandmother for a while, but she and my father didn't really get along that well so we ended up moving to Newark, on Vassar Avenue. My grandfather, my dad's father, was this hard-core Jamaican man, and we moved in with him. We also lived with my dad's brother and some of my aunts and a ton of cousins. The house was full. It was a pretty big house, nine or ten rooms, but there weren't enough beds to go around. I slept on the floor with a bunch of my cousins.

My grandpa had dreams of being rich, so every day he'd give me and my cousin Andre a dollar to go buy the Quick Pick lottery ticket and another dollar to buy bread. My cousin and I were entrepreneurs. We'd buy the Quick Pick, but then we'd buy the cheap, stale bread that cost sixty cents and use the other forty cents to buy gum. We did that a few times before someone in the house said, "How come this bread never tastes fresh?" We got found out and got a whupping from my crazy grandpa.

By that point we were used to having our gum. We *had* to have it. So we stole it. We'd develop all sorts of elaborate plans to distract the guy at the cash register so we wouldn't get caught. One day, Andre and I were chewing our gum and my grandfather said to me, "Where did you get that gum?" I didn't want to tell him I stole it, so I told him a nice lady gave it to me. My grandfather said, "How many times do we have to tell you not to talk to strangers?" So Andre and I got a whupping for that, too.

When I was about eight I started going to the Boys and Girls Club and we played basketball for hours and hours. On the weekends my dad started teaching me the fundamentals. Philip Harrison was a very good city ballplayer, or so all the people in Newark tell me. They say Sarge and my natural father were the two best in the area growing up. My uncle, Mike Parris, once told me Philip Harrison was a cross between Robert Parish and George Gervin.

Philip taught me how to box out and shoot with my elbow tucked in the right way. One of the first books he ever gave me was a story of Kareem Abdul-Jabbar's life. I read the whole thing, and one part of the book was about how Kareem lost all his money investing in soybeans. I told myself, "When I get rich, that's not happening to me."

Looking back, at that age I wasn't very good at basketball. I was clumsy. I hadn't really grown into my body yet, so I fumbled around with the ball at first. Of course everyone expected me to be excellent because I was so big. Good luck explaining to people it doesn't work that way.

Newark was a tough city. You didn't have to look for trouble; it found you the second you got up out of bed in the morning. I think my parents knew we needed to get out of there. The problem was we didn't have any money. My dad was working so hard, but it was never enough to feed and clothe us and pay the rent. He used to drive U-Haul trucks to and from New Jersey and New York for extra cash, and he was just tired all the time.

Then, in 1982, when I was ten years old, my dad came home one day and said, "We're moving." He packed me, my mother, my sisters, Ayesha and Lateefah, and my little brother, Jamal, into his Toyota Corolla, and we drove to Fort Stewart in Hinesville, Georgia. I cried all the way there. I didn't want to go. I didn't want to leave my friends.

And yet, that move was probably the best thing that could have happened to me. I was in trouble all the time in Newark. I was hanging out with the wrong kids.

If it wasn't for us moving around so much, then I wouldn't be the people person I am today. I really believe that. I had to learn how to make new friends, adjust to new places. What if I had to grow up my whole life in the projects of Newark, New Jersey? I would have never seen any white people, Jewish people, Spanish people. Because my dad moved so much, it forced me to learn to live with all kinds of kids.

Hinesville, Georgia, was nothing like Newark. We're living on the army base there and it was very, very Southern. We walked to school from the base, and one day I met this kid named Ronnie Philpot. He's a little guy, and he's very dark skinned, darker than me, so we start ranking on each other about how black we are. He's my first friend in Georgia and I'm going to be his bodyguard. His mother had died and kids started messing with him. They'd say stuff like, "Hey Ronnie, the parent-teacher conference is tonight, too bad your mom can't be there."

I heard that and I was going off the wall. It was just so cruel. This kid is teasing Ronnie about his mom and I shove him and say, "After school. The basketball courts. You and me. I'm going to mess you up." The kid knows he's got to show up because news of the fight is all over the school. Plus, I knew where he lived. He had to go home past the courts unless he went the long way around. So I'm waiting, and he shows up, and the first thing I do is smack him in the head.

My mentality was always to strike first. So I punch the kid in the face and then it's on, and I just start beating him. He can't do anything. All the kids are there watching, so now I'm The Man. I'm the bully in the school and everyone knows it.

My father isn't happy with me because I'm goofing around in class and I'm still getting in trouble all the time. He's taking his belt to me just about every day because I keep screwing up. Finally he says, "If I get one more note from school, I'm going to mess you up." I knew he was serious.

But I can't help it. I'm Shaquille, the funny guy, the bully, The Man. I was so self-conscious about my size, goofing off was the only way I knew how to fit in. So one day I bring my water bottle to school and I've got these tissues my mom put in my backpack, and I start making spitballs and throwing them at the blackboard. I get one big old glob and I fire it and it just misses the teacher. So the teacher whips around and says, "Who did that?" Everyone is cracking up except for me. I'm sitting there real serious.

So class is over and this kid rats me out. He's an officer's kid. I can't believe it. I'm shocked. So I go to the principal's office and I get suspended for three days. I know my father is going to beat the tar out of me so I grab this kid and I tell him, "Three o'clock." I figure I'm going to go home and get an ass whupping anyway, but first I'm gonna give one of my own. I'm gonna kill that kid.

School is over and I'm waiting for him. Three o'clock, four o'clock, and he doesn't come, but I'm still waiting for him on the corner. By then the other kids have given up and gone home. Finally the kid comes out of the school around five o'clock. He's looking around all nervous and then he sees me. I start chasing him. He doesn't realize that I'm pretty quick for a big kid. I track him down and I start punching him and hitting him. I'm kicking him in the ribs so hard he starts having some kind of seizure.

All of a sudden I'm real scared. This kid is foaming at the mouth and his eyes are rolling back in his head and I'm thinking, *Oh no, I really have killed him.* I'm terrified.

One of the officers from the base is driving by and he sees the kid lying on the ground, so he stops the car and runs over and says, "What the hell are you doing?" He runs back to the car and puts a pencil in the kid's mouth because the kid's having this epileptic seizure. The man calls 911. So the cops come and the ambulance comes and now I'm really in trouble. The cops drive me back to the base, and they find my father and they blast him for having such a rotten kid. They come down on my dad pretty hard. I've embarrassed my father *and* I've pissed him off. I'm thinking, *This isn't good.*

My father beat me silly for that. Every time he hit me he said, "You idiot! You could have killed that kid. You'd be in jail the rest of your life. How many times have I told you? Be a thinker! Be a leader!" Then he'd get mad all over again and whack me some more.

I didn't care, because I was terrified about what I did to that kid.

For a long time afterward when I turned out the light, all I could see was his face with his eyes rolling back in his head.

That was it for me. From that day on, I was done being a bully.

Now, I know my dad sounds like a violent guy. I'm sure people have a problem with it, but they shouldn't. My father made me who I am. He always told me, "You are going to be better than me." He did some stuff when he was young. The story he always told me was his friend had a piggy bank, and Sarge stole the piggy bank and broke it, and when his father found out, he tried to kill him. He told me that story a lot. It really stuck with him.

Everything Sarge did to me was for a reason. Now, would I do that to my own kids? Absolutely not. Never. But my kids are coming from a completely different place. They don't live in the projects. They haven't been poor a day in their lives. They aren't coming from the same place as their daddy Shaun did.

Phil Harrison is a good man. He raised me, he loved me, he challenged me. He knows how much I love and respect him.

People like to tell me I need to make peace with my biological father. Those people should mind their own business. I didn't hear anything from that guy for years until I started dunking basketballs and becoming famous. Then he's on the *Ricki Lake Show* telling everyone he misses me and how come I won't have anything to do with him, and he wants me to meet my half brother.

Maybe at some point I would have been willing to see him, but I didn't like how he came at me. On a television program? Really? It was very disrespectful. He's from New Jersey, and all my relatives are there. He could have easily called one of the cousins and said, "Hey, I want to hang out with my son, have him call me." I probably would have done that, but on the *Ricki Lake Show?*

We're too far down the road now. I think it would be awfully disrespectful to the man who made me who I am, Philip Harrison, who raised me from the time I was two years old, to turn around to some other guy and say, "Hey, Daddy!" It's not happening.

One time, when I got to the pros and started playing for the

Orlando Magic, they told me my biological father was at the game and he was waiting on me. When I heard that, I ducked out the back door. That's not usually my style, but I had nothing to say to Joe Toney. Sarge finally went over to the dude's house and told him to leave me alone.

My mom wanted to protect me from all that stuff. She loved me so much, and all she wanted for me was to be happy. When things got bad, she'd always tell me, "Hey, you're going to be fine." My mom and my grandmother were the ones who kept me smiling and believing.

When I got into trouble, my mom kind of stayed back. She let my dad handle the discipline. Even though he wasn't my real father, he paid the bills, took care of the house. He loved my mother to death. There was no question about that. He was crazy about her.

We stayed in Georgia for a couple of years, but being from a military family, we knew we wouldn't be there long. The next move we made was in 1984, to Wildflecken, Germany. I didn't want to go there, either, so I cried all the way to Europe.

It didn't take long for me to find some kids to get in trouble with in Germany. At that point of my life I didn't want to be Shaquille. The kids there started calling me JC, but it's not what you think. I wasn't no Jesus Christ. JC stood for Just Cool.

I was about thirteen years old and I started wanting stuff, but I had no money. My father said, "I'm not buying you anything unless you work for it. So you go out and get a job or you are going to work for me."

I applied for a job at the Burger King on the base in Germany. I lived on A Street, so I had to walk up a couple of hills to get there, but I didn't care because I wanted my own money so I could buy the Air Jordans I had my eye on.

The idea of a job seemed good but I didn't like it. They made me do all the jobs nobody else would do, like mop, clean, wash the counters. I wanted to flip burgers, run the cash register, talk to all the customers, but they handed me a mop and told me to wipe up all the ketchup on the floor. I said, "Screw this," and I quit.

But now I've got to go home and tell my daddy, and he says, "You're not going to be a quitter. Now you will work for me." Uh-oh. That didn't sound good.

So now all of a sudden I'm in charge of my brother and my sisters. I've got to get them up in the morning, get them dressed, walk them to school, then get myself to school. After that, I had to pick them up, get them home, feed them. I became an expert at grilled cheese and Top Ramen, the hard noodles you boil in water. I had to feed them, get them going on their homework, make sure the house was clean. My mom had taken a job to help pay our bills, so I was Mr. Mom.

It was a lot of work. My dad warned me I better do a good job or he was going to whip my ass. In fact, I think the reason I'm so good with kids today is because of all the time I spent taking care of my siblings. Even now I can look at a kid and know what it takes to make him or her smile. I had to make up games for my younger siblings to keep them happy. At night, when there was a bad storm, I knew Jamal would be crawling into bed with me. He was afraid of lightning and he was sure I'd protect him from anything.

I tried. I danced for them, sang for them, made them giggle.

I also would beat up anyone who gave them a hard time.

My dad didn't pay me any money, but if I needed a new pair of shoes, he'd get them for me. I was so excited when I finally got my Air Jordans, but they only went up to size 13, and by the time Sarge bought them for me I was already a size 15. They were so expensive I didn't dare tell him they didn't fit me. I walked around wearing shoes two sizes too small. My feet were killing me. Had to do it, dawg. If you had Jordans, you rated.

Not long after we moved to Germany, I met this white guy named Mitch Riles and he looked exactly like Larry Bird. He had the long hair and the same ugly nose, and he could shoot his ass off.

So he's got the Bird thing down, so now I've got to get the Magic Johnson routine down. That means I've got to learn how to dribble, make the no-look pass, all that stuff. We're out there every day playing Magic vs. Bird, Celtics vs. Lakers, and I'm learning skills that big men don't ever show. I'm developing some moves.

I'm well over six feet tall at this point, but I'm still awkward, still haven't grown into my body. My footwork is good, and I've got my "Magic" moves, but I can't jump that well and I can't dunk. I'm beginning to wonder if it's ever going to happen for me.

So one day the officers on the base are all excited because this basketball coach from Louisiana State University was coming to put on a clinic. His name was Dale Brown and I had never heard of him, but I liked him right away. He had a lot of energy and his message was "Discipline and hard work are both great gifts. If you use them properly, you can be anything you want to be."

I wrote that down and memorized it. I went up to him afterward and asked him if he had any drills for me. I explained that even though I was big and tall, I was clumsy and had trouble jumping. He was very nice.

He said, "I'll tell you what I'll do, soldier. When I get back to Baton Rouge I'll send you a weight-training program. How many years have you been in the service?"

I answered, "I'm not in the service. I'm only thirteen years old."

Dale Brown's eyes opened real wide when he heard that. He said, "Well, son, I'd like to meet your parents."

My dad, I knew, was in the sauna. I could go get him, but what the hell would he say to Dale Brown? I never knew what my daddy was going to say to anybody. Sarge came out and I introduced him to Coach Brown, and he was trying to tell my dad that if I ever developed into a player he would be interested in coaching me, but Sarge cuts him off and says, "That's all fine and good, the basketball business, but I think it's damn time blacks started developing some intellectualism so they can be presidents of corporations instead of janitors, and generals in the army instead of sergeants like me. If you are ever interested in developing my son's academic future, then we'll talk."

I was thinking, *Well, that's the end of it. We'll never see this guy again*, but Coach Brown seemed really pleased with what Sarge said.

Sure enough, when he went back to LSU, Dale Brown sent me a weight program. I started doing it, and when I became a freshman in high school, I tried out for the high school basketball team on the base in Germany.

I got cut.

At the time I was probably six foot eight, but they didn't care. There was another guy named Dwayne Clark who was also about my size, and he was better than me.

They matched me up against Dwayne, and he could do everything. He could dunk, hit fadeaways, dribble. He was an upperclassman and he used to laugh at me. He'd do simple stuff like throw me an upfake, wait for me to jump, then go around me like I wasn't even there. That guy abused me.

The coach of the team never even acknowledged me. He never looked at me, never bothered to learn my name. I don't blame him, I guess. I was terrible. My knees were really bad at that time, and I had one of those brown knee braces with the hole in it on one knee and metal braces on the other because of my Osgood-Schlatter disease. I couldn't do anything. It hurt too much.

Here's the other problem: I was lazy. I liked to do it my way and I didn't use my size. I just didn't know how to play mean. I was going at half speed and everyone else was going a hundred miles an hour.

They had a junior varsity team, but I was too embarrassed to be on it. I came home and told my dad I got cut and I thought he'd be really mad, but he said, "Go back up to the gym and keep working."

I was crushed that I didn't make that team. I pretended it was no big deal, but it was. I didn't cry, but I was devastated. I went into my room, looked at the ceiling, and said, "I'm never going to make it." I was really down on myself.

After a while I tried to put my own positive spin on it. I'm telling myself, *Maybe I'll be a deejay, maybe I'll be a rapper.* But those were long shots. I knew that.

Almost all of my friends made the team, which made it worse. I laughed it off, made a joke about the coach. I was still a funny guy, a great dancer. I was still JC—Just Cool.

My father wouldn't let me quit. He had me play on the base with the enlisted soldiers. He threw me in there with these military guys who were grown men. They banged me and knocked me down and messed me up. If nothing else, I was going to be tough.

I wrote to Coach Brown to tell him about getting cut. He sent me back a nice letter about how I should keep trying, keep working.

Shortly afterwards, this guy named Ford McMurtry, who was the assistant coach of the high school team, quit that job and started a team on the base. He said to me, "Come play for us."

Ford was nice to me. He raised my confidence level. He worked on my conditioning and my footwork. When I got discouraged with my clumsiness, he was patient. "Try it again, Shaquille," he said without ever raising his voice. We got lucky because my friend Mitch Riles didn't play on the high school team, either, because of bad grades, so the two of us were together again, Magic and Larry.

My sophomore year I didn't even bother to try out for the high school team. By then Coach McMurtry had put together such a good team we could have beaten Dwayne Clark and those other guys. He was determined to make me a player.

I got some help from another guy who worked on the base. His name was Pete Popovich. He was watching me in the gym one day and he said, "Why aren't you dunking the ball?" I told him, "I can't jump. It's my knees, I think. I just can't get off the ground."

Later on, when I went upstairs to lift some weights, Pete said to me, "I can help you with your vertical leap." He showed me how to do calf raises and told me do them every day. I did those damn things until my legs felt like they were going to fall off. From the end of my freshman year to the end of my sophomore year in high school, my vertical leap went from eighteen inches to forty-two inches.

In 1987 my father was transferred again, so we moved back to the United States. I was fifteen years old and halfway through my sophomore season in high school with Coach McMurtry, and I just hated to leave. I thought I was finally getting somewhere with the basketball.

We stayed in New Jersey for a few weeks visiting family before we reported to our new base, Fort Sam Houston in San Antonio, Texas. My uncle Mike Parris came by. He hadn't seen me for a couple of years. He took me to a park down in South Orange, New Jersey, to play some pickup. There weren't a whole lot of guys around, but there was this one fairly big dude who played a little one-on-one with me. His name was Mark Bryant. He later became a big star at Seton Hall and played eighteen years in the NBA. I didn't have the skill that Mark had at that point, but now that I could jump, I held my own.

Uncle Mike was impressed with how I improved, I could tell. Whenever we played before, he could shoot over me all day. But now all of a sudden when he pulled up for that jumper, I could actually contest it. My wingspan was always pretty impressive, but I had never used that to my advantage. I was discovering how to block shots. I figured, *If I'm not scoring much, then nobody is going to score on me.*

We were leaving the park that afternoon, and my uncle Mike put his arm around me.

"Something has happened, Shaquille," he said.

He was right. Something had happened. I was finally becoming a baller.

SAN ANTONIO, TEXAS, 1989

S haquille O'Neal was lacing up his basketball shoes when Cole High School coach Dave Madura and his assistant, Herb More, approached him.

Both men were agitated. They told Shaquille about a conversation they'd had with the referee moments before.

"We just heard the funniest thing," the official told Coach Madura. "Those guys from Southside just informed us we're about to witness the biggest upset in high school basketball."

O'Neal didn't even look up. He merely nodded.

In truth, Shaq didn't need any additional motivation. Minutes earlier he had walked into the gym, ducking under the door as a pretty young cheerleader smiled at him. As Shaq grinned in return, her face contorted into a look of disgust.

"Freak!"

She shrieked so loudly, he wanted to cover his ears.

He had grown accustomed to verbal assaults, but he still couldn't fathom why people were so cruel. Did they think because he was so big and so strong that he had no feelings?

O'Neal said little in Cole's pregame huddle. He pointed to his chest and said softly, "Get me the ball."

The first time down, he grabbed it on the block, wheeled

and jammed so hard the rim bent forward. When he got it again, he slammed it with such force the rim drooped to the right.

"By the third time he dunked," More later recalled, "the rim looked like a roller coaster."

The biggest upset in high school basketball would have to wait another day.

Nobody knew where the hell I had come from when I showed up at Cole High School in San Antonio, Texas, in 1987. I wasn't an AAU lifer or a summer camp gym rat. I was a military kid coming from Europe who had some size but wasn't sure what to do with it. That was my self-published scouting report.

I moved there too late to play basketball in my sophomore year. I even wanted to play football at my new high school, but Sarge wouldn't let me. He was worried I'd get hurt. He was planning on my basketball skills paying for my college.

One of the first kids I met at Cole was Joe Cavallero, this little guy who was the sixth man on the basketball team and also the school's starting quarterback. He was a very good athlete, a born leader. Joe saw me in the office when I was registering and he gave me a little crap and that was it—instant friends. Joe got me the job as football team statistician, just so I'd have something to do. I'd walk up and down the sidelines intimidating the hell out of the other team. They'd look at me and say, "Shit. When is that kid coming in the game?"

Even though I wasn't on the team the football coach made me run all the off-season drills. I even did the log drill, which I absolutely hated. You had two logs parallel to one another with ten feet in between, and you had to do bear crawls across them. You were expected to zigzag across, then roll at the end.

I'm almost six foot ten at this point, and they have me rolling around in the mud. By the time I was done I was covered in dirt. I really did look like Sasquatch!

Of course I complained a lot about doing those damn log drills, but it really helped me with my agility and my footwork.

Joe introduced me to the guys on the basketball team, and I liked them right away. Doug Sandburg, who became my best friend, was a smart player, a good point guard who could shoot, too. If he had a little more size he probably could have gone on to play Division I. Robbie Dunn was funny as hell. He was a little guy with herky-jerky moves who didn't get to play a whole lot, but he was still a big part of our group.

Our motto back then was "Fake it until you make it." We used to go to the Eisenhower Flea Market, about two miles from the base. They sold all sorts of junk nobody really needed. Me and Joe would go around looking for the fattest plastic gold chains we could find, since we couldn't afford the real stuff. We'd buy these big-ass plastic chains, then we'd troll around looking for a Mercedes and steal the emblem off the top of the car and paint it gold. Then we'd string the emblem through the plastic chains and there you go. What's cooler than that?

I always wore a Gucci hat back then. Hey, I was already tall, so why hide it? I'd take that hat and make it sit high on my head like a shark fin. I swear, I was about seven foot eight with that thing on.

We used to do a lot of low-level juvenile-delinquent stuff. Outside the base we were surrounded by mayhem—guns, drugs, violence. We stayed on the base, for the most part, and did stupid things like knocking on people's doors and running off. We used to egg people's cars.

One of our favorite tricks was to have three guys on one side of the road and three guys on the other. The speed limit on the base was about thirty miles per hour, but people were always driving too fast. We'd have guys on either side of the street and pretend like we were pulling a rope. A car would come flying down the street and see us pulling this imaginary rope and they'd lock up their brakes. We got them every time with that one.

There was a pool on the base, and on weekends in the summer it would close around ten o'clock. We'd wait until the lights were out and the officers went inside to have their cocktails, and then we'd hop the fence and do cannonballs in the pool.

The officers would hear us splashing around and call the military police. The cops would then come and try to chase us, but they'd have their combat boots on. We were a bunch of athletes, and we knew they couldn't catch us. We'd park Robbie's car on the corner, sprint out of sight, and jump in the car and take off.

Most of the time, they knew it was us. I mean, there weren't a whole bunch of six-foot-ten kids roaming around the base. But we were kind of famous for the athletic stuff we were doing, so they cut us some slack. If the other kids on the base did something like that they'd be lined up and paddled.

I got paddled a few times by teachers on the base in Germany, but not in San Antonio. By then I was too big. Nobody was brave enough to come at me with a paddle—except my father, of course.

The paddles were a part of life on a military base. If you screwed up by breaking a rule or failing an exam or getting in a fight, they'd call the whole school together and line you up in the middle of the gymnasium and have you straddle the line, and the principal or the athletic director would start lighting you up. It hurt, but mostly it just humiliated you. Plus, your parents always heard about it—and if your father was a commanding officer, then look out.

Cole High School was really small and had never won a championship in basketball until I got there. We had seventy-six kids in our class, and we were playing against schools three times that size. I was still learning the game of basketball, still developing my style. My coach, Dave Madura, was a no-nonsense guy. He had me do leg squats in front of a mirror until they were burning. He was trying to improve my flexibility, especially in my hips.

There was only one problem: I still hadn't dunked in a game yet. I was getting close, and physically I finally had the coordination to do it, but part of it was psychological. I just wasn't sure about it. What if I missed? I didn't want anyone laughing at me.

Joe was trying to help me out. We started out by dunking a sock. Once I got comfortable with that, I tried dunking a tennis ball. Next it was a softball, then a volleyball, and then, finally, a basketball.

But dunking in an empty gym with my friend Joe was a lot different than pulling it off in a game in front of fans and family—especially my father.

Early in my junior year we were trying to break the press, so Doug Sandburg threw the ball to me in the middle, and I decided to take it all the way. I'm dribbling up the floor and I lay in a nice little finger roll, only there's a little too much spin on it, so it kind of falls off the rim. All of a sudden I hear my father in the stands yelling, "Call time-out! Call time-out!"

I refuse to look up at him. I know it's him—everyone knows it's him—but I'm not the damn coach, so how the hell am I going to call a time-out?

But Sarge isn't taking no for an answer. Now he's coming down out of the stands, and thank God the other team calls time-out. We're about to get in our huddle but my father grabs me and says, "What's with the finger roll?" I told him, "I'm trying to be like Dr. J."

"What the hell did you say to me?" he screamed. He grabbed my uniform and hauled me through a side door out of the gym. My coach is standing there and all the players are watching, but no one is going to mess with my father.

We are standing in the hallway and the buzzer is sounding because the time-out is almost over but Sarge doesn't care. He's banging me in the chest. "The hell with Dr. J!" he roared. "You start working on being Shaquille O'Neal. Now you go out and dunk the ball!"

He knew. He knew I was afraid to dunk it. He knew the only way he was going to get me to do it was shame me into it.

I went back on the court and I got the ball and I threw down a monster dunk. I mean, it was vicious. And then I realized, *Man, this isn't so hard. I can do this.*

Once I started dunking I couldn't stop. I loved the power of it, and

I was addicted to the looks of terror on guys' faces when I slammed that sucker over them.

It couldn't be the only part of my game, I understood that—but it could be *the* part of my game.

My learning curve was still going up, up, up. When I wasn't in the gym I was stealing a little bit of something from all the great players I was watching on TV.

One of the first guys I can remember paying a lot of attention to is Patrick Ewing. I just loved him because he was so mean. He ran around the court with a scowl on his face, and he always looked like he was ready to beat the crap out of everybody. You could tell people were afraid of him. I'd watch him and think, *Yeah, I need some of that.*

When I was in high school and stuck inside on punishment because I did something Sarge didn't like, I'd sit back and watch Michael Jordan and Ewing and take all sorts of mental notes. Now when I closed my eyes, I wasn't dreaming about the Hulk or Superman anymore. I was dreaming about Ewing and Jordan.

At this point people are saying I'm not going to make it as a basketball star, but they don't know I've decided to kidnap Patrick Ewing's mean streak.

I was a rookie with the Orlando Magic the first time I ever met Patrick. We were playing at Madison Square Garden, and my plan was to shake his hand and say, "Hello, Mr. Ewing," but before I got the chance he punked me. I went to shake his hand, and he wouldn't. So I went to put my fist out and he hit me real hard on my knuckles. Then he said, "I'm going to bust your ass, rookie."

Ewing was mad because everyone was talking about me like I was the Next Big Thing (which I was). I led the All-Star Game in votes my first year in the NBA, and after that happened Ewing told some guys no rookie should ever be allowed to start in the game. Pat Riley was the coach of the East that year, but he was Patrick's coach with the Knicks, and he told everyone it was "ridiculous" that I was the starter. So when we got to the All-Star Game Riley started me because he had to, but he played me and Patrick the exact same amount of minutes.

I didn't like that. I never really forgot it. I was voted in as the starter. Not Ewing. The fans wanted to see me. So give the fans what they want, right?

Ewing wasn't the only guy I was stealing moves from in high school. One night I was grounded and I was watching some ACC basketball, and there was this dude named Charles Shackleford, a forward for North Carolina State, tearing up everybody in his path. I'm watching him play and I like what he's doing, and he's wearing these big knee pads, so I say, "Yeah, I'm going to take that." They called him "Shack," so I show up the next day and I've got big-ass knee pads and I'm "Shaq."

So me and my boys on the base keep watching all the college games we can, and I see Sherman Douglas at Syracuse serving up lobs for this cat named Rony Seikaly. I noticed that every time he dunked he pulled his legs up. I'm watching and I'm thinking, *That's me. I'm taking that.*

One day I'm at the house and these military guys are talking about somebody named David Robinson, so my father goes out and gets a tape and sits me down and I got to watch film of David Robinson. I'm watching him run the floor and I say to myself, *I've got some work to do,* so I go out and I try to learn Robinson's spin move.

My dad is working with me and I'm getting better. I'm in between my junior and senior season of high school when my dad comes home from work one night and punches me square in the face. He's got a program in his hands and grabs me and says, "It's time for you to get serious. See this guy right here? We're going to watch him play basketball tonight, and I'm going to teach you how to destroy him. You know why? Because he makes 15 million dollars—that's why. See how much money you could make if you'd just stay out of trouble?"

The guy he was talking about was Jon Koncak. He was this huge, slow white dude who really wasn't that good, but he signed this contract for $15 million with the Atlanta Hawks. They nicknamed him "Jon Contract."

My dad has two tickets to the Spurs game, so we go to watch Jon Koncak. We are sitting way at the top, the worst seats in the place, but I'm watching this guy and I'm thinking, *I can be better than him.*

So now I've got something to shoot for. And that's when I started to turn it around. When the boys came around looking for fun I told them, "Sorry, I can't mess with y'all right now." Even the girls—I cut back on that, too.

Up to that point I still managed to find trouble just about all the time. One spring I played on an AAU team with Charles "Bo" Outlaw, and we went to Tempe, Arizona, for a tournament. We were playing a team from the state of Washington, and this guy kept fouling me really hard. I told him he shouldn't do that again but he did, so I turned around and I punched him in the face.

The AAU people didn't like that so much, so they kicked me out. Permanently. I messed up that kid pretty bad, so they sent me home. Luckily for me, my father wasn't there. He was in training for a couple of months, so he was out of town for a while and he never found out about it—until now. Sorry, Sarge.

Since I couldn't play AAU, I went to the army base and played with the enlisted men. My dad was running the gym at the base then, and I could always see him in the window watching. He never butted in when those big guys were pounding me, but later that night he'd tell me, "Don't let those men push you around. Stand up for yourself, son."

Ever since I was nine, Sarge taught me all the basics, then told me, "Go play." If I went to the park to work on things, he wasn't trailing along with his head up my butt. It was up to me to get better.

I was going into my senior year, and Bo Outlaw was still playing with my old AAU team. He was probably the best player in San Antonio at that point. They now see how good I've gotten and they figure they have a chance to win the whole thing, so they bring me back.

I have to stay out of trouble because I want to play on that team.

I'm getting letters from almost every college in the country, and this whole basketball thing might work out after all if I can just learn to keep my cool.

Sarge is there for almost all my high school games, and he's not very hard to miss. He's riding the officials so hard my coach doesn't ever have to bother. After a bad call, you could hear my father in the stands yelling, "You stupid ref!"

My dad was going to make sure I didn't blow it. Everything had to be done right. Once, in the middle of a game, he stood up and started hollering at me because my uniform shirt was untucked. That kind of stuff drove him crazy. They practically stopped the game so I could get my shirt tucked in. You could have heard a pin drop in that gym. Everybody knew not to mess with Sgt. Philip Harrison. He spent most of my high school career screaming, "Take it to the hole!"

We played in Class 3A, and everyone was jealous of the Cole Cougars. I was getting all the attention, all the press. Other schools wanted to beat me and our team in the worst way.

There was nothing fancy about our high school program. We dressed in the band room because we didn't have a locker room. I was big into rap at that time and I knew all the lyrics to every song. Plus, we'd make up our own songs. One of our best was when we remixed the school song. It started out like, "Hail to our alma mater, hail to thee, colors green and gold." We added our own beat, threw in a few swear words, put on our plastic Mercedes-Benz necklaces, and had them rolling in the aisles.

Coach Madura was straight country. He'd hear my rap music and yell, "Turn that garbage off!" Coach Madura handled us just right. He was very tough on me, but on the court he let me do a lot of things, which I appreciated. He used me to break the press. They'd throw the ball up to me and I'd bring it up the floor. My ball-handling skills were pretty good. But mostly, I could score.

Besides Doug and Joe, who was all-state football and all-state baseball and had some real speed, we had this kid named Darren

Mathey who could handle the ball pretty well. Our other football player was Dwayne Cyrus, another real athlete who added muscle. We had Jeff Petress, who could shoot the ball.

Then we had Robbie, who we nicknamed the Duke of Juke. Robbie would get the ball, drive to the hole like a madman making all these crazy motions, then he'd kick the ball back out. So one time we're playing and Robbie goes to the hole doing all his Duke of Juke stuff and he's got a layup—I mean, no one is on him—and instead he kicks the ball back to me at the foul line.

I yell at him, "Rob, what are you doing? You had a layup. You gotta take that."

So Rob stops right in the middle of the game and slams the ball down on the court. "Listen," the Duke of Juke screams at me, "I ain't getting no scholarship, bitch. You shoot the ball!"

He was right. I was the only one getting a scholarship. It was all on me.

I ran into some nasty people in Texas. There was a lot of racism. Places like Asherton, Texas, and Plugerville, Texas. Those places held up signs with apes when black kids like me came to town. When you are a kid, that stuff hurts. I was already kind of self-conscious about my size, and that sure didn't help. I had no choice but to learn to deal with it.

When I was playing for LSU against Mississippi State, my teammate Stanley Roberts was shooting free throws and one side yelled "Magilla!" and the other side yelled "Gorilla!" If he was mad about it, he didn't show it. I watched him and I thought, *Stanley's got it right. You can't take it to heart.* If you can't learn to laugh at yourself, then you are going to have one long miserable life, especially if you are seven feet tall.

Mark Cuban, the Dallas Mavericks owner, used to call me Fat Albert when I shot free throws. I thought it was hilarious the first time I heard it. Made me miss the free throw. Not really, because I miss free throws all the time, but it makes for a good story.

My junior year at Cole High we were undefeated and turning the

Texas basketball world upside down. I would walk into practice and never know who would be there. One day, it was Dale Brown from LSU. The next day it was the Shark, Jerry Tarkanian from Nevada–Las Vegas. The day after that it was Jim Valvano of NC State. I was eating it up.

I suppose it went to my head a little bit. I had gone from this clumsy kid who nobody thought could play to a real celebrity. Everyone in San Antonio was talking about me.

Coach Madura wasn't going to let me get too cocky, though. One day we were in practice and he gave us a two-minute water break, and I wandered out of the gym and went to the bathroom and took my time getting back on the court. I was gone only about five minutes, but by the time I got back the team was on the floor running drills.

Coach Madura let me have it. "The rest of the world might think you are some kind of superstar, but we don't deal with prima donnas around here," he said.

I was hot. I was mad, but mostly I was embarrassed. I didn't say anything, but when we started playing again, I started throwing down dunks. One after another. After practice, Coach Madura laughed and said, "Maybe I should yell at you more often."

We made it to the state finals in my junior year. We were undefeated when we played a team called Liberty Hill. They didn't have any post game. They were a bunch of skinny little white guys who ran a flex offense. They were shooting threes from all over the court. I picked up three fouls in the first quarter. I picked up my fourth foul pretty soon after that and had to sit the entire third quarter. It was so frustrating. Sometimes I legitimately fouled those little dudes, but other times those guys were taking a dive anytime I was within two feet of them. The refs didn't know what to do with a guy my size so their solution was, *When in doubt, call a foul on the big kid.*

After a while, when your best player is sitting with four fouls and your team is getting two points every time down and the other guys are getting three every time down, you are in trouble.

Still, we had a chance to win the game in the final minutes. I was at the free-throw line, and if I hit a couple and we went down and got a defensive stop, there was still time to pull it out.

I missed them both.

And that's when it started—the whole free throw thing. Maybe it was some kind of omen. I don't really know, but I've been dealing with it ever since.

Everyone has their theories on why I can't make free throws: my hands are too big, it's all in my head, I've changed my form too many times, I don't extend my arm enough, I need to say a prayer before I shoot, I need to eat three peanut butter sandwiches with the crusts cut off. Crazy stuff.

My mom has her own ideas on why I can't shoot them. When we lived in Germany, I was goofing around and I was climbing a tree and fell out and broke my wrists. I think I had a couple of casts, but I'm not even sure. They just kind of healed on their own, only now I can't bend my wrists back at all. Anyway, Mom thinks that's the root of the free-throw issue.

By my senior season at Cole, we were having problems in practice because there was nobody to match up with me. Coach Madura hired Herb More, a former ballplayer from Cole who still held the single-game scoring record at the school. He was my geometry teacher and the guy I battled in practice. He was about six foot five or six, and he put a body on me, roughed me up a bit. He taught me a little jump hook.

Before long, I am dominating. My senior high school season is about to start, but I've got to pick a college first.

People have always written that it was a slam dunk that I would go to LSU because of my long-standing relationship with Coach Brown, but that wasn't entirely true. I felt I owed it to myself and my family to look around.

My parents didn't come with me on my college visits, even though I'm sure my father wanted to be there. He was worried about the under-the-table payments we kept hearing about.

There was plenty of illegal recruiting going on, but I can honestly say I didn't see too much of that on my college trips. A few guys tried to slip me a hundred-dollar bill. They put it in my hand when they shook it and said, "Here, put this in your pocket," but nobody came at me with a big bag of money or a car. Good thing. If they had, Sarge would have killed them.

I visited five schools. The first one I went to was North Carolina. Rick Fox, who later became my Lakers teammate, picked me up and he was cool, but Coach Dean Smith kind of rubbed me the wrong way. He sat down with me in his office and basically told me, "I'm Dean Smith. Here's what I've done. I'm pretty great and have you ever heard of Michael Jordan? I coached him." He was telling me how much he had won, but I already knew all that.

I also knew something else—Dean Smith liked this other seven-footer from Texas more than he liked me. He had just signed this kid named Matt Wenstrom, and I was UNC's backup choice.

The last thing Dean Smith told me was, "If you come here, you can be like Michael, James Worthy, Sam Perkins." I nodded my head politely but I was thinking, "No. I'm going some place where I'm going to be the first."

And it really bothered me they liked Matt Wenstrom better than me. I didn't like that guy at all. I didn't know him, but I hated him because everyone said he had more upside than I did.

Wenstrom ended up going to North Carolina, by the way. I think he averaged two points a game. Then he went to the pros and played for the Celtics for about five minutes. I'm guessing Dean Smith never told any of his recruits, "Ever heard of Matt Wenstrom? I coached him."

The next weekend I visited NC State because I wanted to see how my idol Charles Shackleford was doing. He came and picked me up, and we got along great. We had the same size shoe. We swapped some funny high school stories. I was liking the "original" Shack and I was liking NC State. But that night Shack got with a girl and left me behind. I ended up hanging with a guy named Avie Lester. He played the four spot and could really jump. We went out and tried to find ourselves some girls but we didn't have any luck.

NC State coach Jim Valvano was very energetic, very enthusiastic. A couple of weeks before I visited, he came to my parents' house and broke our glass table. He was kind of nervous and fidgety, and he had this briefcase and a book, and he dropped it on the table and it broke. He was so horrified. He was saying, "Oh, I'm so sorry. I'll pay for it, I'll pay for it."

Sarge told him, "You are not going to pay for anything. That's a violation."

My father was real clear with everybody about violations.

I really liked NC State and I really liked Coach Valvano. He told me, "We love the way you play. We're going to put you right next to Shack."

That sounded great, but I'll tell you the truth: I had gone from a nobody to a star almost overnight. I liked being a star and I still wanted to be a star, and they already had their own star.

My next stop was Texas University in Austin. Tom Penders was the coach. He was a crazy dude, did the tanning thing, but I really liked him, too. He came to a lot of my high school games. We played our state championship in Austin, so I already knew about the city and Sixth Street, which was where they had all the bars and restaurants and clubs.

The only problem with Texas was it was too close. I needed some space. I needed freedom.

I needed to get away from my father.

From nine years old to twelve years old, I was in the penitentiary—Sarge's penitentiary. Then, from twelve to fourteen, I was in Sarge's halfway house. When I got to be about fifteen and the basketball started working out for me, I was on parole. So, by the time I was seventeen and bigger than my father I was thinking, *I'm a man. I need to strike out on my own.*

Of course, I was still crazy in love with my mother, so I wasn't going to go too far.

The fourth school I visited was Illinois. I got off the plane and Nick Anderson picked me up. He ended up being my teammate and good friend on the Orlando Magic. So Nick grabs me and he takes me to the Maxwell Street Market. It's this big flea market and it's kind of fun, except when we went down there someone picked my pocket. My wallet got stolen. I'm sure if Coach Lou Henson knew about that, he would have crapped in his pants. I never told him. I just smiled and shook his hand and told him my visit was going just fine.

Coach Henson didn't talk with me much. He was friendly, but he wasn't giving me the hard sell. I wasn't confident I could play at Illinois. They were so good back then. They had Nick Anderson and Kendall Gill and the Snake (Kenny Norman) and Kenny Battle, too.

My final trip was to LSU. I'd been writing letters back and forth with Coach Brown for three years, so I already knew him a little bit. I went for my visit and he took me to his home, and I'm looking at this really nice house with a pool in the backyard and I'm saying, "Wow." I had never seen any place that beautiful.

So Coach Brown said to me, "Son, you think this house looks really, really nice? If you listen to what I'm going to teach you, this house is going to look like a ghetto next to the one you can own by the time we're done together."

Hmmm. That sounded good to me.

Coach Brown said, "I've been watching you a long time and I've enjoyed how you've improved. I know you probably aren't going to come here, but I'd love the chance to coach you. You might be able to start here, I'm not really sure."

I was only half-listening until he said that. I was like, "What? He's not sure if I can start here?" I was kind of upset the rest of the day. Everyone else was telling me I was the greatest, and this guy was telling me I may or may not start for his team.

The LSU players took me to TJ Ribs for lunch. It's a restaurant off campus where they have all sorts of LSU stuff, including the Heisman Trophy that Billy Cannon won in 1959. The owner of the restaurant came over and told me if I came to LSU he'd keep an eye on me.

The one mistake the other four schools made was they didn't take me to a football game. Coach Brown had one of his LSU players, Vernel Singleton, take me. I'm sitting in this big football stadium with all the people and the noise and the lights, and then all of a sudden the lights go off and they put a spotlight on me. The PA announcer starts shouting, "Say hello to the number one high school player Shaquille O'Neal! Make some noise if you want him to come here next year!"

The crowd starts going crazy. I'm sitting in the stands and there's about twenty thousand people just going wild and I'm thinking, *Damn, these people know me!* So I start looking around and I'm seeing some of the baddest girls I've ever seen and they're waving at me. I say to one of them, "So if I come here you and I are going to be friends, right?" She winks at me, blows me a kiss, and says, "Definitely."

That's it. I'm signing with LSU.

Coach had me sold—but he still had to deal with my father, who has his own set of very strong opinions. When they sit down Sarge is giving Dale one of his best death stares, but Coach Brown isn't intimidated at all. He tells Sarge, "I'm obviously here because your son is a talented player. Now all the programs are going to tell you about their facilities and how they'll get to the Final Four and all the money they can make for Shaquille.

"I just want you to know I'm recruiting a human being first and a basketball player second, and twenty-five years from now, if your son is willing to listen to what I'm teaching him, I will still be in his life. I will be a big part of his life."

That's how he got Sarge to sign off. I can tell you that everything Coach Brown told me that day came true. After I left LSU in 1992, I went straight to the NBA and made millions of dollars. I have a house in Orlando that is sixty-four thousand square feet and has an indoor gymnasium, a cigar room, a movie theater, and a seventeen-foot-deep pool. And Dale Brown is still in my life. He's part of my inner circle, and it's a small, small group.

Once I commit to LSU I become a rock star at Cole High School. I'm going to be a big college stud so I start acting the part while I'm still playing for the Cougars.

We lose Jeff Petress for a while because of bad grades, but it doesn't matter. This kid named Eric Baker can score a little for us and we are undefeated again, and I'm getting a lot of press and I start thinking I'm The Man. Our games are sold out every night. Little kids are lining up asking for my autograph. My teammates started calling me Shaquille the Deal, or sometimes just The Deal.

It was just an amazing feeling. I had spent so much time wondering if I would ever get to this point, especially after I had gotten cut from the team in Germany. But now, just like Sarge said, it was all coming together. I really thought I was something special, just like my mother always said I would be.

So one day I get to school and I'm walking down the left side of the hall and I notice everyone else is walking on the right. When I sit down at lunch, everyone gets up the minute I put down my tray. I'm thinking, "What the hell is this?" It was Joe Cavallero that did it. He thought I was getting too big. He thought I was forgetting about the team and focusing too much on myself. He was right. I had to humble myself. Joe was going to make sure I did, because if I didn't, he knew we couldn't win.

That shit went on for a week. It was kind of lonely, but I had my Walkman and my princess girlfriend, so it could have been worse. For a few days I was thinking, "Screw you guys. Who needs you? I'm going to LSU in three months."

But I got the message. It was the same one my dad taught me when I was a little boy named Shaun playing YMCA basketball in the championship game. My father was the coach, and the guys on the other side were working their asses off trying to beat me.

We got a pretty big lead, and my father called time-out and yanked me from the game and put in this kid who couldn't play a lick. There were five minutes left in the game and this kid was banging around and just screwing up everything. Next thing you know we were down 10, and I had to go back in to save the game. I'm looking at my father like, "What the hell? Why did you do that? We're trying to win." He said to me, "It's not always about winning at all costs. Everybody deserves a chance. You have to develop the players around you. That's what great players do. It's your job to make sure it comes out okay.'"

So now I'm a senior in high school and it's my job to make sure it comes out okay. Every game I'd take over for the first seven possessions and we'd be ahead 10–2 or 14–4. Once that happened I'd dribble the ball up and start dishing to Darren Mathey or Joe. My job was to be the point center and get everyone feeling part of it. Instead of being a show-off and just scoring every time down the floor, that's what I did. It brought us closer together. My father always taught me team ball. "You can't do it yourself," he told me over and over.

I went through a lot of crap getting through high school. The jealousy was off the charts. People just hated me because I was big and I was good.

We played in Sabinal, Texas, a town about 90 ninety miles east of Del Rio, which is on the Mexican border. We're driving there on a team bus, and I'm looking out the window and I see this huge scarecrow. We get a little closer and I realize it's a seven-foot scarecrow that's supposed to be me. It's got a jersey with my number on it and a noose hanging around its neck. Everyone is so shocked nobody knows what to say, so it gets real quiet on our bus.

Now I'm pissed. I'd never really dealt with much racism in my life to this point. My first thought was, *Maybe they're trying to be funny*. But there's nothing funny about a noose. It was probably racist, but I just didn't want to go there. Maybe I just didn't want to believe it.

So I decided I would take it this way: these people have a noose around my neck so they must want to kill me. So that meant I had to get into my mode where I had my own killer stare going. I told my teammates, "These people are going to pay."

We walk into that gym and I have my headphones on and I'm ready to stare these badasses down—and they're a bunch of small little white guys. Now I'm *really* pissed. You think you puny little dweebs are going to beat me? I don't think so.

I go out there and I give them what they want. I act like a monkey. I'm dunking and I'm swinging from the rim and I'm screaming like a beast. You want it? Here it is. I was acting completely crazy. They think I'm nuts. So now I'm looking into their eyes and they're scared. We got 'em. Easiest forty-something points I've ever scored.

There was a lot of name-calling in my senior year. For some reason, people liked to do that. Southside, the school that I bent the rims against, liked to call me Shaqzilla, Freakzille. I'm the type of guy who takes criticism and name-calling two ways. You can either get dogged by it and hang your head, or you can get motivated and have it make you go up harder.

Here's the thing they didn't realize. My father used to call me names all the time. Crybaby. Softy. I'd heard it all. He started doing that when I was three years old. He knew what was coming. He was getting me ready.

My high school team was still undefeated as we headed into the 1989 states, and I started thinking about the history of our little army base that never won nothing. We had come out of nowhere and could win it all and I was telling myself, *I gotta make this happen.*

A television reporter stuck a microphone in my face after one of our wins and asked me, "What's been the secret to Cole's success this year?" I answered, "The secret is me."

There was a lot of pressure, but I was good with it. I didn't want a repeat of my junior season. We got a rematch with Liberty Hill in the Regional Finals, and I dropped 44 points and 18 rebounds on them, and I also hit 5 free throws in the final minute to clinch it. Consider that score settled.

We rolled over Hearne in the state semifinals, which was highlighted by one of my favorite high school plays. One of my guys had lobbed me the ball for a dunk but I had a bad angle on it, so I threw it off the glass then rammed it through. Check it out—I think it's still on YouTube.

So there we are in Austin, Texas, before the state title game. The place is banged out—a new record for attendance in the 3A championship. We are playing Clarksville and everyone in the locker room is nervous except for me. I'm not nervous because I know we're going to win. We *have* to win. There's really no other option for me.

I look around at my guys and they are tight. Really tight. Every five minutes someone is running out back to go to the bathroom. So now it's my turn and I have to take a dump. I'm cleaning myself up and I get this idea. It's definitely kind of gross, but I think it might work. So I come back into the locker room with a tissue covered in crap. I start chasing all my teammates around the room with it. They are all screaming and howling and laughing, and all of a sudden it's time to go and they are loose. It worked.

Clarksville's game plan was the same as everyone else's—try to get O'Neal in foul trouble and force him to make free throws. They had a post player named Tyrone Washington who kept stepping out to shoot fifteen-footers. He had twenty-four points at halftime, but we made a decision to have me stay home and protect the basket instead of flying out there and trying to guard him from the perimeter.

He kept baiting me, saying, "You can't guard me." I just laughed at him. I told him, "Why don't you come inside where the real big boys play?"

We got an early lead and never really gave it up. Of course I got into foul trouble again and the nine- or ten-point lead we had going into the fourth quarter was disappearing because I was on the bench with four fouls. Coach Madura turned to me and said, "Can you play without fouling?"

I told him I could. I decided I wouldn't go for any blocks and I wouldn't dunk unless it was a clear path so they couldn't call a charge on me. The first time I got the ball when I checked back in, I made a move like I was going to the rim to jam it, but instead I pulled up and hit a jumper.

The crowd kind of gasped, like they were surprised I could do anything other than dunk. The truth was I took jumpers in practice all the time. I had three-point range. Ask my teammates. I drained them all the time. Coach Madura told me once if we ever needed a three-pointer at the end of the game he'd consider letting me take it because I could hit it and he knew no one would ever be able to block it.

It just didn't make sense in games to take those kind of shots when I could just as easily slam the ball through. It was all about high percentage shots. My field goal percentage in my senior year of high school was 71 percent.

We ended up holding off Clarksville to win the state championship. Even though I told myself I wouldn't go after any more blocks, I did swat one more shot away in the final minutes. It was one of Tyrone Washington's jumpers. I couldn't help it. He scored only five points in the second half. When reporters asked me about him I told them, "He said I couldn't stay with him. Obviously, that was a lie."

When the buzzer sounded, I actually lost my breath for a minute. All these guys I loved, my best friends, were on the court with me and we had finally done it. It was an amazing feeling—but, I realized, mostly a feeling of relief. I didn't realize until it was over how much pressure I had put on myself.

Not long after we won, Coach Madura announced he was retiring. He was no dummy. I was graduating and, as he put it, "There will be too many people wanting to get even with me."

Winning that championship meant the world to him. We could all see that.

Right after the game Coach Madura pulled me into one of the stalls in the locker room and grabbed me and hugged me, and then he started to tear up. It was the first time I had ever seen a grown man cry. He told me, "I knew when you arrived at school you were going to be a great player, but I never allowed myself to think we'd win the whole thing. You're going to do great things in college."

I didn't really know what to say. It kind of made me uncomfortable at the time. Here I am, this seventeen-year-old kid who has spent most of his life trying to be cool, and now my coach is crying in my arms. I wanted to say to him, *Get ahold of yourself, man!*

I didn't get it at the time.

I do now.

JUNE, 1990

Baton Rouge, Louisiana

The LSU basketball players were scrimmaging in the dungeon, the tiny, dimly lit basement gymnasium where they congregated in the off-season, when Stanley Roberts unexpectedly sauntered in.

Roberts was a gifted, skilled player, but the amiable seven-footer was perpetually in trouble for missing class or breaking curfew. He rarely showed up for these pickup games, and when he did he only gave, by his own admission, a half hearted effort.

This was infuriating to Shaquille O'Neal, who had just completed his freshman year at LSU. He was tired of hearing about Stanley's "natural ability."

"A Stanley sighting!" exclaimed the captain, Wayne Sims. "Nice of you to join us, man."

Sims quickly divvied up the teams, putting Shaq and Roberts on opposing sides. Former LSU player Ricky Blanton, who came back to work out with his old team in the summertime, whispered in O'Neal's ear, "Go right at him."

Shaq called for the ball on the block, then turned and dunked over Roberts. Unfazed, Stanley set up for a fallaway, then drove to the hole and returned the favor with his own slam.

The big men were fed a steady diet of entry passes as they continued to assault each other with ferocious tomahawks. The other players whooped with delight—until tempers flared, elbows flew, and the two became tangled.

For a split second, the big men squared off before Roberts regained his composure and stepped back.

"I was thinking, 'This really isn't no big deal,'" Stanley said.

"I was thinking, 'I'm going to kill him,'" Shaquille said.

O'Neal glanced around the dungeon for a weapon and settled on a metal trash can. He hoisted it with one hand and began chasing Stanley Roberts with it.

"Easy, big fella!" Sims shrieked. "Put that thing down!"

Roberts sidestepped Shaquille and quickly left the dungeon. He'd played enough basketball for one day.

"Shaq is crazy," Stanley said to Sims afterward. "And you wonder why I don't show up for pickup."

One month later, Stanley Roberts left LSU to sign with the Spanish professional team Real Madrid.

"This is your team now, Shaquille," Coach Dale Brown solemnly informed his eighteen-year-old center.

"Yes, I already know that, Coach," Shaq replied.

I WAS JEALOUS OF STANLEY ROBERTS. IT WAS OBVIOUS THE coaches liked how he *was* way better than how I played. They were always talking about him, even though he was cutting class and getting in trouble and messing up. Stanley was really talented. He could shoot step-back jumpers and turnarounds. He had some great moves. He could even shoot threes. The problem with Stanley was he just didn't seem to care enough.

And I guess you could say I cared too much.

I wanted to be good. I liked the way it felt when I put up numbers and people slapped me on the back and gave me high fives. It was great with the ladies, too. Everybody loved the basketball players on campus. I was only seventeen years old when I showed up at LSU, but I was almost seven feet tall and ready to start my fabulous new life.

Now, before I got to LSU, I was invited to play in the Dapper Dan Roundball Classic, which is a national all-star game for high school players. I'm still ranked number two in Texas behind Wenstrom, only he's not playing in the game because he's hurt.

I get to the game and Sonny Vaccaro, the guy who runs the tournament and works for Nike, is sucking up to the big names like Tracy Murray and Kenny Anderson, giving them Nike sneakers and Nike bags. I'm standing there waiting and finally I say, "Sir, you forgot my bag." He turns and says, "And your name is?" I say, "Shaquille O'Neal." I'm so mad I'm shaking. I go out that night and I own Sonny Vaccaro's stupid game. I'm named the MVP.

The same thing happens when I play in the McDonald's All America game. Dick Vitale is glad-handing all these other players and he's not saying anything at all to me, so I went up to him and said, "Mr. Vitale, I'm Shaquille O'Neal. You might want to remember that name."

The first time I touched the ball in that game I threw it down for a dunk. I was angry and I played like it. There was one sequence where I came up on Conrad McRae, who was one of those New York City high school legends, and I stuffed him. I blocked the shot on one end, then dribbled the ball the length of the floor myself and rammed it through. Vitale went off the deep end. By the end of the night, I'm the MVP of that game, too, and Vitale is shouting, "If this Shaquille O'Neal kid decides to go pro, he'll be the number one pick."

Glad we straightened that out.

Even though Dickie V had signed off on the Shaq attack, I knew, deep down, I wasn't ready for the NBA yet.

LSU was the perfect place for me. It was what I was used to—fairly small, down to earth, not uppity, with lots of nice people. It was also a six-hour drive from my mom. I had to see my mom. But fortunately, back then, a plane ticket on Southwest was $59, so I got plenty of time with her.

The other good thing about LSU was they helped us get jobs in the summer, all on the up and up. We made $15 an hour. We got $7 per hour during the summer and the other $8 an hour was allotted back to us during the school year. I also qualified for the Pell Grant, which helped low-income students pay for school, so for the first time in my life I actually had some cash. I was convinced I was rich. Free food in the dining hall and some pocket money. I had died and gone to heaven.

The time I spent at LSU was the best three years of my life. Dale Brown was an excellent coach and an even better person. He's one of my best friends in the world. He stuck up for me a hundred different times.

One of the things I liked about Coach Brown was he never promised me anything. When I got to campus he said, "If you work hard, anything can happen, but we've got this other guy named Stanley Roberts who is pretty doggone good."

Stanley. There he was again. That damn guy.

But here's the problem: I really liked Stanley. Everyone did. He was a cool dude. He wouldn't hurt anyone, except himself.

He was a Proposition 48 player, which meant his grades weren't quite good enough to play right away, so he had to sit out his first year and not play basketball. When I got to Baton Rouge, even though he had been there a year, it was his first basketball season.

Stanley had a 1979 Oldsmobile Toronado, and it was my job as the rookie freshman to drive him around. I'd take him to the clubs, wait for him outside, and mingle with the people going in and out. I loved it. I got to know so many people that way.

My freshman season in 1989–90, we were expected to do great things. We had Stanley and we had Chris Jackson, who had led the country in scoring the year before. Chris liked to shoot the ball. He could score from anywhere. We also had me, but nobody understood what that really meant yet.

Even though he had these two seven-footers to choose from, Chris still jacked it up about thirty times a game. Chris had Tourette's syndrome. It made him shout out random things for no apparent reason. It took some getting used to. I didn't really understand it. He needed to take some medication, and he hated it because sometimes it made him sick. Chris was off on his own a lot, so I never really got to know him very well.

One day I was in the dorm and I heard this guy screaming at the top of his lungs, "Hey! Hey!" I went running down the hall because I thought somebody was getting murdered.

It was Chris, standing by his door. He had this thing where he had to click the knob on his door to the right three times before he could open it. Sometimes it didn't click exactly the way he wanted it and he'd have to start over. The problem was, he couldn't stop until it was just right, and it got very frustrating for him. He'd waste an hour just trying to open the door.

That particular day I went over and opened it for him. He said "Hey, thanks, Shaquille," and then he was gone. He was very quiet, very isolated. I rarely saw him outside of practice.

I remember one day being in the gym with him and we couldn't leave until he got three swishes in a row. Not three baskets—three perfect swishes. I was like, "C'mon, man, let's go. Party starts at eight."

Chris was All World on our campus. People treated him like a god. He was one of the greatest shooters I had ever seen. He always stayed in shape, always ate right, always did what he needed to do to stay on top.

Near the end of my freshman season I was starting to get a little press, and I got mad at Chris after one of the games because he just wouldn't pass the ball. I said something about it, and the next day Dale brought in this tape on Tourette's syndrome and made us all watch it. Dale's thing was, "Maybe he doesn't know he's not passing. Ease up, okay, Shaquille?"

Great. *Now,* I remember thinking to myself, *I can't dog this kid because there's a chance he doesn't even know he's being a ball hog.*

My best friend at LSU was Mo Williamson. He was from New Jersey and his dad was Super John Williamson of NBA fame, a serious baller. I always thought Mo would go pro. He scored a hundred points in a high school game once. But I think he was overlooked because Chris was there.

Mo was like an older brother to me. He showed me where to go and where not to go. I had no idea what college was like, so he walked me through registration. He told me, "You want that teacher and take this class, and work out your schedule so you have Monday, Wednesday, and Friday classes in the morning. Start at seven thirty a.m. so you can have the rest of the day." All of it was great advice except the 7:30 a.m. classes. Too early for me. I needed my beauty sleep.

I was humbled my freshman year. I thought I was The Man. What I realized when I got to LSU was that everyone there was The Man.

Everyone was on scholarship, so I had to go all the way back down to zero. I had so much to learn about the game of basketball. In one of our first intrasquad scrimmages, Stanley was scoring on me and I was trying to guard him, and Coach was yelling to me, "Shaq, three-quarter him!"

I had no idea what he was talking about, but I was too embarrassed to tell him that. So I came down and I dunked on Stanley thinking that was going to make it all okay. But Stanley rolled out and spun away from me and Coach started yelling again, "Three-quarter him!" Finally I stopped and said, "Coach, I don't know what you mean."

Coach Brown was very patient with me, but he was on me right away about my free throws. He kept telling me how important it was for big men to be able to shoot them.

One day Coach Brown came up to me in practice and said, "You know what I'm going to do? I'm going to get you to shoot underhand. Rick Barry, who is in the Hall of Fame, was the best at it."

"Coach," I pleaded with him, "please don't do that. Please don't make me shoot that granny shot. It's embarrassing."

I really didn't want to shoot them that way. When I was a kid, someone else suggested that approach before and Sarge told me to forget it. "That's a shot for sissies," my father told me.

Coach Brown said, "Okay, I'll tell you what I'm going to do. We're going to chart your free throws every day, separate from the team. You are going to be assigned a trainer, assistant coach, or manager with you at the basket every day. If you keep practicing and can shoot seventy percent or better, I'll let you keeping taking them the way you are."

I shot 72 percent leading up to the season, but once I got in the games my percentage dropped to 56 percent. A lot of it was mental. If I was feeling good, I'd make them; if not, no chance. I could never get comfortable from the line, although I had a habit of making big free throws when it mattered. In our tournament game against Georgia Tech, for instance, I was 9 of 12 from the line. Why? I don't know.

I didn't start the first four games of the season, because, I think, Coach Brown was worried about people expecting too much. But once people saw me play, they said, "Okay, this kid is serious about being great."

What they meant was, I wasn't like Stanley.

Looking back, I realize in many ways Stanley made me who I am. It was good to have someone there who was better than me. He had it all—girls, money, cars. Everyone loved him. What got in his way was his partying. That day in the dungeon when I went after him with the trash can, Stanley was hungover. He was there trying to sweat out the alcohol. I'm thinking, *Imagine how good he'd be if he hadn't been out all night.*

I didn't drink, and after watching what it did to Stanley and some of the other guys, I was pretty sure I'd never be a drinker.

There were plenty of other ways for me to have some fun.

I had a Ford Bronco II. It wasn't much of a car, but I'd move the seat all the way back on the track so I could fit, and I put my own speakers in there, so that truck was rocking. I played that music so loud it was shaking.

Just like every other place I went to when I was the new kid, I told a lot of jokes and did my break dancing at center court before practice. I got everybody loose. When I moved into my dorm, I set up my own little studio with a turntable and a mixer so I could do all my rapping. The guys loved it. My neighbors didn't like it so much, though. I was always getting knocks on my door to turn down the music.

Our team had a lot of fun together. We tended to travel in packs. A few of the guys got together and we called ourselves the Dunk Mob, because me, Shawn Griggs, and Vernel Singleton could all throw one down. We'd show up at the fraternity parties and get in a line with me in the front, and we'd do our Dunk Mob dance. We'd act like we were shooting a jump shot then rock this way, that way, then "do the dunk."

Everyone on campus loved it. It wasn't long before everybody knew me. I was making new friends every day. I loved college. I fit in at LSU. For the first time in my life, I felt like I belonged.

I also knew I had to do well in school or my father would kill me. Even worse, my momma would be disappointed in me, and I never wanted to disappoint her.

I took a public speaking class in my freshman year, and I was a little nervous about it because I had a bit of a stuttering problem. I asked Coach Brown to critique it for me. I did my speech and then I asked him, "Can you come to class while I do this?" He said, "I'll be happy to, Shaquille." The next day I showed up at class and there was Coach, in the back of the room, giving me the thumbs-up.

I had the highest GPA on the team in my freshman season. I think if you ask my mother, she'll tell you that was one of her proudest moments.

We played our games in the Pete Maravich Assembly Center, which was nicknamed the "Deaf Dome" because the fans were so loud.

I spent most of my freshman year at LSU in foul trouble. It was really frustrating. I couldn't really understand how it was that I would take a shot with three guys hanging on me and there was no whistle, but the minute I got near anyone they were calling stuff on me. My dad always taught me, "When you get the ball, be aggressive with it." It seemed like every time I took his advice, they'd call me for charging.

Coach Brown used to go crazy over that kind of stuff. I averaged only twenty-eight minutes a game as a freshman because I spent so much time on the bench in foul trouble.

When I got there in my freshman year, I just wanted to fit in. I was still working on my game. I told Coach Brown, "Don't worry about me. I don't need to score. Let those other guys do that. I'll just play defense and block shots."

That was first and last time I ever said *that*.

I still averaged 13.9 points and 12 rebounds a game, and I blocked a ton of shots—115 of them. That was the first time someone in the Southeastern Conference (SEC) had ever gone over 100.

Stanley showed up out of shape, and since Wayne Sims was a captain he had to get up at five o'clock in the morning and run with him. Wayne was so pissed about that. The two of them were roommates, and once in a while Coach would call Wayne and say, "Is Stanley going to class? Let me talk to him." Stanley hadn't even come home from the night before, so Wayne would cover for him by saying, "He's in the shower, Coach. He'll have to call you back."

In spite of all that, Stanley still managed to average 14 points and 10 rebounds a game.

We had some big wins that season. We were an up-tempo team, so we always had high-scoring games. We beat Texas 124–113, and I had a triple-double. Same thing against Loyola Marymount, when we beat them 148–141 in overtime. It was an incredible game. Loyola's star Hank Gathers scored 48 points in 38 minutes. Both teams were just flying up and down the floor. I had a pretty good game myself— 20 points, 24 rebounds, and 12 blocks.

About a month later, Hank Gathers collapsed and died in the middle of a basketball game in Los Angeles. We were shocked when we heard that. We were saying, "But we just saw him..." For a couple of weeks, we all kind of stopped in our tracks. It put everything in perspective.

But, us being kids, it wasn't long until we were back to goofing off and partying and having fun and loving our lives as LSU Tigers.

We went into the NCAA tournament with a 23-8 record and beat Villanova in the first round. If we won our next game against Georgia Tech, we'd get to return to Louisiana to play in New Orleans the following weekend.

Georgia Tech was loaded with talent. They had four guys who wound up in the NBA: Kenny Anderson, Dennis Scott, Brian Oliver, and Malcolm Mackey.

Stanley and I were close to unstoppable inside, and Vernel played a strong game, but they just kept burying threes over our backcourt of Chris Jackson and Mo. Chris had a bad game. He missed ten of his fifteen shots.

Brian Oliver was all over him. His coach must have told him, "Don't lose Chris Jackson," because whenever Coach Brown called a time-out, Brian Oliver practically escorted Chris Jackson to our bench.

We lost 94–91 in overtime, and we were all pretty disappointed. I was kind of mad at Chris. He had this one herky-jerky move that got him open and he rarely missed, so normally you couldn't say anything, but in that game he kept missing and missing and he just wouldn't pass it. At one point I said to him, "What are you doing? Look inside." He just looked at me. I felt like he sold us out a little bit. He wanted to get big numbers because he knew he was going pro.

We had what they call "exit interviews" after the season, and Chris and Stanley went first. Chris went in to talk to Coach and he came out and said, "I'm gone. I'm leaving."

He was the No. 3 pick in the draft of the Denver Nuggets. He converted to Islam in 1991 and changed his name to Mahmoud Abdul-Rauf. That dude loved the game of basketball. He played in Japan during the 2010–11 season at the age of forty-two. Bet he can still shoot.

When Stanley went in for his meeting, Coach told him, "Stanley, I think you've done just about everything you can do at LSU. Maybe it's time for you to move on." It really was disappointing to Coach Brown that Stanley was out drinking and blowing off class and hanging with his girlfriend.

Stanley was the rebellious type. He told Coach Brown, "I'm not leaving yet."

Stanley thought Coach Brown was trying to run him out so they could feature me in the offense. My dad was talking to Dale Brown all the time, calling him and telling him I needed more shots, more playing time, so maybe that was true.

Stanley had to take a summer course, and when the professor failed him that pretty much decided it. He had already missed the NBA draft, so he went to play ball in Spain.

With Stanley and Chris gone, now I really was the Big Man on

Campus. I spent a lot of time talking with Bo Bahnsen, who worked for LSU and whose job it was to make sure I wasn't breaking any rules that could get us in trouble with the NCAA.

Bo was cool. I gave him a run for his money. I nicknamed him "No Bo," because that was my answer every time he thought I was up to something.

The NCAA was on my case a lot. Everything was under suspicion. They wondered how I got my shitbox Bronco car. They checked my parents' credit and asked, "How can he afford it?"

What they didn't know was I bought that car used. I paid $5,000 for it, and it didn't even have an engine. It cost me another $1,000 to get one. I had what they call a balloon payment. I put a thousand down from my Pell Grant, which was completely legal, and I mortgaged the other $5,000. I paid $50 a month, and at the end I was going to have a huge payment due, but I figured by that point I'd be in the NBA.

Even though I didn't have any money, I wanted people on campus to think I did. I was The Man and I had to act the part, so I took a phone from my dorm room and I put a phony wire underneath my Bronco and pretended I had a car phone. I used to drive around pretending to talk to everybody on it. Of course someone saw me with it and called Bo, and he came down and I had to show him it was phony. "Don't tell the ladies," I told Bo, giving him a wink. He promised he wouldn't.

The other thing I did was when I got my Pell Grant, which was about $2,500, I'd take it in five one-hundred-dollar bills and the rest in ones. Then I'd put it in one fat bankroll and drive around campus with this big wad of cash. It looked like it was a hell of a lot more than it was, because most of those bills were Washingtons, not Benjamins. But nobody knew that because I'd wrap that wad with the big bills on the outside. I'd pull out my stash and wave it around and say, "Should I stay, or go pro?" Naturally, Bo had to come and see me about that, too.

"Bo," I'd tell him again, "I ain't done nothing. It's all an act."

The truth is, it could have been a lot worse and Bo knew it. I kept up academically. He didn't have to jump on me for that. He dealt with all sorts of athletes who couldn't be bothered. He told me one of his athletes gave up school for Lent.

A bunch of us on the team got to be friendly with this guy who owned a bar called The Tiger. We'd go there a lot and hang out and have fun. Once in a while, I'd jump behind the counter and become the bartender. That prompted another phone call and another visit from Bo, who was making sure I didn't have an illegal job and I wasn't drinking any alcohol, since I was underage.

No Bo. No on both counts.

To this day I still don't drink, smoke, or do drugs. I've never been arrested, either, although I was "detained" once in college.

LSU had always been a football school. The football players walked around saying it. But we were winning a lot more than they were, so we walked around saying, "This is a basketball school."

We all used to mess around with the same girls, so you knew that was going to be a problem eventually. There was this one girl named Tiffany Broussard, and everyone loved her. She was bragging about being involved with a football player, and I was trying to be with her, so I said, "Screw the football guys. Check their record. See what we've done. Basketball is king on this campus."

The football player Tiffany liked was Anthony Marshall. He was about six foot three or four, a fairly big guy—unless he was standing next to me. So Anthony wanted to talk to me about what I said to Tiffany.

We all lived in Broussard Hall. I'm in Anthony's room, and he's got about four or five of his boys in there with him. We start arguing about Tiffany, and they start to gather around me, so I follow my motto—hit first, ask questions later—and I pop Anthony Marshall in the mouth. Then I run down the stairs. The basketball players lived on the bottom floor in the corner, and I needed some backup.

The five football guys are chasing after me, and I get to my room and close the door, and now almost the whole football team is outside my door chanting my name. I was scared, because I was in my room all by myself.

Eventually they get the door open, and four or five of them run in and they're about to destroy me when I say, "If Anthony wants to fight, then let us fight. You really need all this help to take me on?"

I got a couple of shots in (and so did he) before I got him in a head-lock. By then the campus police was there and the football coach had come flying in, screaming, "Stop hitting my players!" He's in my face shouting at me, "This is all your fault!" The next thing you know, Coach Brown is on the scene and he grabbed me and got me out of there. There are TV cameras rolling and the football players are getting arrested and it's a big mess.

For my role in everything, I was "detained" by the police. Anthony and I had to shake hands. Everyone was trying to downplay the foot-ball versus basketball thing, but it was real. There was a lot of tension between the two teams.

So Dale said to me, "You need to get your own place off campus." The next semester I moved in with Dennis Tracey, whose claim to fame was that he was an LSU walk-on. One day Dale was having trouble finding someone to shut down Charles Smith from George-town, so he put Dennis in the game. Dennis did a great job on Charles Smith, and Dale ending up giving him a scholarship.

Dennis was a smart guy. He was older than me, and we became good friends. He also became my personal manager for a while. We lived together in this little house with a pool in the backyard. Dennis had a pair of boxing gloves, so we started boxing—with one glove each. Those were really fun days.

During the 1990–91 season I was the first player to lead the SEC in scoring, rebounding, field goal percentage, and blocks. In Decem-ber of that season, we beat Arkansas State and I scored 53 points—including, by the way, 17 of 21 from the free-throw line.

We also beat Kentucky and Arizona, which was the number two team in the country at the time. I was finally on the national radar.

Vernel was our second option, and our guard Mike Hansen also averaged in double figures, but we all knew who was getting the ball when the game was on the line.

Coach Brown was on me to make sure I didn't blow it. I was never late for practice, but once in a while I missed a class. One morning I'm sound asleep in my room and there's this loud knock on my door. It's four thirty in the morning. I get out of bed and there's Coach Brown standing there. He said to me, "Did you miss class yesterday?"

I'm half asleep but I say, "Yes sir."

He says, "Well, then, c'mon, son. Put your shoes on. We're going for a run."

I couldn't believe it. "Right now, Coach?"

"Right now, Shaquille," he said. "Let's go."

After that, I didn't miss too many more classes.

By the end of my sophomore season we had tied for the SEC regular season championship, and we had one game left before the tournament.

I injured my leg and it was really killing me. All we had to do was beat Mississippi State and we'd win the SEC outright, so Coach Brown says, "What do you think?" I told him I could play, but the truth was there was really something wrong with my leg.

Dale decided to sit me out. "Shaq, I don't want you to risk it," he said.

We lost to Mississippi State and everyone was furious. Coach also sat me out against Auburn in the SEC tournament, and we lost that game, too.

Coach Brown and the trainer, Doc Broussard, really got into it. The trainer thought Dale was trying to be a doctor. But Coach Brown told him, "I'm not. I'm just trying to protect his career. I'd never forgive myself if something happened to Shaquille that stopped him from going to the next level."

Doc Broussard was from the old school, worse than my father. I remember once Wayne Sims got popped in the face, and his lip was split open and he was bleeding all over the place and he needed stitches, but Doc said, "You're all right, you sissy. Get back in the game."

He was hard-core, a mean bastard. I kept telling him, "Every time I put pressure on my foot, it really hurts." In fact, I had an MRI afterward and they said it was a hairline fracture.

When Coach Brown told him I wasn't playing against Mississippi State, Broussard said, "This is the first time since Pistol Pete Maravich we can win the SEC championship and this wimp won't go. He's just saving himself to go pro."

Dale said, "No, he wouldn't do that."

While they're arguing our team is on the court warming up. I'm not out there, so the Mississippi State fans started chanting, "Where's your big-lipped African? Where's your big-lipped African?"

Coach Brown went crazy when he heard it. Mississippi State's fans had done this before. The previous year someone wrote an article on Chris Jackson and how he never knew his father, so when our team ran out for warm-ups, they started chanting, "Where's your dad? Who's your dad?"

Dale went to the PA announcer and ordered them to stop. The game hadn't even started and already everyone was all riled up. Coach Brown got on his radio show that night and blasted Mississippi State, their coach, their fans, their president. That's why we loved Coach. He always had our backs.

I was still injured when the NCAA tournament started, but I gave it my best shot. I had 27 points and 16 rebounds, but we lost to UConn. Mike Hansen had gotten mononucleosis, so he wasn't himself, either.

Doc Broussard was wrong about me. I didn't declare for the NBA draft that spring. I wasn't ready. I hadn't even started taking my business classes yet. I knew how to balance a checkbook, but that was about it. I needed to learn about making a living in case this basketball thing didn't work out. I needed an education.

Coach Brown had already started talking to me about playing

professionally. He could see I was going to be dominant and eventually go to the NBA, so he started exposing me to all sorts of different people. I remember one morning I was asleep in my dorm room and I heard some noise and I woke up and I was kind of fuzzy, but I see this old guy talking to me, and it's John Wooden. He was friends with Dale Brown, and he came to talk to me about teamwork and the pride of playing for one's school. I think what he was really trying to do was to convince me to stay in college for all four years. I certainly respected Coach Wooden and everything he stood for, but I still had to do what I had to do.

Another time Dale brought in Kareem to teach me a sky hook. He brought in Bill Walton, who later told reporters I reminded him of Charles Barkley because of my "raw power." My father heard about these visits and wanted to know why Dale was encouraging me to shoot a hook shot.

"He's a power player," my dad told my coach. "I want him to dunk."

Dale got me on the phone with Julius Erving, my childhood idol. He brought Olympic sprinter Carl Lewis in. Coach Brown loved Carl Lewis. Carl told us, "You know, growing up we've all got dreams and we all want to be All-Americans, but wanting that and willing that to happen are two completely different things."

I was an All-American after my sophomore year. The Associated Press and UPI named me National Player of the Year, but I didn't win the Wooden Award or the Naismith Award. Larry Johnson of Nevada–Las Vegas won both of those, so he was on my hit list.

When I started my junior season in 1991, I had an idea it would be my final year of college. I averaged 21 points and 14 rebounds a game, which was second in the nation. I led the country with 5.3 blocks, but again someone else won the Naismith and the Wooden ahead of me. This time it was Duke center Christian Laettner.

The first time I played against Laettner, in February 1991 in Durham, North Carolina, he completely destroyed me. He embarrassed me. He back-doored me to death and walked off with 24 points and

11 boards. I had never heard of him. I remember asking, "Who the hell is this guy?" He fundamentally undressed me, so after that, I was keeping an eye on him.

Coach got us a rematch the next season, my final year at LSU, and a week before the game I strained my calf muscle. I was really sore, but I had to play because people were talking about Laettner and Georgetown center Alonzo Mourning with a little more breath than they were about me, and I couldn't have that. I just had to be the No. 1 pick.

I taped up my calf and I took it to Laettner. Hard. I dropped 25 and 12 on him and I blocked 7 shots, but they came from behind and won. I'll never forget Laettner's face when I was dunking on him. He looked terrified. I was talking all sorts of trash to him, too.

Years later I played with him in Miami and discovered he was a really nice guy. I didn't know. Back in college, I hated everyone from Duke. I knew people who went to Duke had to be smart. I knew I wasn't that smart. Growing up where I did, I never learned all those words they put on those entrance exams.

I broke the LSU school record for blocked shots in my final season, and they presented me with the ball before one of our games. My parents always sat in the same place, right behind the student section, so I turned to my father, pointed to him, and threw him the ball.

The reason I did that was because whenever I was a kid and won a trophy, he'd let me take it home and admire it. I'd get up the next morning and go to school, and the trophy would be gone by the time I got home. When I asked him where it was, he'd tell me, "That's over. History. Go win another one."

The commemorative ball was my latest trophy, so I threw it to him to let him know I remembered.

Some student jumped up in front of my dad and snagged the ball. You should have seen Sarge's face. The kid was smart enough to hand it over to him.

All of our games were sold out in '91–'92. Students were camping outside the gym the night before to get tickets. I was signing auto-graphs all over the state of Louisiana. A family in Baton Rouge named their newborn son after me, so I showed up at their house, unannounced, to take some pictures.

The people at LSU get this great idea to print up these T-shirts with a drawing of me doing my signature dunk where I'm hanging on the rim with my legs kicked up like Rony Seikaly.

They printed up a whole bunch of these T-shirts and were going to sell them during one of our games. I don't really know anything about it, but when Sarge walks into the arena and sees those T-shirts, he loses it.

One thing about my father is he's not going to let anyone take advantage of our family.

We were in our locker room, and Coach Brown was delivering his pregame speech when *boom!* The door flies open, and here comes Sarge. He's eyes are popping out of his head, he's so pissed off. He's got one of the T-shirts in his hands and he's shouting, "What the fuck is this about? What makes you think this is all right?"

He told Dale, "We could be taking money. We've been offered plenty of stuff through the years, but we haven't done it that way. We've done it the right way. And now you're going to make money off my son? I got a big problem with that."

Everyone is quiet. No one is saying a thing. I'm more than a little embarrassed. Everyone knows your parents aren't allowed in the locker room before the game. But Sarge has got a point.

Next thing I know, he's telling Coach Brown that unless the T-shirts are taken down and put away, I wasn't going to play in the game. Now I've got my head down. I want to disappear.

But Coach Brown is really good. He's used to dealing with Sarge. He gets him calmed down. The T-shirts disappear. I play in the game. We avoid a major meltdown.

Bo spends a good part of my final season driving to the mall and handing out "cease and desist" orders to stores who were making and marketing their own Shaq Attack T-shirts.

By then teams were having trouble stopping me, so they were fouling me on purpose. Sometimes, the fouls crossed the line from a "hard" foul to downright dirty. Coach Brown told me, "Don't take all that abuse. If they try to hurt you, I'm giving you permission to hit them back."

We played Tennessee in the first round of the SEC tournament that spring. We were up by 22 points, and I was dominating this guy named Carlus Groves. I got the ball in the post, and he grabbed me and jerked me backward and tried to haul me down. I was so mad I wanted to break his jaw. I went to push him off my back and all hell broke loose.

Next thing I know Coach Brown is out there going right for Groves. When I saw him I thought, *Wow, he's sticking up for me.* After the game he called the NCAA and told them, "Hey, if you don't want these guys to get hurt you better do something, because I'm going to tell Shaquille to play with his elbows up from now on. He's getting killed out there, and you are always blaming him."

Of course, meanwhile he's telling me to keep my composure and don't let these other players goad me into doing something stupid.

The refs threw me, Groves, and nine other players out of the game. Not only that, but I was suspended from playing in our semifinal game against Kentucky. I was hot. Some guy purposely tries to hurt me, and *I* have to pay the price? Tennessee's SEC season was over because we beat them. So what penalty did they get?

Coach Brown was so mad about the suspension he was going to sit out the game and pull our team in protest. I told him I appreciated it, but I thought he should be out there. He really wrestled with it, but in the end he did coach the game. We lost to Kentucky 80–74.

My final season at LSU ended with a loss to Indiana in the second round of the NCAA tournament. They were a higher seed than us, but it didn't stop people from wondering why LSU didn't go further in the tournament with Shaquille O'Neal.

All I can tell you is, in my final college game I had 36 points,

12 rebounds, and 5 blocks. I was also a perfect 12 of 12 from the free-throw line, so what else could I do?

Indiana was the kind of slow-down, motion offense team that always bothered us. They kind of lulled us to sleep. We liked that fast-paced up-and-down style.

Right after we lost, in March 1992, I left campus. I did it quietly, without saying much at all.

There were three months to go before the draft. Three months to get into trouble. Everybody knew I was going pro. It was the worst secret out there. But I've always been what I call Spooky Wook about these kind of things. Kind of superstitious—afraid of what could go wrong.

So, the best thing I could do was leave campus. It kept me away from girls, partying, drinking, weed. I had been successful in staying away from most of that stuff. Why chance it now? I also knew if I was around Sarge and my mother I wouldn't even be tempted, so I went home.

I remember taking one last look at the LSU campus when I pulled out of there in my cranky old Ford Bronco II. I was a little sad, a little nostalgic.

But then I closed my eyes and started dreaming about which car I'd be driving the next time I came on campus. When I opened them up again, I was smiling.

It was time to go.

NBA Draft Lottery

Secaucus, New Jersey

O rlando Magic president Pat Williams stuffed the plastic bag with the Shaquille O'Neal jersey under his seat. He wasn't alone. All eleven men representing their franchises in the NBA draft lottery had printed up a team jersey with Shaq's name embossed in big letters above their respective logos. There was a Dallas Shaq jersey, a Milwaukee Shaq jersey, a Washington Shaq jersey.

With ten of the sixty-six Ping-Pong balls in the mix bearing Orlando's name, the Magic had just over a 15 percent chance of landing the big fella.

One by one, the draft order was revealed. The Houston Rockets were stuck with No. 11 and a Shaq jersey that was instantly rendered useless. The Atlanta Hawks suffered a similar fate when their logo popped up at No. 10. As the Shaq sweepstakes dwindled to five, Mavericks owner Donald Carter caressed his lucky coyote tooth, but it yielded him only the fourth overall pick.

Finally, there were three teams left standing—Charlotte, Minnesota, and Orlando.

When the card for the No. 3 pick was turned over to reveal the Minnesota Timberwolves, Shaquille O'Neal squealed with delight. He was watching the proceedings from the Brentwood, California, home of his agent, Leonard Armato, and while he had no specific preference, his only wish was to play in a warm weather city.

"Excellent," Armato said, once Minnesota was eliminated. "Now we don't have to pull a power play to get you out of there."

"Charlotte and Orlando? I can live with either one of those," Shaq agreed.

When Orlando's number came up as No. 1, Pat Williams's heart skipped two beats. He reached under the table for his Shaq jersey and skipped up to the stage, mindful of the warning David Stern had issued before the draft lottery began.

"Gentle hugs," Stern demanded. Two years earlier, he'd received a crushing squeeze to the ribs from towering New Jersey Nets executive Willis Reed when he landed the rights to draft Derrick Coleman.

Shaq leaned back on Armato's couch. He shook his agent's hand, then embraced Dennis Tracey, his LSU teammate and new manager.

"Orlando," Tracey said. "Home of Disney World."

"Look out, Mickey Mouse," Shaq said, grinning. "I'm coming for you."

A COUPLE OF WEEKS BEFORE THE DRAFT LOTTERY I GOT TO meet Mr. David Stern, the commissioner of the NBA. His question to me was, "Where do you want to play?" Now I don't want to create no conspiracy theory, but I told him, "Definitely where it's hot."

Orlando was hot, and so was I.

I was excited about the NBA—and all the money that was coming with it—but I was also still thinking about LSU. I was kind of scared to tell Dale Brown I was leaving. One night I called him about eleven thirty. He said, "I already know what you're calling about. You are right, you've got to go. They're hammering you so hard out there in the college game you should leave before you get hurt and can't play anymore."

I was so relieved. I really didn't want to let Coach Brown down. The last thing he said was "Please be safe. Drive slowly. Go home and think about it. If you want me to come out there to Texas when you make your announcement, let me know and I will."

Because I left campus without telling anyone, I didn't follow the "proper procedures" of withdrawal from LSU. As a result, my pal Bo Bahnsen confiscated my deposit. All these years later, the first thing I say when I see him is, "Yo, Bo. Where's my fifty dollars?"

Once I got home to San Antonio, we started talking with agents. Coach Brown was the one who introduced me to Leonard Armato. Just before I left campus this guy—I forget his name—came up to me, slipped me his card, and said, "If you sign with me, I'll get you whatever you want. Let's start with $250,000." He was from Southern California and he scared the crap out of me.

Leonard came out to meet my family. He was a former college

point guard and Coach Brown trusted him, but my father warned him, "If you mess with my son, I'll kill you."

"He's serious," I told Leonard. "Don't doubt it."

I was about to become a professional athlete, but my daddy was still standing over me, larger than life, bigger than ever. What I didn't realize was that was never going to change. Philip Harrison couldn't—wouldn't—stay in the background. He just didn't know how.

When I got back home to the army base in San Antonio, I was living with my parents again, and that was an adjustment. It was a flashback. It was "yes sir, no sir" again. It was "turn down the music" again. It was "watch your language, son" again (that's my mother).

But everything was about to change. My parents, who had taken care of me and kept me out of trouble (most of the time), were about to have their roles reversed.

It was finally time for me to take care of them.

In April 1992, even though I hadn't been drafted yet and I had no idea which team I'd be playing for, I got some money from an endorsement for Classic Car. They paid me $1 million. I could not believe it.

I was rich!

I managed to blow through it all in two days.

The first thing I did was take care of some matters on the home front. Both my mom and my dad had terrible credit, so I took out $150,000 and paid that off. I'm rich. I can do these things.

The next thing I did was go to the Mercedes-Benz dealer and buy myself a car. I came home and my dad said, "Where's mine?" so I went back and bought him one, too. And, of course, I've got to make sure my mother is cruising around town in style, so now I've bought three Mercedes-Benz cars in one week.

I then got a call from the bank. The man was very nice. He said, "Mr. O'Neal, I don't want bad things to happen to you like other athletes we've dealt with. But I think you should know you owe us ninety thousand dollars."

At first I was confused, but then he explained to me by the time you take that $1 million and deduct all the taxes, it really is only worth between $500,000 and $600,000. Damn. I hung up the phone and I told my mother, "I need an accountant."

Leonard helped me set up the meetings. The first person, believe it or not, was the actor Wayne Rogers, the guy who starred in the television show *M*A*S*H*. He came in and told me, "We're going to get you this and get you that," and all I could think of was that book about Kareem that my dad gave me and how he lost his money in soybeans and if something appears too good to be true, then it probably is.

Scratch off the *M*A*S*H* dude. Another guy came in wearing a two-thousand-dollar suit, and he was too slick. The next guy was wearing a cheap suit, and even though I'm fresh out of college and I don't know anything about mortgages or money markets or municipal bonds, I still know a decent suit when I see one—or don't see one.

We talked to a lot of people with their fancy brochures and their big plans, but none of them hit me right. I was getting tired and cranky and hungry (I'm always hungry) when this little guy with curly hair and glasses walks in.

We tell him to put his brochure over on the desk with the rest of the pile and he says, "I don't have a brochure." His name is Lester Knispel and he starts talking to me about savings bonds. He talked about potential investments, but mostly he was very conservative in his presentation. At one point he said, "We can learn together how this should work."

Here's what made my mom fall in love with him. She asked every other guy about letting her see the books. She told them I was young and she wanted to help me along. They all said, "Mrs. Harrison, trust us. We do this for a living. Let us take care of it. You don't have to worry or bother with it. It's our job."

Now if you tell that to Lucille you might mean well, but all she's hearing is "Butt out, Mom." And that's not going to work.

Lester was smarter than that. He told my mother, "You can see the books anytime you want. Same with Shaquille. You are the client.

I would be working for you." He was no dummy. He knew all the numbers and figures were complicated and boring, and after a while my mother would learn to trust him and wouldn't want to be bothered with poring over my stuff. And that is exactly what happened.

I liked Lester because he was straightforward and very smart and not too slick. Not only that, he represented some rappers.

We hired Lester Knispel, and it was the beginning of a beautiful friendship. Lester was my sounding board. When I got one of my crazy ideas, he talked me out of it—most of the time. When I started buying too many cars, handing out money to too many relatives, and going off the edge in general, he reeled me back in.

He was very successful and he had saved a lot of money, so I asked him how he and his family did so well. He told me, "We have annuities." I asked, "What the hell is that?" He explained to me, "It's when you pay a life insurance company a single premium, which they will pay back years later in the form of a fixed sum."

That sounded like something I needed. When I started making all the big bucks and I had more money than I could spend, I put big hunks of it into annuities. I bought them for myself, my parents, for my brother, and for my two sisters.

What it meant was when I turned forty years old, which back then seemed like light-years into the future, I would receive a nice monthly sum for the rest of my life that would keep me in excellent financial shape. Thanks, Lester.

My father was very happy with Lester. He was also happy that I was learning how to conduct business. Sarge was proud of my basketball accomplishments, but he always threw the same thing in my face. "You aren't going to be some stupid fucking African dunking basketballs the rest of your life," he'd say. "You are smarter than that."

Well, sure. Most of the time.

I knew the big money was coming, so I told my father, "Get out of the army. Come with me." At that point both of my parents were lucky to be making $30,000 a year. I hired them both to run my fan club at $100,000 each. I said to them, "This is my gift to you."

I bought them a house in Orlando. I did what any son would do when he finally made it big and he wanted to thank his parents for their love and their support.

Lester worries about me sometimes, I know that. He says there is such a thing as being too generous. My feeling on that is you can't take it with you. My parents don't ask for much. I want them to be happy, to enjoy this time of their life. Same for my brother and sisters. My family is everything to me. Now that doesn't mean if some distant cousin from Georgia who claims we've got the same hairline shows up that he's getting put on my payroll. I'm not *that* stupid.

As the actual draft day approached, the people in Orlando were getting nervous because I hadn't said anything about their team, their city, or their players. It was a big moment for them and my silence was kind of spoiling it, I guess.

It didn't help there were rumors floating around that Leonard was going to try to pull off a trade to send me to the Lakers, which wasn't true at all, even though Leonard would have loved that.

Here is the reason I didn't say much. I'm very superstitious, and I wasn't going to talk about being the No. 1 pick until I actually was drafted as the No. 1 pick.

The Magic kept pestering us to meet with them, so finally, a couple of days before the draft, my father, my brother, Jamal, and I flew in to Orlando.

They gave me a tour, and I met with the team officials, and then they ended up having a nice dinner with the owners, the coaches, and some front-office people.

It was fine, but it had been a long day and Jamal, who was only thirteen, was bored. He started messing around a little bit at dinner. He's talking smack to me, he's drinking my water, and the next thing you know we're flicking rolls at each other. My future coach, Matt Goukas, was horrified. To be honest, I was having so much fun with

Jamal I didn't notice. When Pat Williams asked Matt Goukas later what he thought of his No. 1 pick and his brother, he said, "I wanted to send both of them to their rooms."

On draft night, Orlando jammed ten thousand people into their arena for their live announcement that they'd be selecting Shaquille O'Neal as No. 1. They had a platform and Pat Williams was going to make the call to the NBA in front of all these screaming fans, but somehow the transmission malfunctioned. They had only five minutes to make the pick and meanwhile that clock was clicking down, so Alex Martins, the public relations director, called in on his cell phone to let Stern know they were taking me.

When Orlando drafted me, that little Florida city went nuts.

We flew in from Portland, Oregon, the day after the draft and it was insane. I couldn't believe the greeting I got when I landed. People were jamming the airport terminal. The Orlando Magic mascot was there. There was a Dixieland band playing. They had some of the most beautiful cheerleaders I've ever seen lined up on both sides.

There were signs welcoming me to Orlando, signs saying, SHA-QUILLE IS NO. 1.

Pat Williams organized the whole thing. He was there and so was Bob Vander Weide, the son-in-law of Rich DeVos, who owned Amway and the Orlando Magic. Vander Weide was in basketball operations at the time, but he became president of the team a couple of years later. The team did a great job of making me feel welcome, I can tell you that.

It reminded me of how I felt when they turned that spotlight on me at the LSU football game.

Dennis Tracey and I are looking at each other and saying, "Okay, so this is what it's going to be like."

I was twenty years old.

The truth is, before that I wasn't convinced I was going to be the first pick. That was what everyone was saying, but in my mind I was thinking about Christian Laettner and how much more fundamentally sound he was than me. Even though it was supposed to be a slam dunk that I would be No. 1, I kept wondering if it would really happen, because Laettner had it all—the jumper, the footwork, the rebounding, the mental edge. Even at that point of my life, when my career was about to take off, I still wasn't 100 percent sure of my ability. I didn't share my fears with anyone, but they kept me awake at night.

My father's voice was ringing in my ears: "Stay humble, stay humble."

When it all shook down, Alonzo Mourning ended up No. 2 and Laettner ended up No. 3. I was thinking, "They got that wrong." But history tells us they got it right after all.

It was a big step for me to move to a new city, buy my own house, make my own decisions, but I was ready.

Of course my mom wanted to be near me so she could keep an eye on me. In her mind, I was still her Shaquille and she needed to protect her "little warrior." The first thing she did when I moved to Orlando was go to Walmart to buy me kitchen glasses, towels, toasters, and a bunch of other things that I probably didn't need.

I moved into my new house in September. One day we were talking to the mailman and he told us about a cornerback from the Green Bay Packers who had lost all his money and was trying to dump his place. We got my mom over there and she loved it. She would have loved anything, really. My mom wasn't that picky. So Lucille and Sarge moved in—right across the street from Bo Jackson.

My mom is such a kind, caring person and she doesn't get impressed by anything. She's sort of like my grandmother Odessa. When I got my first paycheck from the Magic I wanted to buy my grandmother a $6 million house. She said, "No, baby, there's a nice house down the road there, it will do just fine." So I bought her that house and fixed it up for her.

Same thing with my mother. When I bought her that new Mercedes, emerald green, she said, "That's nice honey, but I don't want a Benz. I'll take that little truck over there that costs twenty thousand dollars." It was a used truck! I said, "Sorry, Mom, but you are going to take this Mercedes."

Now that I had some money I wanted to buy myself some decent stereo stuff, so my mom came along with me to a place called Sound Advice. I got in there and I was like a little kid. I wanted everything! I'm telling the guy, "We'll take that TV and that turntable," and my mom is panicking and she's saying, "Son, slow down!" I tell her, "Mom, it's okay, I've got this. You want something?"

Word gets out I'm shopping in the store, and now there are fans everywhere. I'm off to the side signing autographs, and I see my mom talking to the manager. When I finally get to the counter to pay for my stuff the manager says, "Your mother has signed you up for the Lay-A-Way program." I grabbed her and gave her a big kiss and told her, "Mom, I promise. Those days are over."

Here's what happens when you are the No. 1 pick in the draft and your name is Shaquille O'Neal: you sign a $13 million deal with Pepsi, a $15 million deal with Reebok, and another $20–25 million from Kenner, Spaulding, and Scoreboard training cards.

Leonard was smart. He put us right in the middle of the cola war between Coke and Pepsi and the sneaker war between Nike and Reebok.

Obviously Nike was a giant. They had Michael Jordan, Charles Barkley, and my future neighbor Bo Jackson. They were really successful, but I wanted my own success story.

When I visited Reebok they were all standing out front waiting for me wearing T-shirts that said, WE WANT SHAQ. We had a great day with Paul Fireman, and they wanted me to sign right there. That sounded good to me, but Leonard said, "No, we promised Nike we'd visit."

I'll admit my heart wasn't in it. My father and I met Leonard on the Nike "campus" in Oregon, and I showed up wearing a Reebok jacket. All the Nike people were very friendly, but after about an hour Leonard pulled me aside and said, "Shaq, you have to take off that jacket. It's disrespectful. Phil Knight is going crazy over this."

I took off the jacket, but I was going with Reebok. From that day on, those Nike dudes have had it in for me.

The summer before I reported for my first NBA training camp, I lived in Los Angeles with Dennis Tracey. I was trying to play basketball every day. I used to see Magic Johnson all the time, and he had a little game every morning at ten at UCLA. So I figured, *I better get over there and get busy.*

Leonard knew everyone in LA, so he got me invited into the game. I showed up the first day and I was all business. Let's get to work. Tracy Murray was there and Mitchell Butler, and Magic, and Mike Dunleavy Sr.—not the son who played for the Pacers, but the father who coached the Bucks and the Lakers and the Clippers. At this point he was still playing and he was on my team. The first time down the floor I got a rebound and Dunleavy was calling for me to throw it to him, but I'm saying, "Screw that!" and I went coast to coast. Was I trying to impress people? Yes I was. I wasn't nervous at all. I went in there planning to kick some ass.

Magic was very nice to me. We didn't have a ton of conversations because I'm not a jock sniffer, but he kind of looked out for me. He gave me a lot of "Let's go, young fella." Those basketball games were really good, really competitive, and a great way to stay in shape. I played hard, but I wasn't going to show them everything—just enough so they'd all go back to their teams worried about me.

So life is good. Better than good. I'm soaking it all in. I'm in Los Angeles, but not La La Land. I'm having fun, I'm a millionaire, and I know more is coming, so I'm living on the edge a little bit. I'm buying stuff I shouldn't buy, like cars and clothes and toys.

When I go to those pickup games at UCLA, I'm walking in there thinking I'm a bad dude, but I'm not. I mean, Magic is there. He's in charge. I'm just another guy.

Magic is picking the teams and keeping score. He's there every morning running the show. In the games, he'd come at you with some bullshit move, and when he missed he'd yell "Foul!" We'd all roll our eyes, but he was Magic, so he got the call—just like in the real NBA.

I'd known him a few years, and I was at his charity event, the Midsummer Night's Magic. I had just won MVP, and he said to me, "Big

fella, you don't want to be just a name. You want to own things."
Then he walked away.

I'm driving home and I'm wondering the whole time, *What was he talking about?* And then I realized what he meant. So we got to work on my own shoe. Then my own clothing line. Then my own reality show. Thanks, Magic. Another idea I incorporated into my own unique Shaq style.

I handled things a little different than the other top picks. A lot of them had expensive cars and multiple houses right away. The first summer after I got drafted, Dennis Tracey and I lived in Oakwood Apartments on Sepulveda in Los Angeles. Dennis rented a Volvo, and that's how we rolled all summer.

We lived near all these fabulous clubs but we couldn't get into any of them because I was too young. The Roxy was right there, we drove by it every day, but I never went inside. I had to work my way up to that stuff.

Sarge had warned me about becoming a "sudden celebrity." All of a sudden you have friends you haven't even met before. All of a sudden people like quarterback Doug Williams wants to have lunch with you. Luckily for me, Doug Williams was cool. He just wanted me to know he was there for me if I had any questions.

I was in LA and I was starting to get hot, and I kept running into Arsenio Hall, who had a really popular nighttime talk show out there. Every time I saw him he'd say, "Why don't you come on the show?" I kept saying, "No, thanks," because I wasn't really sure what I'd talk about.

So now some of my commercials are coming out and I've just been named Rookie of the Year, and I'm getting recognized every- where and I go back to Los Angeles for the summer again. Arsenio asks me again about coming on and I was kind of joking around and I said, "Well, if I'm going to be on the show, I've got to do some- thing different. I don't want to be like all the other athletes." Arsenio said, "What do you have in mind?" Up to that moment I didn't have anything in mind, but then this popped into my head: "Can I rap on your show with my favorite group?"

He loved the idea. So we contacted Fu Schnickens, these three rappers from Brooklyn who had a great sound, and we recorded "What's Up Doc." Everyone was surprised how good it was.

Here are my favorite lines:

Forget Tony Danza, I'm the boss
When it comes to money, I'm like Dick Butkus
Now who's the first pick me, word is born and
Not Christian Laettner not Alonzo Mourning

That's okay, not being bragadocious
Supercalifrageltistic, Shaq is alidocious
Peace, I gotta go, I ain't no joke
Now I slam it
Jam it, and make sure it's broke.

Before we performed together on Arsenio's show, Fu Schnickens came to the house and recorded the song. They wanted to write my verse for me, but I did it myself.

So we go on the *Arsenio Hall Show* and I've got this red outfit on that this girl at the mall made for me. It's got glitter and the sleeves are cut off and I'm looking mighty fine. It's a live audience. We're doing this rap and you can tell everyone is really enjoying it. They thought I was going to make a fool of myself. They didn't realize before I do anything I make sure I'm prepared.

Jive Records offered me a record deal the next day. I told them, "I don't want to rap by myself. My concept is to rap with all my favorite artists." So that's what we did.

My first album, called *Shaq Diesel*, had Fu Schnickens, Phife Dawg from A Tribe Called Quest, and Erick Sermon. It went platinum, which means we sold a million records. I also did a song with

Def Jef called "(I Know I Got) Skillz" that made it to number 35 on the Billboard Hot 100.

It was a lot of work, but I loved it. Now I'm a basketball star and a rapper and a movie star (more on that in a minute). My worlds are all mixed together, in some ways. In *Shaq Diesel* I had some fun taking swipes at Larry Johnson, Greg Anthony, and Shawn Kemp. It wasn't anything personal. That's what freelance rap is all about.

The first word I learned in the music business was *recouping*. When we did the first record they wanted to do everything for me—the mixes, the lyrics. We had to record in their studios. Before you get any money for your record, they have to "recoup" all the money for the studio. By the time everyone took their cut, I had a check for sixty thousand dollars left. My album went platinum, but all I got was chump change. I remember saying to Dennis, "Are you kidding me?"

I got smarter after that. I made sure I had control of my masters and my songs. When they said, "Come to this studio to tape," I'd tell them, "I don't want to pay you guys to use this studio. I'll use my own."

My next album, *Shaq Fu: Da Return*, came out in 1994. I got help from RZA and Method Man on that one.

The song that got the most attention was one called "Biological Didn't Bother."

I was in Chicago on business and I was walking down the street and some guy said to me, "Yo, man. That's messed up. How come you don't talk to your dad?" I didn't know what the hell he was talking about, so I called my mother because I figured Phil had gone and said something. I asked her, "What did Daddy do? Was he on TV?" She said, "No, it was the other one."

She meant Joe Toney, the person who insisted he was my father even though I had not seen him since I was a little boy. He had gone on the *Ricki Lake Show* and complained that I wouldn't have anything to do with him and all he wanted was for me to meet my half brother. I contacted the producers and got a copy of the tape and I watched it. I was really angry about it. My thing is, why is this man coming off like he knows me or cares about me? From zero to eighteen I had practically no contact with you. Now you want to tell me about your other kids? I didn't want people to know about my biological father. It was part of my past I'd just as soon have forgotten and a very painful part of my mother's past. I didn't want to talk about it. And now this dude is bringing it up on national television.

My uncle Mike was with me on that trip, and on the plane back to Orlando I wrote a rap called "Biological Didn't Bother." The hook was, "You took me from a boy to a man." It was my way of telling Sarge I appreciated his tough love. It started out this way:

Yo, Yo, I want to dedicate this song to Philip Arthur Harrison
Word up, 'cause he was the one who took me from a boy to a man
So as far as I'm concerned, he's my father
'Cause my biological didn't bother.

I don't know what Joe Toney expects when he walks out on an eighteen-year-old girl and her newborn baby. He's living in an old folks' home now and he still tries to send messages to me but I can't deal with that. I'm loyal. Phil Harrison made me who I am, for better or for worse. That's it. It's nothing personal. Philip Harrison is my father and my daddy. Period. Point-blank. If it wasn't for him, I don't know where I'd be. So leave us alone, okay? Pretty simple, I think.

I loved making rap records and I made some money, but it was tip money compared to my basketball salary. It was a great experience, but I wasn't going to make a living doing it.

People loved my first record and everything was cool, but sooner or later it was bound to happen. The industry hate started to kick in. Rappers started resenting my success. They were saying, "You're a professional athlete, what are you doing in our world?" I could feel the tide turning.

When *Shaq Diesel* came out, everybody played it. But now I've got my second record and I've got to travel to all these radio stations and studios to promote it. They've got a million basketballs lined up for me and if I don't sign them, they won't play the record.

The first time around everyone wanted to record something with me. Now all of a sudden they're calling up and saying they'll do it but they want $200,000.

There were two guys who weren't like that. Biggie Smalls and Jay-Z couldn't have been nicer. They did it for free. They told me, "Man, I love your work. You are a real rapper."

Biggie Smalls was the nicest dude in the world. He was an absolute master in the studio. The other guys would come to the house to record and they'd be there all night. They'd go over it and over it and chop it and change it. I always had my verse prepared ahead of time, because I didn't want to tie them up. I'd be working on my verses on the plane after a game. Dennis Scott, my best friend on the Orlando Magic, would help me with the beats.

When Biggie came, I went in and took about an hour to do my verse. He listened to it and said, "That's tight. That's tight." Then he said, "Are you ready for me?" I handed him a pen and some paper and he said, "I don't write, dawg."

He went in my studio and came out fifteen minutes later with an amazing rap. The problem was, it was too vulgar. I told him, "Hey Biggie, we've got to think about the kids," so he went back in and came out another fifteen minutes later with something even better.

Jay-Z was the same way. A total pro. He appeared on my album *You Can't Stop the Reign*. That album was loaded with major stars, including Mobb Deep, DJ Quik, and Notorious B.I.G., also known as Biggie Smalls.

Biggie was amazed by all I had. By then I had moved into my sixty-four-thousand-square-foot dream house in Orlando, and he said, "I'm going to have all of this one day. I'm going to be the best."

He would have been, too. He was young and talented and ambitious. Every time we saw each other, we gave each other love.

The last time I saw him was on March 8, 1997. We were celebrating my birthday, and I was in a cast. I was riding on Sunset

Boulevard and there was a big traffic jam. Biggie could be kind of volatile, and he was having all these verbal altercations with people, so Uncle Jerome Crawford (he was my bodyguard) and I stopped and got out and said, "Biggie, what the hell are you doing?"

He smiled and said, "Stay cool, Shaq. I'm just getting a tattoo. I'm having a party later. Make sure you come, brother." I told him, "Okay, we're going to roll. See you later." We bumped fists and I took off.

Biggie was presenting at the Soul Train Music Awards and then going to the after-party at the Peterson Automotive Museum.

I had every intention of going to that party. I put on my white suit and my white hat. I was going to be a player that night. But I was damn tired, too. I sat down to watch some television and I fell asleep. I left my pager in the car, so when Dennis and Jerome tried to contact me, the pager was going off in my car while I was upstairs snoring.

My mom was the one who finally got hold of me. She woke me up at 4:00 a.m. and said, "Shaquille, did you go to the party?" I was half-asleep and I didn't know what she was talking about, and then she said, "Your friend's been shot. He's dead."

It took me a minute to process what she was saying. When I finally realized what happened, I closed my eyes and there Biggie was—sitting in the tattoo parlor making noise, smiling at me, banging fists with me, telling me, "See you later, bro."

They never found his killer. With these rap wars, they never do. Biggie left the party and got in the front seat of the car, and some dude wearing a bow tie drove up alongside him and shot him four times. They said it was part of the East Coast versus West Coast rap feud that had been going on forever. Tupac Shakur, one of Biggie's friends-turned-rivals, died the same way—in a drive-by shooting.

I don't usually deal in what-ifs, but after Biggie died I spent a lot of time wondering how it would have been different if I had showed up at that party. If a seven-foot-one Shaquille O'Neal was standing by that car, would the guy still have pulled the trigger? Jerome is trained to make sure he protects me and those around me. I just feel if we were there, maybe something different would have happened. But maybe they were going to get Biggie no matter what. If it wasn't that night, it probably would have been one or two or three nights later.

The rap world is violent. Lots of guys, before they got into the rap game, lived their lives on the edge. Gunplay and drugs are a part of everyday life in their world. You can't hide from it. It's part of them. When you bring groceries up the steps to your apartment, it's there. When you visit your cousin, it's there. When you go to play ball in the park, it's there. I can understand it because I saw the same kind of scene every day in Newark, New Jersey. If you don't break away from it, it will break you.

I really believe people had the wrong idea about Biggie. When he was doing his raps, his art, there was anger and bad language and violence. But a lot of that was an act. His life wasn't perfect. He had some troubles, got mixed up with drugs. But when you met him he was just the sweetest guy, very polite, very humble.

I miss him.

By the time my fourth rap record came out, the critics were after me. They were saying, "If Shaq weren't a superstar his rap albums wouldn't sell." Well that's a brilliant observation. What's your point, brother?

Once the politics of it kicked in, I realized there wasn't enough money in it for me to bother. I didn't need it. It was a dream and I got to live it. I had one platinum record, two gold records, and one wood record. Time to move on.

Of course people were killing me for doing all these things while I was playing basketball. What they didn't understand was it never interfered with my workouts. I was also doing movies, and it was written into my contract that we couldn't start shooting before noon or one o'clock. The morning was reserved for my workouts. Leonard arranged for me to play at a little gym in Manhattan Beach, and we'd go over there and run through drills and shoot. Leonard was a very good shooter. He understood what it took to keep sharp, to stay on top of your game.

That didn't stop people from saying, "There's no way he's concentrating on basketball while he's doing all this stuff." They were entitled to their opinions, but I was trying to build something for the future. I was trying to establish my brand. There are certain opportunities you just can't turn down. If *Esquire* wants you to be on the cover, you gotta do it.

If William Friedkin calls up and asks you to star in a movie, you do it. He was directing a basketball story with the actor Nick Nolte and he wanted me in it. The truth is, I had no idea who William Friedkin was. They told me he did great movies like *The French Connection* and *The Exorcist*, and I'm wondering, "Why does a guy like him want to do a basketball movie?"

He and Nick Nolte came by the house to talk to me about the movie. They said lots of athletes would be in it, but I would be the star. I told them I had never acted before, and they said they would get me a coach. That was important to me, because I didn't want to make a fool of myself.

Actually, I was more than amazed someone would ask me to do a movie, since I had a stuttering problem my whole life. I still do. I'm just cool with it now. I know how to slow myself down and get the words out.

My father stutters, too. I don't where he got it and I don't know how I got it, either. It was a problem for me when I was little. Kids made fun of me. I was self-conscious about it.

I just kept quiet so people wouldn't notice. In class the teacher would say, "Anyone want to read the first paragraph for us? Shaquille?" I would just smile and shake my head.

I'll take the zero. I was too embarrassed to stammer in front of the other kids.

When I got to LSU, I met this gentleman named Tommy Karam. He's still there. I called him the Senator. He was a very smart guy and he was one of my professors. He used to tell me, "You're a special kid, Shaquille. If you ever need help with a speech class or with the media interviews, I'll help you."

One summer I met with him every day. He'd pretend he was from the media and he'd ask me all sorts of tough questions so I'd know what to expect. He was very patient with me. If I started stuttering, he sat there very calmly until I spit it out and then he'd wait and say, "Let's try it again."

He helped me a lot and I've never forgotten it. When I was delivering my lines on the set of *Blue Chips*, all the things he taught me came rushing back: slow down, take your time, relax.

My movies were not what you'd call award-winning. But doing *Blue Chips* was a blast. It's where I met Penny Hardaway, and why I pressured the Orlando Magic to draft him instead of Chris Webber. Bill Friedkin was a very cool guy. He was a Celtics fan, and back when all the fans could own stock in the team he bought some. He was very excited to show me his stock certificates.

Friedkin told me, "Whatever you need. Just ask." They put me up at the Beverly Hills Hilton, and it was nice enough but a little run-down. So when Bill asked me if everything was okay, I told him I wanted to change hotels. He put me up at the Four Seasons. That worked, because I had found out Arnold Schwarzenegger was there, and I wanted to meet the Terminator.

Bob Cousy was on the set and he was amazing. He plays an athletic director in the movie. In one scene he's talking to Nick Nolte and he's shooting free throws and he's hit twenty in a row, and Nick Nolte says, "Do you ever miss?" and Couz deadpans, "No," and then he hits another one. They did it in one take. He got a standing ovation. Now there's a Hall of Famer for you.

Thankfully they only asked me to hit one free throw in the movie, not twenty-one. Hell, I didn't have that kind of time.

The next movie I shot was called *Kazaam*. I played a genie who lives in a boom box and grants a little boy three wishes. The critics absolutely destroyed the movie, but every single person I met on the street told me they took their children to *Kazaam* and they absolutely loved it. I'd go through airports, and kids would run up to me and shout "Kazaam!" with the biggest ole smiles on their faces, and it made me laugh. Every time.

After I finished *Kazaam* I get a call from the legendary Quincy Jones, who wants to turn me into the first black superhero. So I did a movie called *Steel*. I wasn't allowed to tell anyone at the time, but I did all my own stunts, which included running through fire and jumping across a couple of buildings.

I'm not even twenty-five years old and I'm a basketball star, a rapper, a movie star, and an endorsement king. It happened so fast, sometimes I couldn't believe it.

Ahmad Rashad has this show called *Inside Stuff*, so my first summer as a pro he asked me to come on. We're at the Sports Club in Los Angeles, and Dennis Tracey is with me and Ahmad is playing me one-on-one and he's barking at me, "Let me see your best. Let me see your best!" So I blow past him and dunked that thing so hard and the whole backboard shattered. It knocked me right on my ass. For a second, I wasn't really sure what happened. I got up and I had some blood on my elbows. Dennis looked like he was going to pass out. He was petrified that his meal ticket had just shredded both of his arms! I waited a second and then I started smiling. It's cool, dawg. I'm fine.

Pretty soon everyone is watching that dunk on the Internet.

They hadn't seen nothing yet.

APRIL 23, 1993

The Meadowlands

Newark, New Jersey

Orlando shooting guard Anthony Bowie dribbled the ball down the left side of the floor, aware that Shaquille O'Neal was filling the lane on the weak side and advancing to the basket. As he released the pass to his rookie big man, he noted, "They've lost track of him. What a mistake."

Shaq took one hard dribble to the hole past Nets forward Derrick Coleman, then rose up to dunk the ball. Seven-footer Dwayne Schintzius grabbed his arm as he rose up to slam it through, requiring O'Neal to drag New Jersey's big man along for the ride.

Shaq hung on the rim for a split second before he realized what was happening. The entire backboard was collapsing and the shot clock was about to drop on his head. He ducked as the shot clock grazed his shoulder, and the rim broke free from the stanchion and crashed in a heap.

Orlando president Pat Williams, watching from home,

winced as his prize player narrowly missed serious injury. "He's lucky he wasn't killed," Williams said.

Across the country in Los Angeles, Leonard Armato, Shaq's agent and marketing guru, couldn't contain his glee. "This is perfect!" he exalted.

Shaq feigned indifference over his show of strength, yet inside, he was seething. The dunk was a message to Coleman, who had been talking trash to him all night and threatening to dunk on his head.

"When Shaq pulled that backboard down, it was all about respect—and one-upmanship," explained his friend Dennis Scott.

Within days Armato and Pepsi were on the phone, concocting ways to capitalize on the big man's demonstration of dominance. Pepsi drew up a commercial that would feature a bigger-than-life Shaq reaching through the roof of an arena, grabbing the basketball rim, and tearing it off.

When apprised of the story line, O'Neal rejected it immediately.

"I only do what's real," Shaq explained. "Like tearing down rims and playing with kids."

WHEN I FIRST GOT TO ORLANDO, I WANTED TO ESTABLISH myself as a dominant force. I felt it was important to intimidate the other big men out there with my size and my strength. I wanted them to think twice about coming after me.

I was Superman, just liked I had dreamed about when I was a little boy in Newark, New Jersey. The Magic was an expansion team and needed some credibility. It was my job to bring it.

But first I had to get settled in my new community. Lester found me a house that he thought was just perfect for me. Wrong. When I sat down on the toilet my knees were up to my ears. The shower had to be ripped out because I couldn't even stand up in there. That house was a temporary holding tank for Superman. I had much bigger plans for myself.

That was my mentality back then. Buy something, then make it bigger and better. I went to a place on Lee Road in Orlando and bought a Ford Fairlane convertible. I turned it into what Dennis Tracey and I called my first Hoop-D. I put about sixty thousand dollars into it to get it the way I wanted.

By the time I was done with that car, it could jump up and down and shake side to side. There were speakers inside every available panel. That car was literally rocking.

I saw it at this little old used-car lot one day when I was driving by. The guy wanted ten grand for it. I walked out of there having paid $3,800. Even then I was a good businessman.

There was this fairly new community called Isleworth sprouting up in Windermere. It had a gate and that was good, because it was becoming obvious I needed some place where people couldn't just ride up and hang with Shaq. It was a beautiful spot, right on the water. The house was furnished, and when I went upstairs to look around I saw this amazing round bed in the master bedroom. It was huge. It fit thirty people.

I told Lester, "I gotta have this house."

It was the bed. I wanted that bed.

We made an offer and I told them I wanted it furnished. The guy wanted three hundred thousand dollars extra for the furniture. Now I was so in love with that bed I would have paid that much just to get it, but I'm a businessman, so I got him down to seventy-five thousand. As soon as that bed was mine, I had a custom-made black comforter with a Superman logo for it.

We had to throw in a couple of signed jerseys, some tickets, and a signed picture with me after a game. It was amazing how the price dropped if I would just stop and take a picture with someone.

Of course, if you were a kid, I was going to do that for free anyway. I did just about anything for kids. Now those pushy grown-ups? That's another story.

Once Dennis and I moved into Isleworth, we used to tell our friends, "Welcome to Disney World." It felt like it. I had everything I ever wanted. But the minute I walked outside those gates I'd say, "Well, here we are back in the real world again."

Years later someone asked me why I insisted on living my life like I was still a little kid. I told him, "Sometimes I feel like the Tom Hanks character in the movie *Big*. But my life is not a movie. I never have to go back to Coney Island to find the fortune teller machine so I have to grow up again."

One of the things I invested in when I first got to Orlando was some coin-operated car washes. We were doing really well, making a lot of money, but one day Lester called me up and told me the numbers weren't matching up. The profits we should have had were not the same numbers that were being deposited in the bank.

"Don't worry, Lester," I told him, but he was freaking out about it. He even flew to Orlando to discuss it with me. He calculated we were missing almost a quarter million dollars.

It took me a while, but I finally came clean with him. I showed Lester my bedroom, where there were a whole bunch of wooden rain barrels—full of quarters.

Lester said, "Shaquille, what the hell is this? Is this the missing money?"

"Yes," I admitted. "Lester, I can't help it. I like *seeing* my money. Come here, run your fingers through all these quarters. It's awesome!"

Lester called the bank and told them he had $250,000 worth of quarters to deposit. It took weeks to put it all in there because they didn't have enough coin machines to sort it all out.

Even though I had all that money, I was determined to keep it real. I had two Rotweillers, Shaz and Thor, and I used to walk them all over town. I wasn't going to be a shut-in just because suddenly I was famous. One day I was driving my new SUV and I had the music blasting and they could hear me coming from five miles away. *Boom da boom da boom*, must be Shaq.

I was driving past Turkey Lake Park and there were a bunch of guys playing some ball. I slowed down a bit and I was watching them play, and they weren't half bad.

They looked like they were having fun, so I pulled over, and me and my Rotweillers got out and I shot around with those guys for about an hour.

I liked doing things like that. I liked talking with people. And once they put their tongues back in their mouths and got over the shock that it really was me, Shaquille O'Neal, star of the Orlando Magic, we had ourselves a few laughs.

It's hard for celebrities to get around. That's what you always hear. Well, it's only as hard as you make it. I'm a people person, so I like to be out and about. It's what makes me happy. I'm not the guy who is sneaking out the back door. Never.

One of the things I loved doing when I was in Orlando was riding the SkyCoaster. It was this skydiving and hang-gliding ride, all in one.

I always took the same route home every day and I was mesmerized by what looked like this upside-down triangle. I always wondered what it was. One day I'm driving and I see these people swinging back and forth up almost over the highway. I was so curious about it. At first, I used to go at night and watch people do it.

So one night I finally got on it and I was hooked. I was addicted. I did it thirty times in a row. They put you in this harness and they tie you in and when pull this lever the cord springs you up in the air.

The last time I did it I was with my bodyguard, Jerome, and another friend. All three of us are big. There was a lot of weight on it and when we started swinging up the damn thing buckled. We were up so high I thought we were going to tip over. I looked at Jerome when the ride was over and said, "I'm never riding this thing again." Too bad, because that ride was a lot of fun.

One thing that got a little complicated was all the people who came out of nowhere once I signed my contract. All of a sudden everyone wanted a piece of me. Old "friends" who I never liked in the first place. New "friends" who didn't love me, only the sight of all my money. Even people I really cared about, all of a sudden everyone had an opinion on what I should do and how I should do it.

My first couple of years in the NBA, I tried to please everybody. Unfortunately, it just doesn't work. I wish it did, because I like to get along with people. I was raised by the Sarge to respect authority and to never question the people in charge.

But that became hard to do after a while.

We went 41-41 my first season in Orlando, which was 21 wins better than the year before. I was still learning my way around the NBA, but I still managed to be the first rookie in eleven years to have 1,000 points and 1,000 rebounds in a season. We missed making the playoffs because Indiana, which had the same record as us, edged us out in the tiebreaker, but then the most incredibly lucky thing happened.

Even though we had only a 1 in 66 chance of winning the draft lottery, we did it again. We got the No. 1 pick. The Magic was going to take Chris Webber, but I went in to talk to Orlando general manager John Gabriel and flexed my Superman muscles. I told him, "Listen, I understand you want Webber, but this cat Penny Hardaway is the answer. I got to know him doing the movie *Blue Chips*, and if you put us together we could be like Magic and Kareem."

I waited a second for dramatic pause. Then I told him, "If you don't bring Penny in here, then maybe I've got to think about doing something else."

So they bring in Penny and everything is great. We're cool, we're playing ball together, we're going to win the whole thing.

Penny was a lot of fun. He wanted to be a star, and he had some grand ideas on how to pull that off. I liked his style. We got involved in this little game of "anything you can buy I can buy better." It was a competition, but not in a negative way. We were just two young, stupid, rich athletes showing each other up.

It went something like this. Penny would go out and buy a Ferrari, so I had to go out and a buy a nicer car. We were young and cocky, and we all wanted to be The Man in every category. Girls, cars, houses. I figured since I was single and had a lot of money and a lot of responsibility, I had to be The Man on the team. I'm a bit of a show-off, so if anyone tried to one-up me, I had to do something outlandish to respond to it.

So Penny would come in with a Ferrari, and I'd go out and buy two Ferraris. I'd cut one in half and superglue it together with the other one, and I'd have a Long Ferrari.

When Horace Grant joined our team, he got this house with a really nice pool in the backyard, so I had to tear down my guest house and gut it and build an even more fabulous pool than his.

It was all in good fun. No animosity. It wasn't ever a negative thing. It was more like, "Yo, Penny. Check out my new Long Ferrari when you get to the valet."

By the time Penny came on board, Matt Goukas had stepped down and Brian Hill was the coach. He was a very nice man, one of those basketball lifers. We gave him a run for his money.

Like a lot of teams I was on, the Orlando Magic had cliques. It was me, Dennis Scott, Nick Anderson, and later on Brian Shaw. We always hung out together.

Then there was a group led by Scott Skiles that included Jeff Turner, Greg Kite, and Larry Krystkowiak. Now I'm not big into the racial thing, but it was true my group was all black guys and Scott's was all white. There weren't any bad feelings between the groups, but we had absolutely nothing in common. Can you see Greg Kite coming to the clubs and rapping with me? I don't think so.

It kind of came to a head eventually. I was having a blast living large in the NBA, and we went on a West Coast trip that started in Seattle. We flew from Seattle to Los Angeles after the game, and me and my guys went out and partied our asses off. For me that meant staying out late, mixing some rap music, having some fun. I didn't drink, but other guys did. So we're playing the Clippers and we lost.

Brian Hill was the coach and he was ticked off. He had a right to be. Skiles was our team leader, a guy who was a little older and on his way out, and I was the young leader coming in.

We were still in LA the next day practicing and BHill was making us run. Everyone was a little slow except Skiles. He was running us ragged, swearing at us, telling us, "All you damn guys do is party."

He was right. He was telling the truth, but he was puffing his chest out a little too much for my taste. It was a little too phony as far as I was concerned. If you're a leader, then be one. Don't try to show off and embarrass the rest of the guys. Skiles kept yapping and yapping and I finally told him, "Shut the hell up. We've heard enough of you."

All of a sudden the son of a bitch came right for me. Now Scott Skiles is a foot shorter than me. He looks like a little old man at this point. He's going bald, for crying out loud. But he's charging me so I've got no choice—I gotta slug him with an uppercut to the jaw. You know my rule: Don't wait for someone to hit you.

Next thing I do is put him in a headlock, because if I have to hit him again I might hurt him, and that wasn't what I planned on doing when I showed up to practice that day. At that point Kryst-kowiak tries to jump me, but DScott elbowed him in the back of the head and now we've got this mini brawl going on. If anyone had seen it they would have sworn it was a black-white thing.

It wasn't, really. Anyhow, the coaching staff broke us up and Brian Hill said, "Practice is over," and that was it. You'd think something like that would carry over, but it really didn't.

Actually, I wish I would have gotten Skiles a little earlier in his career. He was a tough guy and a great passer. He had some range, too. I really did have a lot of respect for his game.

The summer after my first NBA season Reebok asked me to do a clinic in Brazil, so I went along with Brian Hill. I remember seeing Phil Jackson there, but I didn't really say much to him other than hello.

Dennis Tracey is my manager, and he's supposed to be organizing this trip for me, but he forget to take into account it was on the other side of the globe and it was winter there, so we had all the wrong clothes. I'm thinking I'm going to this warm South American city and instead I was freezing my ass off.

I had to get Dennis back for that, so we're driving down the street in Sao Paulo and we're at a red light and I say to Dennis, "Hey, dare you to jump out and run to the light and back with no clothes on." It was probably about fifty yards away, tops. Dennis says, "What's it worth to you?" I told him, "I'll give you five thousand dollars." So Dennis whips off his clothes and jumps out of the car, and of course the light changes and we lock the doors and take off. So Dennis is running after us for about a mile and a half and he's naked. We finally let him back in—but only if he agrees to forfeit his five grand.

I did a couple of overseas trips that summer, including one to Tokyo. I did one appearance where there were about fifteen thousand fans, and they kept pushing closer and closer, and when they announced I'd be signing autographs it was like a dam broke loose and these people were all coming straight for me. They had to bring out the riot police so the fans wouldn't rip me to pieces.

My favorite part of that trip was when I got to meet a genuine sumo wrestler. He gave me a samurai sword as a gift, but they wouldn't let me take it on the plane.

My early years in Orlando were a great time in my life. Our team was getting better, but we were still young and foolish and having fun. I was a real practical joker. Guys would come out of the shower and I'd completely ambush them, tackle them, take them to the ground.

Butt naked, of course.

Guys started to realize they better stay sharp on the plane, otherwise they might wake up with pink-painted fingernails.

I was in demand all the time. I did a lot of endorsements, but I also made sure I made time for the community. That was very important to me. Whenever there was a sick kid or a terminally ill person who wanted to meet a Magic player, I was their guy. I had a soft spot for the kids in particular.

I started a Shaqsgiving Dinner for homeless people in the area. One of the most vivid memories of my childhood is when I was with my dad. We never had any money, but he was going to take me out for a burger. We're heading there and we see this homeless guy on the street, and my dad calls him over and he gives him our money for the burgers. "You always help those less fortunate than you," said Sarge.

I know, but geez, I really wanted that burger.

Because I was so visible in Orlando, I started becoming really popular in the community. Leonard described me as "a cross between the Terminator and Bambi." Pat Williams told *Sports Illustrated* I was "sucking the marrow out of the bones of life."

Most of the time, everyone was good with it. Once in a while, though, they didn't dig Shaq being Shaq.

Somehow it just worked out that when we played Atlanta it always hit on the weekend of Freaknik, this big spring break party they had in Buckhead with students from all of the black colleges. It was party city, and me and DScott and the guys always made certain we participated. What that meant was when it came time to play the Hawks a lot of us were suffering from the "Buckhead flu."

Brian Hill got so upset he told us, "I'm never taking you guys to Atlanta the night before the game again. From now on we're flying in on the same day." NBA regulations require you to fly into the city the night before the game, but he didn't care. He paid the fine rather than give us another crack at Freaknik.

Even though I was having fun my first couple of years, we weren't winning enough, and everyone around me in my inner circle was frustrated. My father complained constantly about our point guards to just about anybody who would listen. Leonard called Pat Williams all the time about it. He'd say, "Get the big man the ball." Pat would tell him, "We'll get right on that." It wasn't until they brought in Brian Shaw and we established the Shaw-Shaq Redemption that we had a point guard who knew how to throw up that lob.

Brian was one of those final pieces that helped us bring it all together during the 1994–95 season. The other piece was Horace Grant, who had won championships with the Bulls and knew what it took to get over the top.

We had a strong nucleus with those two guys and me and Nick Anderson and Penny, who was turning into a serious star. He had raised his game to an incredible level and made the first All-NBA team that year. We made it to the NBA Finals, and we did it by beating MJ and the Bulls, which was a big deal for Horace.

Hell, it was big for all of us. We were jumping on top of the press tables at the O-rena and soaking in the love from the crowd. All of a sudden our city was on the basketball map. It was loud, vibrant, crazy.

We got too happy too soon. After we beat the Bulls we had ten days off before the Finals. Me and DScott flew to Atlanta and just partied. We were hitting the clubs and finding some girls and dancing and gambling and listening to music all night long.

They had a Disney parade for us before we even went to the Finals. It was a mistake. The whole way we approached it was a mistake.

When you get to the point where I am now, retired and looking back, you recognize the 1995 Finals as a lost opportunity. You wish you had a chance to do it over, but it doesn't work that way.

So after four days off, we start practicing and we are terrible. We're sluggish but we're still cocky, because we beat Houston twice that year and in our minds, we've got this.

At night after practice, DScott and BShaw and Anthony Avent would come to my house. Anthony could sing a little, so we decided to go in my music studio and make our own rap championship song.

We figured if we had it all done before the Finals started we could capitalize on it once we won the whole thing.

Game 1 was in our building and we came out flying. We led by 20 points in the second quarter. Hakeem Olajuwon and Clyde Drexler brought Houston back, but we had a three-point lead at the end of the game and all Nick Anderson had to do was hit some free throws. He missed four straight.

I couldn't believe it. I wanted to knock him out after that game— not so much because he missed the free throws, but because he was laughing and pounding his chest after he did. I know he was doing it because he was nervous, but the way he behaved made me sick.

I've never said this before, but one of the reasons I was mad at him was because I really felt he disrespected the basketball gods. He missed two free throws and he was banging his chest like he won the lottery.

All that bullshit he did drove me crazy. All he had to do was hit one free throw. Just one.

The other thing that upset me was they were running a pick-and-roll with Hakeem and Clyde Drexler and I kept telling BHill we shouldn't help on it, but that was how he wanted to play it.

So what happens? Clyde blows right past Nick and I've got to help, and Nick doesn't drop so my guy Hakeem gets a tip-in. So now because Nick can't guard his own damn guy it looks like I can't guard mine, either. Number one, just make a free throw; and number two, when I come over to help because your guy abuses you, at least drop down and do what you're supposed to do. I swear. I wanted to kill him.

After the game he was at his locker and I went right for him. I was about two inches from his face. I said, "What the hell are you doing? You're playing like a wuss." He didn't say a word. He just sat there with his head down.

I wanted to hit him, but I knew if I did, we would have gotten swept.

Turns out we did anyway.

The problem was we all knew Nick was done after Game 1. He was shook and he couldn't recover. Couldn't look at any of us. He was afraid to go to the line. Done. Completely done.

Looking back, it was probably my fault for jumping all over him like that. I was probably too hard on him. I was still learning how to be a leader.

After we're down 0–2 I could see which way it was going. I was so angry, so upset. I just couldn't understand it. We had dominated Houston during the regular season, yet here we were, blowing the damn series. I got into my Hoop-D car and I took off.

I drove all night—to Miami and back. That's how I relieve stress. I drive and listen to my music. I got to Miami in about two and a half or three hours, looked at the water, then came back.

I was trying to think of a way to turn it around. I had all sorts of questions rattling around in my head. *Am I playing hard enough? Can I do something else? Are we coming back, or is it over?* I thought I might come up with some answers. Instead, I just came home exhausted, having burned up a ton of gasoline.

I was trying to tell Brian Hill to just let Hakeem score. I'm going to score on the other end. It will all balance off. But he wanted to double-team everybody. We're double-teaming Clyde Drexler and we're doubling Hakeem. It's really ticking me off because I felt it was the wrong strategy, and if we lose, it's all on me.

That was when I realized that if we win, I'm going to get most of the credit, and if we lose, I'm getting all of the blame. That's how it works when you are the CEO, the superstar.

Once I caught on to that, I was like, "Give me the fucking ball. If it's going to be on my head, then throw me the ball so I can get the job done."

But Hakeem just dominated me in that series. Looking back, I was too respectful to him. I held him in such high regard I forgot I was supposed to be kicking his ass.

After they swept us, the fans smacked our charter bus with brooms on our way out of Houston. Coach Hill said, "Remember how this feels."

It took me a while to get over it. Dennis Tracey and I took our girlfriends on vacation to St. Pete, and we were sitting on the beach at night talking about what went wrong and everyone was having a drink and I decided, *Well, maybe if I have a drink it will make me feel better. I'll have some of that pink Zinfandel.*

I drank two bottles of pink Zinfandel in about ten minutes' time. Then I threw up, and that was the end of that experiment.

You'd think since I was only twenty-three and Penny was only twenty-two we'd have plenty of chances to win a title for Orlando, but the following season, in 1995–96, it seemed as though everything that could go wrong did.

Penny decided he wanted a new contract. A big contract. I was like, "Hey, he deserves it, he's a great player," because I'm figuring the DeVos family owns Amway and everybody is always buying the stuff they sell, so there's enough money for everyone to get paid.

Penny holds out for a few days and the media is killing him, and I'm the only one who sticks up for him. So he finally gets his, but then when it's time for my new deal at the end of the year, Penny is nowhere to be found. I find out that he wants to make sure he's the highest-paid player on our team. He's telling people in the front office, "This is my team. It's a guard's league now."

I can't believe it. Craziest thing I've ever heard. Because I knew

Penny was kinda soft and he'd be screwed if he wasn't playing with me. I could take the heat. I could handle the pressure. He wasn't wired like that.

The bad thing is when you have two alpha males on the team that don't have the same understanding, things can go haywire. That's what happened with Penny and me. I was the AA alpha male and Penny was the AB alpha male. Somewhere along the way he decided he could do it without the big dawg.

It didn't help that I broke my thumb and missed the first two months of the 1995–96 season. It happened in an exhibition game against Miami. Matt Geiger karate-chopped me. I said, "I blame [Coach Pat] Riley for my broken thumb, not Matt Geiger. That ain't defense Miami is playing. That's just chopping. I have no idea how his team gets away with it. I guess when you've been in the league thirty years you can do it. Respect—Riley gets it—he's like John Gotti."

Horace was hurt that year, too. We were winning, but the chemistry had changed.

Whenever we went to New York to play the Knicks or the Nets I always went by to see my grandmother Odessa. I was looking forward to seeing her because every time I called for her, she wasn't around. I should have known, looking back, that something was wrong. She was sick, dying of cancer, but nobody was going to tell me that in the middle of my NBA season. All I knew was Grandma wasn't feeling well and was tired a lot.

When I showed up to see her it was obvious she was in her final days. We were playing the Knicks on April 3, and I got there on April 2. She was very frail. I think she was waiting on me. I held her hand, talked to her awhile, and then she said, "You want to fight me?" After that she closed her eyes. She slipped into a coma later that night.

I went back to see her the next afternoon around two and the nurse there said, "She's going to die at eight o'clock." I'm ticked off at this lady and I say, "Well, if you think that, you better get somebody over here. I have money. Call whoever you need. Money is no object."

This nurse just said, "No, it's too late. She's going to die at eight o'clock."

I swear to God, my grandmother Odessa died at eight o'clock on the dot, right in her home, in her own bedroom. I don't know how that lady knew, but she did. My cousins and I were all sitting with my grandma. When she left us, we all started crying. My cousin Brian started kicking tables, breaking things. My mother was there, so I had to man up and take care of her. I was hurting, but I had to console my mother.

We called the nurse, and they came and they put my grandmother in a bag and they zipped it up, and we all lost it again. I had to carry her outside and put her in the van. Hardest thing I've ever done.

I was sitting with my grandmother, watching her die, while my teammates were beating the Knicks. They went back home and played the Celtics the next night, on a Thursday, but obviously I stayed behind.

My plan was to take the week off. My grandmother's death hit me hard, and I was in no shape to play basketball.

Her funeral was beautiful but very sad. Grandmother Odessa had planned it all herself, right down to the flowers and the music. I tried to hold it together, but I couldn't. I was so mad she was gone I took it out on the church door. I hauled off and punched a hole right through it. I was lucky I didn't break my hand.

Our team was playing a nationally televised game that Sunday against Mike and the Bulls, so that Saturday Brian Hill told reporters, "I don't know where Shaq is, so if he comes, he's not going to play."

I had gone to Atlanta right after the funeral, because I didn't want to be around anybody. Dennis Scott was the only one who knew where I was. He called me and said, "Yo, man, they're looking for you." I said, "Why are they looking for me?" He told me what was going on. I was ticked off. Why were they acting like they had no idea what was going on in my life? I woke up Sunday, chartered a plane, got there in the second quarter and played 33 minutes. I had 21 points and 9 rebounds, but we lost.

I called Brian Hill on his bluff. I knew if I showed up he'd play me. I don't know why he disrespected me like that in the papers when I was dealing with something so personal and so serious. It's not like I was on vacation. I was grieving. I had lost one of the most important people in my life. To be honest with you, I think that was when my relationship with the Magic started breaking down.

They knew how much my grandmother meant to me. It was the first time someone so close to me had died, and I was struggling with it. She was such a special woman. I was always trying to do something nice for her, but she never wanted it. I'd tell her, "Grandma, I've got a nice mansion picked out for you, right next door to Eddie Murphy." She'd just say, "Nope." I'd say, "Grandma, stop working. I'll take care of you." She'd say, "Nope."

We started a foundation in her memory. It's called the Odessa Chambliss Quality of Life fund, and it helps nursing students further their education. You should think about making a donation. (That's what we in the business world call "cross-promoting.")

Both Penny and I had a good year in 1995–96, but we got swept in the playoffs by that Chicago Bulls team that went 72-10 and will probably go down as one of the best teams ever.

Now my contract is up, and that's when I learn there is no loyalty in this game. None whatsoever. Zero.

You just have to develop a thick skin and accept it. I knew there was no loyalty when I watched Patrick Ewing get traded, and Dominique Wilkins, too. Even Michael Jordan switched teams. Ewing made the Knicks. 'Nique made the Hawks. Jordan made the Bulls. I know they were at the end of their careers and they thought it would be best for them to go somewhere else, but it should never come to that.

I wanted to stay in Orlando. Leonard wanted me in Los Angeles because of Hollywood and all the opportunities, but also because he knew right away Orlando wasn't going to pay me.

I was naive, I guess. I didn't really believe that. I loved the DeVos family. They were great people. I think it was John Gabriel's call. He started low, too low. And we probably started too high. I was saying I wanted $150 million, but everyone knew I wasn't serious.

The Magic offered me seven years at $69 million. Leonard had already started talking to me about $100 million because he thought I could be the first guy to get that kind of money. It sounded like a lot to me, but I was the best young player in the game at that time and I figured, *Why not me?*

Back then, after your first contract expired, you became a free agent. You could sign with anybody. But right after I left Orlando they changed the rules. Now after your first contract you are what they call a "restricted" free agent, which means the team that drafted you can match any offer. That wasn't true in my case.

We were keeping an eye on the other free agents in the league. Leonard called me up and told me Juwan Howard had signed for $105 and Alonzo Mourning had signed for $110 million.

Now the market was set. Orlando *had* to pay me $100 million. In fact, we asked for $115 million. But they wouldn't. They came back with four years, $80 million. I asked John Gabriel why they wouldn't pay me what he knew I deserved and he said, "We don't want to upset Penny. We can't pay you more than Penny."

I couldn't believe that. It was like they had punched me in the gut.

In the meantime, Jerry West, the general manager for the Lakers, is calling and telling us, "Listen, I know you deserve more than Juwan and Mourning, but right now all I can get you is $98 million."

I was so glad to hear that I told Leonard, "Let's take it. Let's take the $98 million and get this over with. I want to be somewhere where I'm wanted."

Right about that time, the *Orlando Sentinel* came out with a poll. The first question they asked was "Is Shaquille O'Neal worth $115 million?" Ninety-one percent of the people said no. The other question they asked was "Should the Magic fire Brian Hill if that is Shaq's condition for returning?" About 82 percent of the people said no to that one. I wasn't calling for Brian Hill to be fired. I had my issues with him, but they had the wrong superstar. It was Penny who had issues with BHill, not me.

At the time the poll came out, I was playing for the 1996 Olympic team and we were training in Disney. I heard about that poll from all the fellas. Charles Barkley and Scottie Pippen were ragging on me. They were saying things like, "Your own fans don't want you." I won't lie to you—it was embarrassing.

My mother was very upset by all the negative publicity. She called me up one day and said, "Are you being a little greedy, son?" I told her, "Nope, there are guys out there getting $100 million, and I'm better, so I need $120 million." She said, "Well, okay, I won't tell you how to do your business, but I was just wondering. That sounds like so much money."

She was looking at those numbers and she couldn't make sense of it. Remember now, this is the same woman who wanted to put my stereo system on layaway.

Everyone else in Orlando was doing what my mother was doing. They were looking at all that money and saying, "The hell with Shaq. Nobody is worth that kind of money."

They didn't understand the business of the NBA. Meanwhile, I was getting my own crash course on the economics of the league.

I'm ready to take $98 million from LA, but Jerry West calls back and he's excited because he had just traded George Lynch and now he can give us seven years and $121 million. I loved Jerry West before, but now I loved him even *more*.

I was in Atlanta when all that news came down, because the Olympics were about to start. By that point I just wanted it done. That poll bothered me. The fans seemed like they had turned on me. I had worked my ass off for that city, and this was how they repaid me?

At that point the Magic realized they had totally blown it, so they made a last-ditch effort to salvage the deal. John Gabriel and Bob Vander Weide hopped on a private plane to Atlanta. They went to see Leonard, who was shagging volleyballs for USA star Holly McPeak.

He ended up marrying Holly, actually. John and Bob were in suits and ties, and Leonard was dressed in a pair of gym shorts.

They told Leonard they would match what the Lakers were offering. Leonard said thank you and sent them on their way, but it was too little too late. I hadn't signed anything, but I had given Jerry West my word I was going to play for the Lakers and I wasn't going back on that.

Gabriel knew it was over. Bob Vander Weide said to him as they flew back to Orlando, "I thought that went well." Gabriel answered, "Bob, we've lost him."

When Jerry West flew into Atlanta with the contract, he was so nervous he was actually shaking. He was telling me, "We're going to win a lot of championships. We've got you and I've got this eighteen-year-old kid coming in. Wait until you see him. He's going to be the best player in the game some day."

I had met Kobe Bryant once in our locker room in Orlando, but I hadn't really ever heard of him. To be honest, I was barely listening. I was thinking my usual Spooky Wook stuff, so I wanted to say to Jerry West, "Okay, can I just sign this in case something happens to me?" You know, like the Unabomber or something. I just wanted it done.

So now the contract is signed and I'm the highest-paid player in the game, but I don't say a word. I go to my Olympic practice and I'm looking around at Penny, who is now my former teammate but he doesn't even know it, and I don't say anything.

For one thing, I didn't want to brag. We were training for the Olympics and talking every day about being one team, not individuals. It just didn't seem right to be puffing my chest out about my salary. Besides, I knew we were going to hold a press conference the following day.

We did it right in Atlanta. Penny was really pissed. I didn't care. Penny wanted to be the highest-paid player on the Magic. Good luck with that, bro.

The reaction from Orlando was ugly. People were angry. They felt betrayed, Well, join the club. That was how I felt, too.

I said some things they didn't like. I called the city of Orlando a "dried-up pond." Obviously I didn't mean it. My entire family lives in Orlando, and it is where I live *today*. I was hurt and it just came out. I wish I could take that one back.

Of course a big salary like that was going to be big news. I was called greedy, a mercenary, a traitor.

Reporters asked me about the contract. I told everybody, "I'm tired of hearing about money, money, money, money, money, I just want to play the game, drink Pepsi, and wear Reebok."

But first I had to help the US win a gold medal in the Olympic Games. During the Olympics I had a few things going through my mind. The first was signing with the Lakers and knowing my whole life was about to change. That was the most overwhelming feeling. It kind of overshadowed the Olympics for me, in a way, because there was so much going on and it was happening so fast and it was a little distracting.

There was never any doubt our 1996 US team was going to win the gold medal. We had Charles Barkley and Hakeem Olajuwon and Karl Malone and John Stockton and Reggie Miller. We were stacked. I knew I wasn't going to shine, but I was hoping to give the world a little peek at what I was all about.

I had some extra motivation heading into those Olympics. They called us "Dream Team II" because we were following the 1992 Dream Team, which had Mike and Magic and Larry and all those guys. I was the final cut of that team. It came down to me and Christian Laettner, and they gave it to him because he had more international experience, whatever the hell that meant.

So now here it was, four years later, and I was starting to dominate in the NBA, and it was clear they'd made a mistake in 1992. They picked the wrong guy.

Our coach for the '96 team was Lenny Wilkens, and early on he did a pretty good job of getting us all in there. We pretty much rolled over everybody. I remember Penny and I took over in the quarterfinals against Brazil, and Charles and Reggie started dumping on

Penny, saying, "Shaq used to be your boy, but not anymore. He left you!"

Anyhow, we got to the gold medal game and we were playing Yugoslavia and Vlade Divac, one of the guys they traded away to make room for me in LA.

I was pretty revved up for the game. Having a military background, I was looking forward to standing up there on the gold medal platform and hearing our national anthem being played. It was a moment I was really looking forward to. I knew my dad was going to be very proud of me.

What happened pretty much ruined it for me. Before the game Lenny Wilkens came up to me and said, "Shaq, you will go to many more Olympics, but this will be David Robinson's last one, so I'm going to give him most of the minutes." Lenny is a very smooth talker, and before I could say anything he just walked off.

I barely played in the gold medal game. I played about five minutes total. Wilkens put me in for the final fifteen seconds. I think I had 2 points. It was David Robinson's third Olympics and my first. So you can't give me some time? I was really disappointed. After we won, I took my medal and I jumped in my car and I drove home.

That was the beginning and the end of my Olympic experience.

I didn't have time to really dwell on it, though. I had to find a house in LA. It wasn't a whole lot of fun going back to Orlando to get my stuff. I tried to block out all the negative stuff coming out of there, but it wasn't easy. All these people who loved me were now trashing me. Some of it was pretty vicious. It destroyed my mom, it really did—and I don't like it when people upset Lucille.

I didn't know it at the time, but the Orlando Magic ended up doing me a favor. Once I hopped that flight to LA and put on that Lakers uniform, my life was never the same.

DECEMBER 23, 1996

Los Angeles, California

Shaq-a-Claus shifted his Santa hat on his head, gleefully clapping his hands together as he approached the community center in Watts.

"Just like a little kid would," recalled his uncle Mike Parris, who accompanied him on the trip.

Shaquille O'Neal was no stranger to the center. Over Thanksgiving he served dinner to nearly eight hundred low-income children who found refuge there from the drugs and crime that infested one of the poorest neighborhoods in Los Angeles.

And now, Shaq happily took orders for their mostly routine Christmas wants: computer games, bicycles, a talking dolly.

Yet it was the wish of one small boy that resonated with him.

"What I'd really like for Christmas is snow," he said. "I've never seen it. I asked my momma about it once, and she said I never will see it because we're going to be stuck here for the rest of our lives."

During the car ride back to his Mulholland Drive mansion,

Shaq was mostly quiet. That, Mike Parris knew, meant the wheels were turning.

"Uncle Mike," he finally said. "We need to get those kids some snow."

Parris was used to fulfilling Shaq's unusual requests, often on the spur of the moment and almost always for children. He nearly caused a riot at a Toys R Us one Christmas when he bought every video game in the store to fill the Shaq-a-Claus quota.

But snow? In LA?

"People ski here, don't they?" Shaq reasoned.

One month later, the rumble of three dump trucks thundering down Central Avenue sent the startled children of Watts flocking to the street. Their community center parking lot had been transformed into a winter wonderland, blanketed with mounds and mounds of snow, all imported from Bear Mountain.

Shaq had not yet arrived at the center. He was just minutes away when he passed a gas station with a line of bicycles displayed out front.

"How many bikes do we have?" Shaq asked his uncle.

"About eighty," Parris answered.

Shaq then pulled into the gas station and purchased the owner's entire inventory. The additional fifty bicycles were delivered within the hour.

By then Shaq was knee-deep in a snowball fight, frolicking with his tiny friends dressed in T-shirts and shorts, squealing with delight each time one of them knocked his sizable Shaq-a-Claus hat askew.

My PARENTS TAUGHT ME TO GIVE BACK. IT WAS UNDERSTOOD that if I became rich and famous like we thought I would, then I would share the wealth. Some of my happiest moments have been doing that.

One of the best things about having money is doing something nice for people who don't expect or want you to do anything. For example, we had this fellow who worked for the Lakers. His name was Rudy Garciduenas, and he was in charge of cleaning our practice gear. You were supposed to take your stuff and put it in the net, and he'd wash it. I'd leave my crap everywhere, but for some reason Rudy would take care of me.

One day I needed him to take a bag of stuff somewhere for me but he said, "I can't. I don't have room in my car." I'm leaving and I see him driving out in this dumpy little Hyundai with a million miles on it and I said, "That's your car?" Rudy answered, "Well, you know, Shaq, we don't all make twenty million a year." The next day I grabbed him after practice and we went to a truck dealership and we got out and I said, "Pick one." He said, "Really?" The look on his face was priceless.

For the rest of my time in LA, I always made sure that Rudy had a new truck. He bought himself a vanity plate that said, THNX SHAQ. You're welcome, Rudy.

My only complaint with some of my fellow NBA players is they don't give back enough. Yeah, some of them have foundations, but if you ask them, it's just a tax break for them, nothing more. Some guys are generous, but not enough of them. One time I was in the Lakers locker room and I got this letter from this handicapped woman. I shout out to the guys, "Hey, this lady needs help. She's in a wheelchair and she needs a van. It costs sixty thousand dollars. Anybody want to chip in?" Silence. Not one guy. I bought the van for her myself.

When those things come up, my mother is the first one I think about. She's so sweet, so big-hearted, I'd never want to embarrass her, so when I can do something I know will make her happy and proud, I do it. And, if I can, I usually talk some other athlete into doing it with me.

When I first got to Los Angeles, Jerry West was very hands-on with me. He sat me down and gave me the "I want you to focus on basketball" speech. I knew it was coming. Leonard Armato warned me, but he didn't have to. I understood they'd be concerned that I was spreading myself too thin because people were always telling me that. What they didn't understand was I could do twice what normal people did. I always could. I had a ton of energy and my mind was going all the time.

Of course Jerry West commands a lot of respect, so he's telling me, "Now there's a lot of distractions out here in LA, so you've got to stay away from the limelight because people are going to target you. There's a party every night, so you've got to control that. And watch out on the movies—they take more time than you think. They'll tell you it will only take an hour but they'll have you on your feet all day." I'm saying, "Yes sir, yes sir," but deep down I already knew I could handle both.

Whenever people criticized me for doing all my "extracurricular" activities, I wanted to ask them, "What, twenty-nine points and thirteen rebounds a game aren't enough?" It's not like I was slacking. I'd do my movie stuff and my rap stuff, but that never stopped me from getting into the gym and putting in my work on a daily basis. Leonard and I were in the gym two to three hours every day working on shooting, passing, free-throw shooting. That was the only beef, really, anyone could have—my free-throw numbers weren't good. And believe me, that wasn't from lack of practice. I shot so many of those things I'd have to ice my wrists afterward.

The summer before I reported to the Lakers I got really serious about my training. I worked out with Billy Blanks, the fitness guy who invented Tae Bo and got me interested in martial arts. I was in great shape.

I met Lakers owner Jerry Buss and he was certainly nice enough, but I have never made the mistake of getting too close to the owners.

Dr. Buss had his cronies reach out to me a lot in the beginning. It would be, "Hey, the boss is having a party, come down to Malibu." I would say, "Hey, thanks, but I can't tonight." After a while, they stopped asking.

Now don't get me wrong. It's not like I was sitting home every night. I still managed to have a lot of fun.

When I got to LA I bought myself a silver Ferrari. I couldn't fit in a regular Ferrari so I had the guy take the engine out of the back so he could adjust the seat and create some legroom for me. That meant he had to put the motor in the front. It was a nightmare—cost me around $350,000, but I had to have it.

When you are a big guy like me, people are always telling you, "Well, you can't have that. You won't fit. You are too big." Even though I was big, I just wanted all the things all the little guys in the world had. I just wanted to be like everyone else. Really. Why is that so hard?

By the time the guy fixed that Ferrari up for me, the only gas tank he could fit in the car was one—and I'm not kidding—from a lawn mower. The most gas I could put in at one time was about nine dollars' worth. The guys on the team never let me forget it.

The next car I tore apart was a Benz. It was a burgundy 600. I put air bags on it, like hydraulics, and I put a fish tank in the back through the speakers. They were clear speakers with the tank on the top. I usually had practice at 10:00 a.m., so my bodyguard, Jerome, would put some goldfish in there and I'd drive to practice, and by the time I got there all those fishies were dead.

The problem was there was no air filter system—just water. And I think I played the music a little too loud for those poor little goldfish. They probably died of shock.

There's no question I certainly had a car fetish, but I actually bought my first Bentley by accident. One day after practice, I'm wearing my flip-flops and my sweats and I'm all sweaty and looking a little raggedy, but I'm driving by the Rolls Royce place and I decide to stop in.

I'm looking at this beautiful Bentley and this old, stuck-up white guy, a classic car salesman, is giving me the evil eye, so I say to him, "How much is this car?" He looks me up and down and says, "Are you sure you can afford it, sonny boy?" I was so ticked off. I was really, really offended.

While I'm standing there I hear this kind of squeaky voice that sounds familiar and there he is—Mike Tyson, the boxer. He's looking at Bentleys, too. Next thing I know Tyson has picked out two. He's buying two of these cars, so you know what I've got to do. I've got to buy three! I grab the salesman and I say, "I want that silver hardtop one, and I want the green one, and give me that red one over there, too."

I can't remember exactly how much they cost, but I think they all ran me about $200,000 each. So there's $600,000 for three cars that I can't fit into. I had to get my guy to come in and move the seat back, so that's a few more grand, and of course it was an absolute nightmare when we tried to trade it in after I got tired of it, which was about a year later.

My moneyman Lester Knispel was so mad at me he didn't talk to me for two weeks. After a while, I think he realized I just had to get these things out of my system. Honestly, the cars didn't even really mean that much to me.

It was really more about the idea of coming from zero to eighteen years old and having absolutely nothing and being a dreamer and fantasizing about having all these things—and then all of a sudden, it's not a fantasy anymore. It's real. I could afford almost anything I could think of. And what you realize later is, you don't really even want most of it.

Lester had this filthy-rich client who made hair products and he wanted to meet me. Lester told him, "Okay, but it's going to cost you." The guy told Lester, "Whatever he wants. I just want to meet Shaq." So Lester calls me and says, "What would you like?" I think about it and I say, "I've always thought those diamond Rolex watches were cool."

The guy buys me a $150,000 Rolex watch for shaking his hand and spending fifteen minutes with him. I put on the watch and I'm looking mighty fine, and I'm quite pleased with myself.

A few months later I see Lester again and I'm not wearing the watch. He asks where it is. I tell him I gave it to my cousin. He goes nuts over that. "After all that trouble!" he said, throwing his hands up in the air. I put my arm on his shoulder and tell him, "Lester, I wanted that watch because as a kid I never had anything like that. I didn't even have shoes to wear half the time. So I wanted it. But once I got it, the thrill was over. It didn't mean anything to me. So now my cousin has it and he's showing it off to everybody, and someone will probably steal it from him because he's bragging so much about it."

The money was a tricky thing. There were a lot of negatives tied to it. People started putting their hands out, and no matter how much you helped them, they seemed to end up disappointed. They see in the papers you are making $20 million a year, so they figure, what's a few thousand dollars here and there?

What I liked most about having all that money was being able to do things I wanted to do. One day I was shooting baskets with my brother, Jamal, and the Boys and Girls Club. The pavement was cracked and sloped and we couldn't even have half a decent game of one-on-one. I was so disgusted I called up Lester and said, "I want to donate $1 million to the Boys and Girls Club."

Lester said, "Okay, slow down, Shaq, what for?" I told him, "We've got to fix these courts. It's ridiculous to ask kids to play ball in conditions like this." Lester's trying to tell me, "It won't cost a million dollars to fix some blacktops," but I didn't care. I had made up my mind.

When the LA riots broke out in 1992, I called up Lester and told him, "We've got to buy those cops some new cars." He said, "Shaq, they have a budget for that."

I didn't care. I love law enforcement, and I love cops. I was already starting to go through the Police Academy, so I figured it couldn't hurt from a public relations standpoint. I had a deal with Ford, so I said, "Hey, here's what we're going to do. We're going to have these cars and you can stand up on the stage with me when we give them out." Ford paid for one, I paid for one, and the LA Police Department paid for one. It was good for me, good for Ford, and good for the LA cops. A win-win-win, I think they call that.

Now, in the back of my mind I knew I had to be smart about not going crazy with my spending. But, in those early years, in the front of my head I was thinking, "I'm making twenty million dollars a year. Screw it!" I wish I was a little wiser at a younger age, but that's why you get old, right? So you can be wise. That means now I'm Nostradamus.

I was a great dreamer—what you'd call a fake dreamer. What I mean by that was when I was a kid I didn't really have the confidence or the know-how to make my dreams happen. My life wasn't really all that great sometimes. It was the same old cycle—screw up, get a beating from my father, spend the whole day in my room. But instead of being sad and depressed and upset about having just taken another brutal ass whupping and being stuck in my room on punishment again, I'd force myself to be happy. I'd watch TV and there would be a beautiful woman on the screen smiling, and I'd say, "Oh, she's smiling at me! I'm going to marry her!" I'm picturing my wife and my beautiful house and my fabulous kids and my glamorous cars, and it made me feel better.

I never stopped dreaming. Not even after I got to LSU and things started to go well for me. I remember being in the dorm room one night and we were watching the movie *Jungle Fever* with Halle Berry in it, and I thought she was so stunning, so I wrote her a letter. I was just kind of kidding around, telling her I was a big fan and I'd love to meet her sometime.

The guys totally goofed on me for doing it, but I didn't care. A few weeks later, no lie, Halle Berry wrote me back. She sent me a signed picture that I still have hanging in my office. Turns out she's a basketball fan. She wrote, "I'm a big fan of yours, too. I can't wait until you get to the NBA."

I finally got to meet her in person in 1999. I told her, "You know, I wrote to you when I was in college." She said, "I remember. I told you that you'd be in the NBA!" Halle Berry is a beautiful person—both inside and out. Sometimes I still can't believe she knows who I am.

That's LA for you. All your dreams come true—except, when I first got there, we couldn't win a championship.

Hell, we couldn't even get to the Finals.

When I first got there Kobe was just a skinny teenager. He had plenty of confidence but not a whole lot of life experience yet.

It's funny to look back on the fact that Derek Fisher and Kobe were rookies at the same time. Derek always seemed so much older than him. He was one of those guys who knew how to keep his cool at all times. He had a certain way about him that made you respect him.

So here's how I met DFish:

It's my first season with the Lakers and I've just finished up with the Olympics in Atlanta and I get a call from my bodyguard, Jerome. He says, "You've got to come down and work out for Del Harris." Del was the coach of the Lakers at that point. I said, "Work out? Why? For what?" Jerome said, "I guess he wants to see what you can do."

I'm thinking to myself, *If you want to see what I can do, why don't you replay the highlight reel of my first four years in the league?* But I'm new, and I've just signed this big contract, so I'm going to do what they want.

So I show up and the first thing they have me do is take some shots. There's this little bald-headed guy passing me the ball, over and over. I say, "What's up dawg, you a coach?" He said, "No, I'm Derek Fisher. I'm on your team." I was a little embarrassed, so I said, "Hey, great to meet you, bro. Looking forward to it."

Next thing I know Del starts putting me through all these conditioning drills. He's got me running and jumping and dunking. He had me running stairs, suicides, all that stuff for about an hour and a half. I'm saying to myself, *I just signed for over $100 million and I used to come to this town and bust Del Harris's team every night, and now I have to audition for this guy?*

But I didn't say anything. I'm thinking that because I have all this other stuff going on he's trying to see if I'm in shape or not. I wasn't—not in basketball shape, anyway—and I was sucking wind a little bit, but I'm a player. I knew how to fake it.

For example, if Del told me to shoot 10 hard jump hooks, the first two I went at really hard, then 3, 4, and 5 medium, then 6, 7, and 8 slow, then the last two real hard again.

Of course, when you run the wind sprints, there's no faking that. You have to go all out because there's really no other way.

I was pretty ticked off Del put me through all that, but I did it because I didn't want to be labeled as one of those disgruntled, know-it-all superstars.

Del Harris is a nice, nice guy. He knows basketball, too. He was just the wrong guy for the job.

One thing I admired about him, though, was he didn't care if you were Shaquille O'Neal or Kobe Bryant—he was hard on everybody.

If Kobe came down and threw it between his legs ten times and then made a pass, Del would call a time-out and tell him, "Pass the damn ball!" and then Kobe would talk back and Del would sit his ass down.

That was impressive, until one of Buss's cronies would come up in the middle of the game and tap Del on the shoulder. He'd tell Del, "Put the kid back in the game." I never knew what the guy's name was, but there he was, always lurking around our bench, talking to our coach while we're trying to beat San Antonio.

Meanwhile, the fans are all chanting "Kobe! Kobe!" so Del Harris didn't have much of a choice. He'd have to put Kobe back in.

You knew even then Kobe was special. He was just different from everyone else, from Day One. I remember the first practice he was there, I walked in and here was this skinny kid doing all this "And One" crap; high crossovers, between the legs, palming and carrying and all this other trick street stuff. Eddie Jones and Nick Van Exel were laughing at him, but all I kept noticing was he never stopped working. He worked harder than all of us. So I started thinking, *Damn, this kid is going to be all right.*

He was so young and so immature in some ways, but I can tell you this: everything Kobe is doing now, he told me all the way back then he was going to do it. We were sitting on the bus once and he told me, "I'm going to be the number one scorer for the Lakers, I'm going to win five or six championships, and I'm going to be the best player in the game." I was like, "Okay, whatever." Then he looked me right in the eye and said, "I'm going to be the Will Smith of the NBA."

It would be one thing if the kid was all talk, but he was always trying to add something to make his game better. If practice was at 10:00 a.m., I might show up at nine once in a while to work on something, and Kobe would have been there since seven shooting. Sometimes, he'd be working on his moves without the ball. You'd walk in there and he'd be cutting and grunting and motioning like he was dribbling and shooting—except there was no ball. I thought it was weird, but I'm pretty sure it helped him.

Kobe and I were fine in the beginning. We didn't spend a lot of time together because he was a quiet kid, too young to go out to the clubs or anything. I don't know what he did because he kept to himself.

One thing we had in common was our first year with the Lakers was a struggle.

We didn't have the right guys to win. Nick Van Exel was our point guard, but he was too busy trying to be a star, and you could see that before long Derek Fisher, the quiet cat, was going to take over.

Eventually it happened, and after that Nick stopped caring. Eddie Jones was supposed to be another veteran to help us win, but he spent most his time looking over his shoulder at Kobe. He knew it, I knew it, and Kobe knew it. Eddie Jones was done in LA. Kobe was going to take over his position.

And if you listened to Kobe, he was going to take over the team, too. My reaction to that was "Not so fast, young fella."

My first year with the Lakers I missed twenty-eight games with a knee injury. I hyperextended it, fracturing a bone and partially tearing a ligament. I was in a bad way for a while. When I came back I played with a brace, but I had no confidence in my leg. The team went 16-12 without me. Even so, my first season in LA I was in the top five in the league in scoring, rebounds, shooting percentages, and blocks.

In the fall of 1996 they picked the top fifty NBA Players of all time, and I was on the list. I was kind of surprised because it was still early in my career, but it was obviously a great honor. The plan was to have everyone who was chosen to go to the 1997 All-Star Game in Cleveland for a big ceremony to celebrate the NBA's fiftieth anniversary.

Because I had the knee injury and I was in a cast, and flying would have caused it to swell, I got strict orders from Jerry West not to go. He said, "Shaquille, you have to do what's best for the Lakers, and we can't afford to aggravate that injury any further." That sounded right to me. The only way I could have possibly done it was if I flew privately, and the Lakers weren't going to sign off on that. Jerry really didn't want me pushing my injury.

Jerry was also chosen as one of the top fifty players of all time, but he didn't go, either.

I didn't think it was a big deal, but all of a sudden people are saying, "Who does Shaq think he is? Why didn't he go?" Instead of stopping for a minute and realizing I was injured they all said, "Shaq's arrogant."

All the criticism kind of blindsided me. It wasn't like I lobbied to be on the list. I don't even know who voted for it. I agree there were a couple of players who should have been ahead of me. Dominique Wilkins, Sidney Moncrief—they were great players who put in the work before me. But I had no say at all in how it was done.

They gave Jerry West some grief, too, about not going. He had scheduled some surgery on his nose, which was messed up from all the times he had broken it during his playing career, so that was his excuse.

I didn't find out the real reason Jerry West didn't go until a whole bunch of years later. Turns out the Orlando Magic had filed tampering charges against the Lakers for signing me. When Jerry heard about it, he went ballistic. He told the guys in the NBA office, "You are questioning my integrity and Shaquille's integrity and Jerry Buss's integrity. I can tell you no one will ever tamper on a team owned by Dr. Jerry Buss." David Stern said he understood, but they had to investigate.

Jerry West was so annoyed about it he decided, "The hell with the NBA. You can have your top fifty without me."

And without his young star center, as it turned out.

Here's why I love Jerry West: he wasn't afraid of Stern or anyone else. Afterward, he admitted to people the way he acted was "a little childish."

I didn't think it was childish at all. Once I found out what went down, I was saying, "That's why Jerry West is the best general manager there ever was." I'm big on loyalty, and Jerry West was loyal from start to finish.

My first year with the Lakers we won fifty-six games but lost to Utah in the second round of the playoffs. We just weren't ready to beat a veteran team like the Jazz that had John Stockton and Karl Malone. For some reason their center Greg Ostertag thought he had something to do with why Utah won, which I would have found to be hilarious if I wasn't so irritated that we lost.

Nick Van Exel was getting into arguments all the time with Del. Usually it was in practice, but in Game 4 of the series against Utah it spilled over to the game. They were yelling at each other on the bench while John Stockton was tearing us apart.

We took the Jazz to overtime in Salt Lake in Game 5, but Byron Scott got hurt and Robert Horry got thrown out of the game and I fouled out, so that left the Kobester to pull it out on his own.

It was the moment he had been waiting for. I'm sure he had replayed it a thousand times in his mind, only Kobe wasn't ready yet. He threw up three air balls in the final minute and a half of overtime. Forced one shot after another. I'm standing along the bench and I want to vomit.

We lose 98–93 and the kid is shaken, maybe for the first and only time in his life. I put my arms around Kobe as we walk off the court. I tell him, "Look at all these people laughing at you. One day we're going to get them back." I knew eventually he was going to be a great player. I told him, "Don't worry. Someday everybody's going to be screaming your name. Take this and learn from it."

What did he learn? I'm not sure. Maybe that no matter how many air balls he throws up, he still has the green light to shoot. Hey brother, how about learning to pass? Me and Rob Horry tried to explain to him he could still get his 20, but instead of coming out, putting it between his legs and shooting, he could pass it to me and cut, and I'd give it right back to him.

We were victims of expectations that season. I was only twenty-five and Kobe was still only a teenager. I told reporters, "We'll be back."

Our potential was unlimited. Everyone in Los Angeles was dialed into the Lakers. I was in the white-hot spotlight and I loved it. I spent a lot of time entertaining the media. When a reporter asked me, "Do you have a special routine before the playoffs?" I told him, "Yeah, I rub your mother's feet."

When the '97–'98 schedule came out and I saw we played Utah in the season opener, I put a circle around my calendar. I had some unfinished business with Ostertag. I didn't like how he spouted off after they beat us in the playoffs, and I planned to take it up with him.

I saw him at the shootaround and I went over and confronted him. I told him, "You should stop talking and stick to playing. Watch what you say." He said, "Fuck you, man. You watch what you say." So I said, "Oh, you bad now?" We got into it and he was mouthing off again, so I turned and slapped him upside the head.

I know. Stupid. But Ostertag hit the deck like I had slugged him or something. I got him with an open hand. He was curled up on the ground moaning, "My contact lenses." It was embarrassing. I was embarrassed for him. I wasn't playing in the game that night because I was recovering from a torn abdominal muscle, but I knew right away I had just gotten myself into some trouble.

The league suspended me one game and fined me ten thousand dollars. But that was nothing compared to what Jerry West did to me. He got right up under my chin and blasted me. "I won't tolerate that kind of childish behavior. Ever. Do you hear me?" he said. "You embarrassed yourself, your team, your parents, and this organization. How do you want people to perceive you? As a bully who does stupid things, or a champion who is a serious ballplayer? You better decide. Now you will apologize to Greg Ostertag and the Utah Jazz, and you will apologize to the Los Angeles Lakers. And if you do something like this again, I'll trade you."

Whoa. Okay.

We won sixty-one games in '97–'98, but once again we lost to Utah, only this time it was in the Western Conference Finals, and this time we got swept.

I averaged 30 points, 10 rebounds, and almost 3 blocks in the play-offs that spring—good D, Ostertag—but nobody cared about that. The new knock was Shaq couldn't even win a game in a big series. First the Rockets had swept us while I was in Orlando and now the Jazz with me in LA.

As soon as we got into our locker room, I lost it. I knew what was going to happen. The papers were going to say I didn't know how to win, that I was a choker, that I didn't care enough. After all the work I put in, all the numbers I put up, it was Orlando all over again and I just couldn't take it.

Just thinking about it got me so damn crazy. Some of the guys were pissed off, like I was. Kobe, for one, wasn't happy. But then I heard Nick and Eddie talking about going to Vegas. They were already on to the next thing, so now I'm even more revved up.

The TV and video equipment are against the wall and I whack it off the stand and kick the crap out of it. Then I go to my locker and I start ripping all my stuff out. My clothes, my shoes, everything. It's flying all over the place.

Then I go into the bathroom and I tear the stall off the door with one hand. I smash that to the ground. Next, I grab the urinal and rip it right off the wall. They say sometimes people don't know their own strength. I knew mine. I was in a complete rage and I wanted to destroy everything in my path.

Nobody is trying to stop me because they know better. They are terrified, and they should be. Jerome is outside the locker room because he's the team security guard, so someone runs out and grabs him because they figure he can talk some sense into me.

But Jerome knows me. He knows how I think. He tells them, "Just stay away from him. It will only last about thirty seconds. Let him blow it off and then he'll be back to normal."

So everyone is staying as far away from me as possible until Jerry West comes flying into the locker room. He grabs me and says, "What the hell do you think you are doing?"

"I'm tired of losing," I told him. "I'm busting my ass every night and I'm tired of it always being my fault."

"And this is how you expect to win?" West said. "Listen to me. I went to the Finals nine times before I ever won a damn thing. Nine times and I *never* acted like this. You're supposed to be our leader. You're supposed to be the one they look to when things go bad. And this is what you come up with? If you want to win so badly, then learn how to be a leader. Stop trashing the bathroom and get back in there and sit down."

I did what he told me to do. I went back and I sat down. Jerome was right. My rage passed after about thirty seconds.

Jerry West wasn't done talking to me. He explained to me how every player is different. Some guys care too much and some guys act like they don't care at all, even though they do. I said to him, "If I'm getting all the blame, they better fucking care."

Back then guys who were too cool to care drove me crazy. Nick Anderson was like that in Orlando, and Eddie Jones was the same way in LA. He'd freeze up in a tight situation, then act like it was no big deal. So, as a young player, the way I tried to get guys like him to perform was to threaten to put my hands on them.

My dad had always motivated me with the threat of physical violence and it always worked. So I guess that was all I knew. I can tell you it didn't work with Eddie Jones at all. When I towered over him and challenged him, all it did was (1) scare the living shit out of him, (2) make him conclude I was nuts, and (3) ultimately make him decide to ignore me.

Jerry West had a lot of different conversations with me. He knew I had big shoes to fill. He talked with me a lot about Kareem, how he took such great care of his body and never got hurt because of things like yoga and his diet. He told me what set Abdul-Jabbar apart was his focus.

"You could learn a lot from Kareem," Jerry West said.

I agreed, except Kareem was never around. And, whenever I did see him, he usually ignored me. The disappointing thing to me was, being in LA all those years and trying to fill those shoes, I would have liked to have a conversation with him.

He'd say hello, but I was looking for "Hey, do this" or "Watch out for that." He knew everyone was comparing me to him. He knew better than anyone what I was up against, but he gave me nothing.

Being mindful of the history of the game, one of the first commercials I ever did for Reebok as a rookie in 1992 was one that included all the great centers.

The commercial opens with me standing on a court, knocking on this imaginary door to the hallowed kingdom of the big men. Bill Russell is looking through the slot and he says: "Password." I answer, "Don't Fake the Funk on a Nasty Dunk." Russell barks, "ID." I show him my Shaq logo. He says, "You're early." I say, "I'm ready." I walk in and there's Wilt Chamberlain, Bill Walton, Bill Russell, and Kareem wearing suits with their arms folded, waiting and watching. I start at the foul line and throw down a nasty, nasty dunk that shatters the backboard. I'm standing there holding the rim in my hands, then I give them one of my very best Shaquille The Deal grins. Kareem says, "That's not enough," and hands me a dustpan. The commercial fades with my voice saying, "I guess that's some kind of rookie thing."

It was my idea to have the legends in the shoot. It was a sign of respect, and I made sure they all got a nice paycheck for doing the commercial. You'd think it might have led to a relationship or something, but it really didn't, except for Bill Russell. He was cool then, and he's cool now. We hit it off and have had many conversations through the years. He has always treated me with great respect, and I've always valued his opinion and his guidance. I'm humbled that he bothered to take an interest in me.

A few years after we filmed the commercial I saw Wilt in a restaurant in Beverly Hills. He was sitting there with his back to me, and Jerome said, "Aren't you going to say hello?" I said I didn't want to bother him, but I kept hoping Wilt would come over and say, "Hey, big fella." He never did.

He died right after that. I loved Wilt. I used to call him my godfather, and I wanted to buy his house sort of as a tribute. It was nice, but it was kind of old and it would have cost too much to fix it up, so I ended up passing on it.

Once I got to the Lakers I saw Kareem all the time, but he just didn't want to deal with me. It went on like that for years. We were at the All-Star Game in 2006, and I saw him in the parking lot and I said to my uncle Mike, "Watch this." He walked by and I said, "Hey, Cap." He muttered hello and kept on moving.

Jerry West said one of Kareem's biggest weaknesses was he had trouble relating to his teammates. He kept reminding me that was one of my strengths.

"People like you," Jerry told me. "They're drawn to you. You are a natural leader. That big personality of yours is one of your biggest weapons, unless you use it the wrong way."

And, whenever I did use it the wrong way, I knew Jerry West would be coming for me. My first season we had a couple of rookies, and we hazed them pretty badly. We were dogging them out constantly. It was "Go get my bags, go get me something to eat." It was kind of a rite of passage in the NBA that a lot of teams do, but we probably went a little too far with it. One of the rookies—Derek Fisher—just took it. The other rookie—Kobe Bryant—ratted us out to Jerry.

Talk about a bad start with your veteran teammates. Jerry called me into his office and absolutely crucified me. He was really ticked off about it. "The kid is eighteen years old, and the two of you can win five championships if you just work together, and already you're down his throat," he said. "What the hell are you thinking? Be smarter than that. Be a leader!"

If I closed my eyes, I could have sworn it was Philip Harrison talking to me.

Just like Sarge, I couldn't get anything past Jerry West.

In the summer of 1998 we were locked out while the owners tried to squeeze some money out of us. We were all told it might be a while before we played any basketball. It was. Our first game that season wasn't until February, and when we got the call that the games were on again, most of the guys were out of shape—except for Kobe.

They fired Del Harris after twelve games into the shortened season and hired Kurt Rambis for the rest of the season. He quickly aligned himself with Kobe.

Kobe was starting to get comfortable in the league. He started doing too much and taking everyone else out of their rhythm. I told him, "Hey, you've got to play team ball," and he always had an answer back. Anything you told him or suggested to him, he always had a comeback. I don't think he ever said, "Yeah, sure, thanks. That's a good idea."

Rambis had made Kobe the golden child, so everyone was afraid to question the kid. I wasn't afraid of anyone. I was going to say what was on my mind whether people liked it or not.

We were in Sacramento and we were losing, so we called a team meeting. No coaches—just players. Every time Kobe started with his one-on-one nonsense, we were tired of hearing "He's just a kid—let it go." Guys were saying stuff under their breath about him, and that's never good.

In the meeting one guy after another stood up and said they were tired of the "golden child" getting special treatment. Kobe just sat there. He didn't say anything.

Kurt was eavesdropping outside, so he busted in and threw in his two cents' worth which was, "Well, you guys were young and selfish once."

Right, Kurt. And how is that working out for Kobe? Three air balls in a row. Three of them.

Once Kurt said that it became clear to all of the veterans we weren't going anywhere with this guy as our coach.

At that point the media starts writing about the "problems" Kobe and I are having. A couple of guys suggested I was jealous that Kobe's jersey was selling more than my jersey. Please. DFish came to my defense right away. He told them, "Man, all Shaq wants to do is win."

Stop me if you've heard this before: the Lakers won a lot of games in the regular season, then got swept in the playoffs. It happened again in 1999. This time we got swept by the San Antonio Spurs, who went on to win the NBA championship.

The Spurs won because of Tim Duncan, a guy I could never break. I could talk trash to Patrick Ewing, get in David Robinson's face, get a rise out of Alonzo Mourning, but when I went at Tim he'd look at me like he was bored and then say, "Hey, Shaq, watch this shot right here off the glass."

You gotta love that. I used to say Duncan and I were like two mafia bosses. I was the loud East Coast boss, taking names, knocking heads. Tim was the laid-back, one-hundred-acre farm don. Nobody knows what he does, he's the chill mafia guy, but we both know how to carry out a hit.

I was jealous of guys like Duncan and Kevin Garnett, who got to do stuff like face up and shimmy. I could so some of that myself, but I was such a power player and the double teams came so quickly, in order for me to get mine I had to go with the boom-boom-bam move. Meanwhile Timmy and Kevin are out there dribbling, shooting off the glass, fading away.

Anyhow, after Duncan and the Spurs swept us out of the playoffs, I was hurting really badly.

All that self-doubt that used to wear me out was coming back. What if I can't win a championship? I was really beginning to wonder if I could. It just wasn't happening. What was wrong with us?

Jerry Buss and Jerry West must have been wondering, too. They fired Kurt Rambis. When the media asked me what I thought the Lakers should do, I told them, "We need someone we can respect, like a Phil Jackson."

Hint hint.

Jerry West had the same idea. He told the owner the coaching carousel had to stop. We needed someone with some juice.

So they hired Phil, and right after the press conference they tell me, "He wants to meet with you."

Phil didn't mess around. He told me he expected big things from me. He told me there was absolutely no reason why I shouldn't be the MVP of the league. And then he went right into it: no more movies, no more rap records, no more parties.

"I know you've heard this before, and you've said, 'Yes sir,' and 'Okay, sir.' But you ignored it. This time you better not," he said.

I told him he had my word. For one thing, the man's résumé spoke for itself. For another, I was getting older and I wanted to win. I was so tired of people talking about me not being a leader.

That summer I went to see Phil Jackson at his lake house. I was booked to do a benefit rap concert in Montana about twenty miles away, so I told him I was going to drop by.

Phil was at a doctor's appointment with his daughter. When he got back I was jumping on his trampoline with all the neighborhood kids. But then I got hot, so I threw on my bathing suit and started to do gainers off Phil's dock into the lake.

Phil kept asking me, "Shouldn't you be wearing a life vest?" Maybe he thought I couldn't swim, because most white people think black people can't swim. Not true, dawg. I'm an excellent swimmer.

We sat down and had a conversation, and he reminded me he expected me to concentrate on basketball and basketball only. Then his kids came to my concert and that was it. I didn't see Phil Jackson again until training camp.

I couldn't wait. I wanted that ring, and I'd finally hooked up with the guy who could get me one.

JUNE 19, 2000

Staples Center

Los Angeles, California

The first person who got to Shaquille O'Neal was Kobe Bryant, leaping into his arms like an excitable little boy who couldn't wait to celebrate with this big brother.

Their embrace was emotional, prolonged, and the big man didn't bother to conceal the tears that streamed down his face. Shaq had just won his first NBA championship, yet his were not tears of joy. They were tears of relief.

They were the by-product of eight years of frustration, criticism, and self-doubt, emotions one person in particular would completely understand. And that was why, in the biggest moment of his professional life, Shaquille O'Neal went looking for Lucille Harrison.

"Once that buzzer sounded," he said, "all I wanted to do was give my mommy a kiss."

Since he was eight years old his pregame ritual hadn't wavered. He found his mother and pecked her on the cheek, a homage to the woman who had fortified him with the emotional strength to withstand the withering disappointments that had clouded his career.

Lucille was the one who reminded him, "Michael didn't do it the first time. Michael didn't do it the second time. Stay with the mission."

"Everything with Shaquille was, 'He's a great player, but...'" Lucille said. "After a while, what people say about you starts to influence your thinking. It can overwhelm you. And it started to overwhelm Shaquille."

On the eve of the 2000 playoffs, Lucille corralled her oldest son and attempted to eradicate the doubt she knew was lurking.

"Turn your ear off to the naysayers," she said. "Don't let them crush you with their words. You have to change your way of thinking. You were the happiest, most positive little boy I've ever seen.

"Now draw from that positive thinking as a grown man."

He caught glimpses of her in Game 6 of the Finals against Indiana, resplendent in pink, the stress of her son's journey etched in her face.

He scored 41 points in the final game against the Pacers to smash an exclamation point on a truly dominant season. He was named the All-Star MVP, the regular-season MVP, and the Finals MVP, only the third player in league history to receive all three in one season.

All the past failures in Orlando and LA and LSU were washed away by a deluge of purple-and-gold Laker confetti and the impassioned chants of "MVP!" meant only for him.

A succession of well-wishers embraced him: Phil Jackson, Glen Rice, Magic Johnson, his uncle Mike Parris, his bodyguard, Jerome Crawford. Yet Shaquille O'Neal, the most happy-go-lucky superstar in the league, remained stone-faced.

"I guess I just wasn't sure it had finally happened," he said.

He clutched the Larry O'Brien trophy with one of his massive hands and used the other to wrap it around his mother's waist. He celebrated with John Salley and Rick Fox and Ron Harper and Kobe, too, but they had not walked in his shoes. Although they were his teammates, they were not his confidants.

"Mom," he whispered in Lucille Harrison's ear, "this one is for you."

Trust is a beautiful thing. We had it on my first championship team in Los Angeles. I admit I wasn't always good about trusting my teammates in the past. I felt I had to get it done myself.

But we had made some big changes, starting with Phil Jackson.

The first day of workouts he asked me, "What's the most impressive thing about Wilt Chamberlain's career?" I knew it was a trick question. I thought he wanted me to say scoring 100 points in a game, but I went with the fact that Wilt averaged 50 points and 27 rebounds one season. "That's not it," Phil said. "It was that he played almost every minute of every game. He averaged 48.5 minutes a night in 1961–62, when his team played in ten overtime games. Do you think you can average forty minutes a game?"

I hear myself saying, "Sure, I can do that."

Phil was a smart guy. He understood me. He knew I liked to have fun and I liked to do things my way, but if he showed me respect and asked me to do something, I would do it.

One of the things he told me was he was going to mess me up if I missed free throws, so I started working on it five hours a day. When I was in Orlando, I worked with a guy named Buzz Braman, who preached routine. If it goes in, follow the routine. So my routine became bounce it one, two, three times, elbow straight, elbow at the rim, take a little deep breath, shoot it, then forget about it. I tried it, but I got the same results. Sometimes it went in, sometimes it didn't. It was mental with me—had to be. I often shot 80 percent from the line in practice.

Right before the season started there was an article in the paper quoting Phil saying, "If Shaq concentrates he can be the MVP of the league this year. If he doesn't, it will be like all the other seasons. We'll win fifty-six games but we'll go home early."

I didn't want to go home early.

We added John Salley and Ron Harper to our roster, two guys who had rings already. They brought in Brian Shaw, my old teammate from Orlando. Suddenly we had veterans who had seen it all, who really truly cared only about winning. I had help all around me, and I'm not just talking about Kobe.

Take a guy like Rick Fox. He's standing there in the corner and you know he's deadly from there, so I've got the ball and I'm thinking about muscling it in, but then I say, "Let me kick it to Rick and see what he can do," or "Let me kick it to Glen Rice and give him a look. I've already got 25, so let's get them involved." It was my way of showing them "Hey, I believe in you."

It worked. The triangle gave us ball movement and the trust gave us the chemistry we needed to succeed. That's not to say there still weren't conflicts once in a while. But we had guys on that Lakers team who knew how to handle it, like Ron Harper. Harp won championships with Phil in Chicago and he commanded respect from everyone.

He was old school and I was old school and Harp knew Kobe was new school, so if Kobe and I were having a beef he'd have a conversation with Kobe then he'd come to me. He'd calm us down. He'd tell me, "Shaq, meet me halfway on this. Kobe's a young guy, you've got to understand that. And we need him. You know we do. You're getting under his skin, so lay off a little bit."

I won't lie to you. That was hard for me. I was under so much pressure, and Kobe took so many bad shots I wanted to scream at him, "Miss another shot and I'm getting you traded!"

BShaw was another guy who ran interference. He had no problem getting in Kobe's grill and telling him, "Stop being so selfish. We're playing team ball here." BShaw knew how to get me the rock. Our Shaw-Shaq Redemption move was unstoppable. We had an eye contact thing. Brian wasn't a traditional point guard. He's not just looking at where you want the ball, he's looking at how the defense is playing. A defender might be in one spot, but only a smart guy like Brian would know to throw it to a different spot. Once I saw his eyebrow go up I knew the lob was coming. And it was perfect, every time.

We were lucky to have Robert Horry on our side, too. Every coach has their whipping boy and Rob was Phil's. He would mess with Rob all the time. He'd tell Horry, "When you hear me whistle, that's the sound of your master calling, so you better come." Rob would say, "You ain't my goddamn master," but when Phil whistled, Big Shot Bob came running.

Man, Horry hit a ton of big shots. He was a guy who understood his role and didn't worry about anything else. Hit game winners. That was what his calling card was. Everything else was gravy.

Phil Jackson knew how to treat us like men. If I went out and gave him a 29-point and 20-rebound game, he'd come in the next day and say, "Hey, go find Danny. Get a massage."

Danny Garcia was our massage therapist. He's one of my closest friends, and he's been with me ever since I went to Los Angeles. When I played in Boston during the 2010–11 season, he lived in my house in Sudbury with me. He knows the pounding my body takes. So I'd get my massage, and then Phil would put me on the exercise bike for thirty minutes, and then he'd send me home. I remember thinking, "I love this dude."

You know I was going to give my coach everything I had in the next game because I wanted Phil to believe this arrangement was going to work.

Naturally we were going to run the triangle because that was Phil's signature offense. I didn't know anything about the triangle before Phil got there. The good thing about Phil was we did the same thing every day. We did this little hip-skip-hop thing. He said "hip" and we went forward. Then it was "skip" and we hopped back.

We'd run through each option of the triangle seven times each.

We did it over and over so guys would memorize it, almost like muscle memory, only this was brain memory. After a while it became second nature.

He's telling me, "Shaq, you will be like a point center in the triangle. You are going to touch the ball every time down."

Phil was definitely a different sort of cat. He was into his Zen mode a lot. Being from the 'hood, I knew what certain drugs smelled like—weed, for instance. Phil wanted us to meditate, so he'd put us in a room and dim the lights and he'd burn sage. It smelled like weed. We'd call him on it and he'd tell us, "No, it's not weed. It's the cousin of weed."

We had this fifteen-seat theater at the practice facility, and he'd start pounding this Indian drum. When he hit that thing, it meant "Get your ass to the theater." You could be anywhere, but when you heard that *doo, doo, doo* sound you better get moving—or else.

Once we got in the theater he'd turn out the lights and it would be pitch-black. So here comes the weed—oh, sorry Phil, the "cousin of weed"—and then he'd tell us to lean back in our chairs and relax. Then he'd start talking to us about whatever was going on with our team.

He'd say, "Right now there's some negativity going on, so let's release that," or he might say, "Tomorrow we're playing a team that is going to be coming for you, so concentrate on your safe place, your positive thoughts. Remember to share the ball, move the ball, trust each other."

A lot of days you'd hear guys snoring, usually the ones who had been out late the night before. Certain days even I'd fall asleep because I was tired, and other times I'd try to listen to what he was saying, and other times I really would meditate.

When Phil was done, he'd tell us to take ten deep breaths, then blow each breath out. As we blew those breaths out we were supposed to blow away our stresses. Some days it felt good. Some days I really think it helped me. Other days it was a chance to catch a good nap.

Either way, you knew Phil was dead serious about this stuff. No one dared make fun of it.

The other thing Phil did was after being there awhile and getting to know the guys, he'd hand out books. It was his way of saying, "This is the type of person I think you are. You should read this." Every year he gave me a book on Friedrich Nietzsche, a German philosopher who questioned the value and objectivity of the truth. Phil told me Nietzsche was a guy who was so brilliant everyone thought he was crazy.

So he's giving me these books, but I'm a busy guy and I really don't have time to read, so I sent one of my assistants out to get me the CliffsNotes version. Hope you don't mind, Phil.

People ask me all the time if Phil Jackson ever talked about Michael Jordan. I don't remember him doing that a lot. He talked about the Bulls in general, but rarely about Black Jesus. I would have liked to known a little about MJ. He was the greatest player I had ever seen, and it would have been kind of cool to hear what made him tick, but Phil didn't go there. He wanted us to develop our own identity.

But there was a guy who was around our team a lot who did bring up MJ. His name was George Mumford, and he was Phil's guy. Because of Phil's résumé I listened to everything George said, even though I thought some of it was just wacky. George was sort of like a psychologist. The craziest thing about him was every problem we had on our team the Bulls also had, so he had an answer for everything.

I'd say, "Yo man, I'm tired of people coming after me in the paper," and he'd say, "Well, you know what Mike did in Chicago..."

He sat down with me one-on-one a lot. When I read something that some self-promoter like Ric Bucher or TJ Simers wrote, he would tell me, "Channel that anger. Get rid of it."

I would have liked to have gotten rid of Bucher and Simers, but that wasn't an option, so I did the next best thing—I ignored them.

Because of George Mumford, I don't read newspaper articles

anymore. I'll glance through stuff now and then, but in order for me to react, someone will have to draw my attention to it. I sleep better at night now. That stuff bothered me, so I eliminated it from my life. People say I'm too sensitive. Well, I'd like to see how all of you would deal with someone drilling you in the head every day, questioning your work ethic and intelligence and your manhood.

It's not like I treated reporters badly. Hell, I was a quote machine for them. Had a lot of fun with them, too. Once a reporter asked me, "Let's say a snake bit your mom right here, in the chest area. Would you be willing to suck the venom out to win the title?"

"No," I answered, "but I would with your wife."

I got in the habit of creating "Shaqisms." If you went on a glamorous vacation with me, it was Shaqapulco. If I was a painter, I was Shaq-casso.

Then there was the nickname game. After one stretch where I had completely dominated Vlade Divac, Rik Smits, and Arvydas Sabonis, I started calling myself the Big Deporter. By January 2000 I was in the middle of the most incredible stretch of my career, so I told everybody my new name was The Big Stock Exchange. When they asked me why, I gave them my full-strength thousand-watt smile and said, "Numbers, baby, numbers."

I was putting up some big ones. I dropped 61 points and 23 rebounds on the Clippers on the night of my birthday in March. I was terribly disappointed by the Clippers, who refused my request of about twelve complimentary tickets, so after I destroyed them I warned them, "Don't ever tell me no on the tickets again."

The best thing about Phil Jackson was he didn't give us any panic room. We'd have some games where we'd have five or six turnovers in a row, and we'd be looking to the bench and he'd say, "I'm not wasting one of my time-outs on you guys. Play through it. Do what we do every single day in practice and you'll be alright."

Just like Phil asked me to, I was logging around forty minutes a game. I was getting pounded. The Hack-a-Shaq strategy, which was to foul me on purpose so I'd have to go to the free-throw line and, the other team hoped, miss my free throws, was in full swing a lot of nights. Whenever I felt like I needed a little break, I'd tell John Salley, and he'd go to Phil and say, "You know, Shaq is feeling a little run down…"

Phil had fun taking his digs at me. I didn't mind, because I knew he cared about me and he did it to motivate me.

The two of us would get into it once in a while. He'd say, "Get over there sooner." I'd say, "I'm trying, man." He'd come back with, "Well try harder, fat boy." He called me that all the time. I'd get 39 points and he'd say, "That's all you could come up with, fat boy?" Anyone else says that and I'm punching him in the face. But Phil had earned my respect.

The free throws were a constant topic of conversation with us. I had the key to the Mira Costa High School gym so I'd go there and practice after the team workout. I usually went late at night. I told Phil, "Don't worry, I'll make them when we need them."

Everything about the Lakers during our title run was fun. The guys, the team, the city.

We used to rap on the bus all the time. We'd freestyle. We'd see something and go off. It could be anything—a guy with a big nose walking his dog, a guy on our team with a zit on his cheek. Kobe wouldn't usually say anything, but he was sitting there observing. You could tell he wanted to join in, but he hung back. Maybe he was afraid he wasn't a good enough rapper. Who knows? We spent a lot of time wondering what was going on under that retro afro he had.

Kobe was a very intelligent guy. One day we're on the bus rapping, and he starts in with his own rap. He's using all these big words, and the damn rap sounds like a movie script or something. That was when we realized he was going home and writing stuff up, then memorizing it and coming back with it on the bus.

He would pretend to be freestyling, but he'd throw all this metaphysical and metabolical stuff in there, so we'd call him on it. We'd tell him, "That ain't no freestyle," and he'd get all defensive and say, "Yes it is. Yes it is. It's off the dome. It's off the dome."

We'd all just laugh and say, "Okay, brother."

Kobe hated the triangle, but I never understood why. He got a ton of shots from running it. BShaw used to say the triangle was really just a way to take everyone's attention away from what was really going on, which was me and Kobe running a two-man game. If they doubled Kobe off the pick-and-roll, then here I am, rolling to the basket. If they don't double Kobe, he comes off in a one-on-one situation and you can't stop him. And, if you really want to make the mistake of concentrating too much on the both of us, then Big Shot Bob Horry or Glen Rice is going to knock down open shots.

Here's what I didn't like: when the media tried to climb inside my head and Kobe's head and make something out of nothing. Perfect example: at the 2000 All-Star Game I was warming up and goofing around, and I mimicked one of his next-generation dribbles and threw the ball into the stands. Some guys wrote I was taking a shot at Kobe, that I was dissing him over his turnovers.

Wrong. Kobe was in on it. We had this joke that every time anyone on the team committed some kind of crazy turnover, we used to call him Tragic Bronson. It was a takeoff on Magic Johnson. In 1984, when he coughed up the series to Boston with some bad plays, they started calling him Tragic instead of Magic.

We were picking up on that and having a little fun with it. So when Kobe would drill Brian Shaw in the chest with one of his no-look passes we'd call him Tragic Bronson. Some days, when I tried to take it coast-to-coast and lost it out of bounds, I was called Tragic Bronson.

It was becoming obvious the whole Shaq-Kobe deal was the biggest story in town. We were both smart enough to put that aside once we got inside the gym.

I wasn't the only guy who got frustrated with Kobe. Very early in that '99–'00 season, we were scrimmaging in practice and Kobe was being so selfish with the ball that some of the older guys like Rick and Brian and AC Green decided, "Okay, Phil's not saying anything to him, we've got to have a players-only meeting."

Phil always said he was against meetings like that because he didn't think anything positive ever came out of them, but we decided to do it anyway. So we get everyone in this tiny room, and naturally everyone is going off on Kobe, which is exactly what Phil didn't want to happen.

Next thing you know the coaches come busting in and Phil is trying to stick up for the Kobester, saying, "C'mon, now. This isn't all on Kobe. Let's not turn this into a witch hunt."

DFish interrupts him and says, "Hold on, Phil, you're new here. We've been putting up with this for three or four years. It's time to get to the bottom of it."

The weird thing about that meeting was Kobe was sitting in the back of the room saying, "I love you guys." Only he wasn't saying it like that. He went into this street talk, saying, "Y'all my niggers, y'all like brothers to me." I was looking at him and wondering, *What the hell is this?* Maybe he was trying to fit in. After all, the kid was only twenty-one years old. But if he wanted to fit in, he should have taken off his headphones once in a while and tried to talk to us.

I asked Phil why he wouldn't get on Kobe. He said it was because he wanted Kobe in attack mode all the time. That was how he was most effective, and if Phil was on his case all the time Kobe might start to hesitate, and that would be bad for our team. That made no sense to me, but really, it didn't matter.

The way I was playing that season, Kobe wasn't going to mess up our chances.

We won sixty-seven games in '99–'00, and I was named the Most Valuable Player. I called my father, Sgt. Philip Harrison, and when I told him I had won it, he broke down and cried. The guy who had told me my whole life "No tears—they are a sign of weakness" was bawling like a baby. Once he regained his composure, he reminded me I wouldn't be able to enjoy my new big-ass trophy unless we won a championship, too.

Nothing had changed since I was a kid. My father was still challenging me, still living and dying with every game. He still felt he needed to stand up for me. Sometimes he went a little overboard. One night I swear I heard him yelling to Kobe, "Get it inside!" just like when I was at Cole High School in San Antonio.

Sarge was getting better about letting me fight my own battles, but once, when we were beating the Spurs pretty easily, Phil Jackson left me in the game. The Spurs backup center at the time was Felton Spencer, a big dude who started hammering away at me. My dad was furious. He was screaming for Phil to take me out. "They're going to break his arm!" Sarge was yelling.

After the game, I'm doing an interview on the court, and all of a sudden I see him. He's coming onto the court right for Phil Jackson. There's nothing I can do. I can't get there in time. It was like I was watching the whole thing in slow motion. Sarge goes up to Phil and starts jawing at him about leaving me in the game. Phil whipped around and said, "Get off this court. You don't belong out here." Jerome had the good sense to pull Sarge away.

My father was right about that '99–'00 season. It was championship or bust. We had a tough series with Sacramento in the first round, which back then was a best-of-five series. It went all five games. The two teams were developing a real dislike for one another. Vlade Divac was on that team, and he was the guy they traded to get Kobe, so I'm sure he had all sorts of motivation. Then you had Chris Webber, the guy I convinced the Orlando Magic to pass over in favor of Penny, so there was some history there, too.

When we lost Game 4 in their place to tie it 2–2, that meant we were looking at a winner-take-all Game 5 in our building. The Sacramento fans were all over us after the game, so Ron Harper turned around and flashed one of his championship rings at them to shut them up. Instead they started chanting, "Not with Shaq! Not with Shaq!"

Ouch. That stung. I'm thinking, *Okay, dawg. You gotta make it happen in Game 5.*

My dad called me beforehand and told me, "You've never played well in Sacramento. Put it behind you." That was good advice. We went back home and I dropped 32 points and 18 rebounds on them. No sweat, right? If I tell you the truth, those guys worried me, and I was glad we got past them. Good-bye, Sacramento.

We breezed past Phoenix in the next round, but then we got hung up in this killer series with Portland. That was the one where we found ourselves down 15 points in the fourth quarter of Game 7, the one where I went to that "safe place" in my grandmother Odessa's lap, and we ran off the now-famous run to beat the Blazers and advance to the Finals. I had 9 points in that fourth quarter, including the monster dunk from Kobe, but what I was the happiest about was hitting two free throws to tie it 77–77 with about two minutes to go.

Playing the Pacers in the Finals was almost anti-climatic. They were a scrappy team. Larry Bird was the coach, and he did a good job of preparing them, but we were just better. By that point, no one was getting in our way. Here's the other thing: I couldn't believe they decided to try and stop me with single coverage. Please. You know better, Larry. In Game 1, I had 43 points and 19 rebounds. Afterwards they asked me, "How would you guard yourself?" I answered, "I wouldn't. I'd just fake an injury and go home."

In May of that season I coined myself the Big Aristotle, because, as I explained, it was Aristotle who said, "Excellence is not a singular act, but a habit."

My plan was to make winning championships a habit.

What I realized once we finally won was that title wasn't just for us. After kissing my daughter, Taahirah, and sharing hugs with family, teammates, and friends, all of a sudden there's Jack Nicholson and Snoop Dogg and Will Smith. All of sudden, all of LA wants to give me a hug.

Everybody loves a winner. And nobody could say ever again that Shaq couldn't win the big one.

There was one disappointing thing about that 2000 championship. When we won it, Jerry West was nowhere to be found. I asked about it and they said he was superstitious, that he was too nervous to go to the games. But I later found out the real reason—Jerry and Phil didn't get along. It was a power thing, I guess. We'd have team meetings and Phil would ask Jerry to leave. That really hurt Jerry West. After all, he was the guy who built that team.

I've never been a brownnoser. Even though I loved Jerry West, the only times we really had any meaningful conversations was when he was giving me a hard time. He'd chew me out, tell me a story, then tell me to beat it. I loved that. Once in a while he'd say, "Good game," or "Do this and do that," but I never hung out with him.

But there came a time when I guess Jerry Buss didn't want to pay him, so I got on TV and said, "If Jerry West isn't going to be there, I don't want to be here." I meant it. So Jerry West got his money, but eventually he left anyway.

To be honest, the day Jerry West quit was the day it all started going downhill.

He called me and told me, "Shaquille, I'm leaving. Things just aren't working out here for me." I asked him, "Is there anything I can do?" He said, "No, it's just time for me to move on." He sounded kind of sad. If you go back and look at the championships that we won and the ones Magic won, Jerry West was the guy who put together all the pieces.

Mitch Kupchak took over for Jerry, and I just never felt like he had my back. Once you deal with someone like Jerry West, you better come up with someone pretty special to keep my attention. Unfortunately, Mitch wasn't that guy for me. We never got along. Mitch looked out for two people: himself and Jerry Buss. The rest of us were afterthoughts.

The Lakers were instantly the favorites to repeat in '00–'01, and we weren't backing down from that. I told everyone, "We have to repeat. Anything else would be uncivilized."

As hard as it was to win that first one, it's even harder to repeat. Everyone who gets that ring thinks they're special (including me). We all started thinking we were The Man.

Well, there could only be one Man and that was me, the big dawg.

Kobe missed the memo. He thought it was his time to take over our team.

Naturally that caused some problems for us. Kobe still hadn't warmed up to the triangle, and once in a while he'd get out there and freelance, and nobody was happy with it. The dude didn't get it. So what if the shot went in? You busted the play, man.

Phil decided we needed more defense, so Glen Rice, who had made the mistake of getting in a public contract squabble with the Lakers, got traded and Horace Grant came in. He knew the triangle in his sleep, and it was great to be reunited with him, but we lost DFish for sixty-two games with a broken foot, and it hurt us more than you'd know.

We started the '00–'01 season with a 23-11 record, and Kobe was on my nerves. After one game, when he scored 38 points and refused to even look at anybody else, I asked for a trade. I was kidding— sort of.

The best thing that happened to us that season was Kobe got injured and had to sit out nine games. Like I've said before, he's a smart guy, so while he's sitting there and he's watching us win eight out of nine games, he notices that when the ball is moving and everyone touches it, we're a better team.

Give him credit. When he came back after his injury, he was a different guy.

That meant we were a different team. We finished strong and beat out Sacramento by one game for the division crown.

People asked me about the roll we were on and I told them, "Our offense is like the Pythagorean theorem. There is no answer."

The media had a blast with that one. Of course some wise guy comes back at me later and challenges me, so I said, "There is no answer to the Pythagorean theorem. Well, there is an answer, but by the time you figure it out, I got 40 points, 10 rebounds, and we're planning for the parade."

I was planning for a big parade. I was feeling invincible, like

Superman. The only thing that can stop Superman is Kryptonite, and there's no such thing as Kryptonite.

What we did next was the most satisfying stretch of my entire career.

We played our old nemesis Portland and swept them in three straight. Just dominated them. Next up, the other team I couldn't stomach, the Sacramento Kings, who I started calling the Sacramento Queens. Here are my numbers for that sweep: Game 1—44 points, 21 rebounds; Game 2—43 points, 20 rebounds; Game 3—21 points, 18 rebounds; Game 4—25 points, 10 rebounds.

See ya, Queens.

So now we've got to play the Spurs in the Western Conference Finals, and that means Tim Duncan again. Tim was injured in 2000, so we didn't get a chance to see them in the playoffs. In my mind, I had to win at least one title that included getting past my most worthy opponent.

We took Game 1. In Game 2 they were up 15 in the third quarter and Duncan was terrific, and I was like, *Damn, we can't let this happen.* Kobe was thinking the same thing, and he just took over the game. He went nuts. He was spectacular and the Spurs had no answer. He brought us all the way back, and after we won I said, "He's my idol."

And I wasn't even kidding.

We went on to sweep the Spurs—did you hear that? We swept the Spurs!—so we still hadn't lost a playoff game yet.

We're going to play the Sixers in the Finals, which means a lot of Allen Iverson, who stole my second regular-season MVP trophy from me. He was a talented little bugger and we knew we'd have our hands full, and when they beat us in Game 1 we started hearing the hoots from all the Lakers haters. They said their center Dikembe Mutombo, who was the Defensive Player of the Year that season and a Georgetown guy (you know how those Georgetown guys bother me) was going to "negate me." That's a fancy word for "stop me."

Don't bet on it. It became my goal not just to beat the Sixers, but to destroy Dikembe. He was complaining about my elbows and my "aggressive play," and I figured, *How's this for aggressive?* I dunked on his head, again and again. I completely undressed him.

We needed only five games to get the job done. What I remember most about that 2001 championship is my father on the court with me, looking up at me and saying, "I love you." The old man didn't say that too often, and it kind of choked me up for a minute.

Jerry West called me after the series to congratulate me. He said I had "shredded" the morale of the Sixers and Mutombo. "Shaq, your quickness, your footwork, your balance, your power, it was like watching a one-sided boxing match," Jerry said. "They should have stopped the fight. You dominated Dikembe so completely, at times I was thinking, *This almost isn't fair.*"

Getting that kind of praise from one of the best ever, the logo, was really special. I was on top of the basketball world.

Before the '01–'02 season I had some minor surgery on my toe. I had this arthritic toe that was giving me major problems. There was a more serious, more involved surgery that I probably should have had, but we were winning and I didn't want to interrupt that with too much time missed, so I went for the quick fix that would only keep me out of training camp.

It didn't work. My toe was killing me all season, and it made it difficult for me to push off. That year we finished second in the division behind Sacramento. Our rivalry had heated up, and of course I was fanning the flames every chance I got.

During one of our preseason games against Sacramento we're staying at the Palms in Las Vegas and we go to hang out at this club called Rain. It has three levels; there's about two thousand people in the club and we're roped off up on the top floor. It's me, BShaw, and DFish, and I start rapping about Doug Christie's wife, who had popped off in the papers about how her husband was being treated. I mention Kings guard Mike Bibby and CWebb and Vlade in my rap, and I'm having some fun at their expense.

Of course the Kings players were all there. They were on the second level and they heard everything I said, but I didn't care. It was all in fun. It was freestyle rap—whatever comes to you, you say it. I'm dumping all over them in this rap but they're laughing, because what else are they going to do?

Naturally we ended up playing Sacramento in the 2002 Western Conference Finals. It was a bloodbath, a lot of smack talk going back and forth. Three of the games ended on last-second shots.

Their coach, Rick Adelman, kept complaining I was stepping over the line too soon after I shot my free throws. So, after Game 3 I sent him a little rhyme that went like this: "Don't cry / Dry your eyes / Here comes Shaq / With those four little guys."

In Game 4, I hit 9 of 13 free throws, and we won at the buzzer on a shot by Big Shot Bob. In Game 6, I was 13 of 17 from the free-throw line. We won, which forced a Game 7.

As I've said before, I happen to be a big "conspiracy theory" guy, but I can't sign off on Sacramento's charges that the league wanted the Lakers to win instead of them.

When we won Game 7 (11 for 15 from the line, because I know you were wondering), we got on our bus and got the hell out of there. I couldn't resist, though. On the way out I mooned their fans.

My mother didn't like that. If I had thought about Lucille before I did it, it would have stopped me in my tracks. Sarge wasn't too crazy about it, either, but he has a temper so he understands sometimes your emotions get the best of you.

We played the New Jersey Nets in the Finals, and just like the previous year it was kind of a letdown after the series we had just had with Sacramento. We won the first two games, and in Game 3 the Nets were making some noise about winning a game, but I sent Jason Kidd's driving shot into the third row of the seats and Kobe hit a spinning jumper and it was over. We went on to sweep them to lock up the three-peat.

I got myself another ring, another series MVP. Kobe came up to me and said, "Congratulations, greatest," and I said, "Congratulations, most dominant."

This time I didn't guarantee a four-peat because I was still having some serious issues with my toe. The doctor told me I had hallux rigidus, which is a disorder of the joint located at the base of the big toe. It's a form of degenerative arthritis, and mine had gotten so bad I needed more surgery. There were three options. I could have the quick-fix surgery again that hadn't worked the first time, or another surgery that would keep me out two to three months, or a third, more involved surgery they perform on ballerinas. If I had chosen that one, I would have been out six months and I wouldn't have been able to come back until January or February. Phil Jackson was pushing me to have the more involved surgery. He could tell my toe was so painful and so stiff that it was affecting my lift and I was putting strain on the rest of my body.

He told me, "If you get this done right, you can play until you're forty."

I wish I had listened to him. I was too nervous about being out six months, especially since the Lakers were stalling on the extension we had been negotiating. So I had the surgery that would keep me out three months. It helped me some, but my problems with my toe have never gone away.

It took me a while to make that decision, and to find the best surgeon, so I didn't have the surgery until later in the summer. I missed the first twelve games of the season. When someone asked me why I put if off so long, I said, "I got hurt on company time, so I'll heal on company time."

Phil wasn't happy with me after I said that. Neither was Dr. Buss. It probably wasn't the smartest thing I've ever said, but I was injured and worried about my future, and I was getting no love from the Lakers.

We started that season 11-19. We recovered enough to win fifty games but we lost to the Spurs in the playoffs. The series was tied 2–2, and we had the ball in Big Shot Bob's hands to win it in Game 5, only this time, the ball went halfway down...and out. We were all shocked. Rob's shots always went in.

Our locker room was pretty quiet after we were eliminated. We
had won three championships in a row, and all of a sudden we were
yesterday's news. I remember Kobe and I sharing a black bro hug and
then going our separate ways for the summer.

Even with all the back-and-forth crap between us, we understood
we needed each other to win. Go back and look at any criticism I
ever had of Kobe. Never once did I ever say the kid couldn't play. It
was never about that.

The crazy thing about Kobe and me was, we never had a problem
in practice. Once we got on that court, whatever issues we had disap-
peared.

I just never looked at it as a big deal, although I know everyone
else did. I heard Doc Rivers say once our relationship was the "biggest travesty in sports" because we should have stayed together and
won at least five championships. Maybe, maybe not. We'll never
know.

The media was constantly asking me about Kobe and they were
constantly asking Kobe about me. They kept poking us, prodding
us, but in the end, what were the results? Rings. Championships.
Legendary status.

At one point they asked me: are you and Kobe the most powerful duo that's ever played? I put on my blank face and said, "I can't
answer that question. I didn't have a TV growing up and I don't
know how to read."

Kobe and I went at it a different way. He was driven, obsessed with
being great. I wanted to be great, too, but I had other things in my
life. I didn't have that tunnel vision that made Kobe so special and
so annoying at the same time.

The other thing Kobe didn't understand was I wasn't born with his
body or his metabolism. If the two of us spent a month in the weight
room and did the exact same program, he'd be ripped, defined. Not
me, no matter how much I lift. I don't ever look that way.

Some guys are what I call natural salad eaters. Kobe, LeBron
James, Dwyane Wade, they're salad eaters. Their bodies are fabulous,

chiseled. I don't know what they eat but they look like he-man dawgs. It's a genetic gift.

Then you look at guys like me, Zach Randolph, Kevin Love. We don't have those bodies, but we're still going to do magical things. Dwight Howard and Blake Griffin? They're salad eaters.

Me, I'm going to McDonald's, buy a Big Mac, and then I'm going to bust your ass. I don't look like the others, but that doesn't mean I can't get the job done.

I'd say three championships in a row proves my point.

2002

Los Angeles, California

S haquille O'Neal was in training, but not for a fourth NBA championship. For years he had been enrolled in the Los Angeles Police Academy, a challenging physical and academic regimen he took on in addition to playing professional basketball.

His goal was to be a member of the SWAT team. The specific requirements for the specialized unit included the ability to scale a rope one hundred feet in the air. O'Neal had completed the conditioning tests, the sit-ups and the push-ups, had endured the verbal assaults and disciplinary penalties, but that rope climb kept crossing him up.

"I was too big," he said. "I'd grab onto that thing and haul myself up, but I wasn't able to hang on."

Without completing the task, a spot on the SWAT team was out of the question.

Dozens of times, he tried to shimmy up that rope at the Academy. Each time, he failed. Finally the supervising officer told him, "Shaquille, I don't think this is for you."

A few weeks later, Mike Parris went to visit O'Neal at

his Los Angeles home. He couldn't help but notice the one-hundred-foot rope dangling from the roof.

"Police training," said Shaq, when asked for an explanation.

For weeks the big man tested his will against the rope. One morning, Shaq decided to add some small knots so his grip was more stable. Within days, Shaquille O'Neal had scaled it to the top.

He skipped into the house and called Philip Harrison.

"Dad," he said excitedly. "I did it!"

The following morning Shaq removed the knots and attempted to elevate himself without them. He made significant progress and was almost three quarters of the way up when he lost his grip and toppled seventy-five feet to the ground. He landed with a sickening thud squarely on his back.

For a moment, he thought he'd fractured his pelvis. He crawled into the house, calling for help. His injuries proved to be minor, but he was so bruised and sore he missed a couple of practices and a game with the Lakers.

"I could climb that rope with the knots all day, every day," said O'Neal. "But without them... it was just too hard."

The rope was taken down. The SWAT team dream was crossed off the list. The NBA superstar continued on with his chosen profession of dunking basketballs, but the disappointment lingered.

For the first time in his life, Shaquille O'Neal discovered there were some things a big man simply cannot do.

My FATHER'S VOICE FOLLOWS ME. SOMETIMES, I REALLY don't want to hear it, but I know I should listen. One of the things Sarge always told me was, "What if you break your knee? What if you can't play anymore? You better have a backup plan."

One of my aspirations when I was done playing was to be a sheriff somewhere. Sometimes when you are a big-name star and you cross over to another entity, people think that whatever you want is just going to be handed to you.

So, in order to be a sheriff, I had to learn what the police force already knew. Rather than just being Shaq, basketball hero, the star of a couple of terrible movies and best-selling rap artist, I needed to gain some credibility in law enforcement.

I enrolled in the Police Academy in Los Angeles, and it took me three years to get through. In LA the definition of a reserve police officer is you have another job. Level 4 gives you security guard status. Level 3 gives you minor police status, which means you can ride around with the police but you can't carry a gun. Level 2 means now you are a real police officer but you always have to be accompanied by a cop. Level 1 means you are a full-time police officer on the force.

I was reaching for Level 1, but it took me a while. After practice I'd put on my uniform and go straight to the Academy. I did that because I wanted the respect of the troops. People used to offer me badges all the time. "Hey, come to our precinct, be chief for the day." That was not what I was after.

I wanted those other officers to respect me, not to look at me as just Shaq the basketball player. So that meant I had to go to the Academy and get tased and maced like everyone else.

I went to Sheriff Lee Baca in LA County and asked him if he'd sign off on my training. He was kind of skeptical at first because he had given gun permits to a couple of other celebrities who had been irresponsible. He didn't tell me their names, but it took me almost four years to get a permit because of Baca's concerns of celebrities carrying guns. He wouldn't let me enroll in his Academy, so I went around asking some of the smaller outfits if they would take me.

I found this little department, the Los Angeles Port Police. I used to wind up at Jerry's Deli at around 2:00 a.m. after almost every game. Every night I was there I saw this black guy with a bulge in his jacket. He'd look at me and I'd look at him and finally one night I went up to him nicely and said, "Are you a gangster or a cop?" He was a cop and his name was Duane Davis. I asked him if he could hook me up at the Academy. So now I had a sponsor, and I went to the LA Port Police Academy, and Sheriff Baca found out and tried to shut it down.

My sense was that Sheriff Baca just wanted me to be a trophy piece. I kept telling him I wasn't interested in some DARE campaign. I wanted to be a real cop.

I'd have my uniform hanging in my locker, and after practice I'd wait for everyone to leave before I put it on, but Kobe was always there, watching me. He said to me, "Why do you want to be a policeman?" and I said, "I don't. I want to be a sheriff."

Because I had grown up in a military home, some of the stuff they required was second nature to me. My boots had to be clean, my lines had to be straight, there were a lot of salutes and "Yes sirs" and "No sirs." No problem. That was my childhood.

If I screwed up or got yelled at I had to write these essays. One time my belt line was off, so the sergeant made me write something about appearance. I had to write a little paper about strength and honor and representing yourself in the proper manner.

The cops went out of their way to treat me like shit with their abuse and their orders and shouting in my ear, but since I grew up like that, it was nothing for me.

When they got all tough with me and yelled, "Drop and give me twenty push-ups!" inside I was laughing because I was thinking, "My father would have made me do a hundred."

I had to go through basic training, but it was a special program because I was in the middle of basketball season. I didn't have to go to the Academy on game days or when I was on the road. Let's say I was in town Monday, Tuesday, and Wednesday. The Lakers would practice from ten to noon. I'd eat lunch at the practice facility, then go to the Academy from 1:00 p.m. to 10:00 p.m. There was a lot to learn. I needed to be an expert on the law, arrest tactics, civil rights.

It was a lot of work, but I absolutely loved it. Anyone who has been through the Academy understands the commitment.

Once they realized I was serious about what I was doing and once I met the necessary requirements, they let me go along on some raids and some busts.

I had a patrol where I was pulling over about a hundred people for speeding. I was handing out tickets, and they decided it was too dangerous for me to be in uniform in public and getting out of my vehicle, so they moved me to a specialized unit. It was a stolen car unit.

We'd go into the office and they'd give us a piece of paper with a list of all the cars that had been stolen and we'd patrol the area looking for them. There were about fifteen of us, and we called ourselves the Cargo Cats because we also went out looking for stolen cargo.

So one night we get a call about a car that was on our list, but we had to notify the homicide detectives because there were two dead bodies in the car. I'm riding with Duane and he asks me if I've ever seen a dead body. I told him, "Of course. I'm from New Jersey."

We get over there and we rope everything off, and this is a big test for me. Anyone who comes in after that has to be recorded. It's called a chain of custody, and you have to keep track of who comes in just in case any evidence is missing. The forensic guys come in and take pictures.

We get to the car and there's a guy, about nineteen or twenty years old, with a piece of his head blown off. It was gang related. He still had a shotgun sitting in his lap, but a good chunk of his head was gone. I wish I could tell you I've never seen anything like it, but I have.

One day I was in the house in Newark on punishment, and it was raining really hard. I went to the bathroom and I opened the window because it was hot, and I see these two guys fighting. One of the guys pulls out a gun and shoots the other one right in the face—*boom!* Only the guy that gets shot doesn't die. He gets up and he's bleeding all over the place and I can't believe what I'm seeing. I'm just a kid and I'm on punishment and I'm a compulsive liar because of what my mother called my "active imagination," so I'm all worked up and I run to get one of my cousins and yell, "Someone just got shot!"

My cousin runs to the window and he doesn't see anybody so he said, "Screw you, Shaquille. Get back in your room." No one believes me. After a while even I'm wondering if I made the whole thing up, but then about three days later some of the gang guys from the neighborhood come by and tell my cousin, "Yeah, our boy got shot in the face."

Most of the time when I was working with the Cargo Cats, we'd be tailing stolen cars. Sometimes they'd pull over and get arrested peacefully. Other times we'd have to chase them down. You had to be careful where you did that because you didn't want to go after a car at high speeds with lots of people around. The trick was to wait until they got on a highway. We'd be coordinating with a couple of other cars, and we'd chase them down and pull our guns. I did that countless times without anyone knowing about it, but one time people found out about it because I had my Shaq sneakers on instead of my boots.

One of the most memorable busts for me was in Baton Rouge, somewhere around 1998 or 1999. It was a drug bust and nobody was supposed to see me. We were wearing masks, and we went into the house with a warrant and we're asking questions and we've got our guns drawn. This guy looks over at his refrigerator, which has a picture of me from LSU on it, and then back at me. He says, "You're not a cop, you're Shaq!" But he was really drunk, so I said, "You're crazy. Shut up and put your hands behind your back."

I've assisted in more than five hundred arrests. Some go smoother than others. I was in Virginia working with a federal task force—the ICAC, which stands for Internet Crimes Against Children. We had to go up there for training. It was a three-day course, sixteen hours each day, and then we graduated.

The US Marshals and the FBI were conducting a child porn raid and invited me to assist. The street address was something like 1336, but this house had those little numbers that you hammer in with a little nail and when the nail comes out, the nine flips over and becomes a six. So we ended up going to the wrong house.

And this was no little bust. We had helicopters overhead, the whole thing. So we hit the house and it's a big spectacle because we've got the wrong place, so I get across the street and I take off my mask and someone recognizes me, so of course the story comes out that Shaq was on a raid and he crashed the wrong house. Give me a break. It wasn't even my bust!

I learned a lot about law enforcement and the tendencies of criminals. I saw a lot of horrible things, some disgusting crimes against children that still makes my stomach turn every time I think about it. It was a six-week course and they show you all the horrible things you can't possibly imagine anyone would be sick enough to do. I had to take a step back from that kind of work because I love children, and those kinds of crimes really fill you with rage.

What you realize when you get involved in police training is you don't really know people. You think you do, but you don't. The innocent couple walking their baby up and down the street could be embezzling millions of dollars for all you know.

We all have secrets.

And, as we all found out in the summer of 2003, that included Kobe.

I'll be honest with you. I thought the kid was a geek. He got a perfect score on his SATs or something, so I figured he was always in his room studying or reading.

That's why I was so shocked when the Colorado thing happened. It was the summer of 2003, and Jerome came in and said, "You aren't going to believe what I just heard." He told me a nineteen-year-old girl had accused Kobe of raping her in a hotel. I couldn't believe it. I kept saying, "For real? Are you busting me, Jerome?" because I just never figured Kobe would ever be involved in something like that.

The most amazing thing about the entire incident was that when Kobe finally walked into camp, it was like nothing had happened. He just showed up with an extra bodyguard or two and played a little harder. He's the type who never shows his cards. He has a serious poker face.

As soon as I heard the news, I got a message to Kobe through Jerome that he was welcome to stay in our gated house with his family if he needed to get away from all the media attention. I told Jerome, "See what he needs. See what we can do." Jerome put in a couple of calls, but we never heard anything back.

When Kobe showed up at the practice facility, I didn't say anything to him. Maybe I should have. In truth, I was waiting on him. I was trying to respect his privacy. I was told later on that he was unhappy I didn't offer him more support. I thought at some point he'd fill me in on what happened, what he was going through, but he never did. So I left it alone.

Publicly I didn't say much. It was a serious charge, and without any knowledge of what went on I made a decision not to get in the middle of it. I didn't need every women's group in the country coming after me. I had already experienced my share of special interest groups gunning for me. Let me explain.

One time I did a commercial for Taco Bell with Jerry West. The idea was that I loved Taco Bell tacos and I'd crane my neck to eat the taco. I did it so many times my neck was stuck sideways. Next thing you know, people with a certain neck syndrome are picketing the game with a picture of the commercial stuck on the sign. What the hell? I didn't know there was such a thing as a "neck syndrome."

Another time I did a Taco Bell commercial where I bit into the taco and my body was on fire. Next thing you know, burn victims come to the game and they're picketing.

And, of course, I always had PETA on my case because of my fur coats and the stuffed wild game I had displayed in my house.

The last thing I needed was to have the women's groups on my case. They can be tough. So when reporters asked me about Kobe, I tried a "no comment." They kept pushing so I finally said, "I'm a big believer in the process of the law and hopefully he's exonerated of all charges."

That didn't work for him, I guess. All those years of the little nit-picky stuff we'd been trading back and forth started escalating. For the first time, there seemed to be real animosity between us. It didn't help that I heard that Kobe mentioned me in his statements. According-ing to the newspapers, he had told the cops that when I got myself in trouble, I just bought people off to stay quiet. That was curious to me. First of all, what trouble? Second of all, how would you know, Kobe? You never ran with me—ever.

When we started training camp in '03–'04, Kobe was coming off knee surgery. I told reporters he should be more of a passer than a scorer until he heals. Looking back, it was kind of a dig. Old habit. Kobe fired back I should leave the guard play to him and go set up on the block where I belong.

So that was how the season started. There was tension. We were sniping at each other a lot.

I had my own issues at that point. We had been trying to get an extension from the Lakers on my contract and certain promises were made. They told me if I could convince Karl Malone and Gary Pay-ton to come to LA for less money, they'd take care of me on the other

end with my contract. So I'm on the phone begging these two future
Hall of Famers to come. It wasn't an easy sell. Karl had his legacy
in Utah and he was leaving a couple of million dollars on the table.
Same for Gary in Seattle.

But I held up my end of the bargain and convinced them to
join us.

The Lakers didn't. The extension wasn't materializing. We're in
Hawaii for a preseason game and I'm going off. I've got about 30,
I'm interacting with the fans, I'm *feeling it.* So I turn around, hit a
deep fadeaway, then run past Jerry Buss and shout, "Pay me." Buss
didn't like it. I could tell he was ticked. He thought I showed him up.

By that point I had a new agent named Perry Rogers. He called
me up and said, "Man, you can't do that."

I said, "Hey, I was just playing," but Perry was really angry at me.

"You messed this up," he said. "Being disrespectful is not going to
help these negotiations."

So I'm on edge because I don't have a new deal, and Kobe is on
edge because he might be going to jail, so we're taking it out on each
other. Just before the start of the '03–'04 season the coaching staff
called us in and said, "No more public sparring or you'll get fined."

Everyone knew it was simmering, but Mitch never came down.
Magic Johnson, who was around all the time, never said anything.

But Phil was tired of it. Karl Malone and Gary Payton were sick
of it.

I said, "All right, I hear you. I'm done."

So what happens? Immediately after that Kobe runs right out to
Jim Gray and does this interview where he lets me have it. He said I
was fat and out of shape. He said I was milking my toe injury for more
time off, and the injury wasn't even that serious. (Yeah, right. It only
ended my damn career.) He said I was "lobbying for a contract extension when we have two Hall of Famers playing pretty much for free."

I'm sitting there watching this interview and I'm gonna explode.
Hours earlier we had just promised our coach we'd stop. It was a
truce broken. I let the guys know, "I'm going to kill him."

That night Brian Shaw gets a call from rookie Devean George. BShaw had retired and was a scout for the Lakers in Northern California, but Devean told him, "They're going to want you down here. The shit hit the fan today. Shaq is going to destroy Kobe."

Sure enough, a couple of hours later Brian gets a call from Phil and Mitch Kupchak. They ask BShaw to fly down and intercept me at the practice facility the next morning. My bodyguard, Jerome, got wind of what was going on, so the next morning he went by my house early to pick me up, but I was already gone. He knew if I was up that early that I was a dangerous man.

BShaw was waiting at the training facility for me when I pulled in. He had been around me for a lot of years. He knew when the talking was done and it was time to knuckle up.

I said to Brian, "Did they bring you down here? It won't matter. I'm going to kick his goddamn ass."

Brian convinced me to go inside to the theater at the practice facility with Jerome and wait.

A few minutes later Kobe pulled up. Brian said to him, "Shaq is going to kill you. He's going to fuck you up on sight." Kobe grinned and said, "Ooooh, am I supposed to be scared?"

"Yes," Brian told him. "This is no joke."

Meanwhile Horace Grant and Karl Malone have joined me and Jerome in the theater. They were backup in case they had to physically restrain me from going after Kobe. GP was too small for that job, but he wasn't about to miss all the great Shaq-Kobe drama, so he was in there, too.

They get me and Kobe into the theater and instantly it's a shouting match. We're cursing each other and calling each other names and I'm making a move for Kobe when BShaw steps in and tells us both to sit down.

Brian starts with me. He says, "Shaq, you are being childish and immature. You dunked on Eric Dampier in preseason and started acting like a goon and yelling at Jerry Buss, 'Pay me,' and now that's coming back to bite you in the ass."

I wanted to tell him, *I did that because Jerry Buss said he was going to give me an extension and it hadn't materialized, yet,* but before I could say anything BShaw held up his hand.

"And Kobe," he said. "Shaq takes a beating every season. You know that. Phil told Shaq to take the summer off and let his body recover. He's always told Shaq to take his time getting back in basketball shape."

So now Kobe starts saying, "But I work so hard every summer..." but BShaw has his hand up again.

Then BShaw hits us both across the bow. He starts telling us how after we lost in '03 we told the media we needed to get younger and more athletic, and that ended up costing him and Robert Horry their jobs. "You guys are so worried about yourselves that you didn't even think about us," he said.

I was kind of shocked. BShaw was right. I'd never considered that what we had said had anything to do with him or Rob not being asked back. I was just trying to give the politically correct answer. I hadn't meant to undercut Brian or Rob.

Kobe is trying to hear BShaw out but he can't contain himself. He stands up and goes face-to-face with me and says, "You always said you're my big brother, you'd do anything for me, and then this Colorado thing happens and you never even called me."

I did call him. Everyone knows Jerome is me. I had Jerome call for me—twice. But Kobe never picked up. I told him, "We reached out to you but you didn't accept that. You kept us all out. You didn't tell any of us anything. None of us in this room have any idea what went on in Colorado."

To this day, I still don't know what happened in Colorado. Kobe never came clean. He came in very quiet to practice and stayed away from the topic. The only details we knew were what were reported in the papers. Kobe eventually admitted to having a sexual relationship with the girl but said it was consensual.

So here we are now, and we find out he really was hurt that we didn't stand behind him. That was something new. I didn't think he gave a rat's ass about us either way.

"Well, I thought you'd publicly support me, at least," Kobe said. "You're supposed to be my friend."

BShaw chimed in with "Kobe, why would you think that? Shaq had all these parties and you never showed up for any of them. We invited you to dinner on the road and you didn't come. Shaq invited you to his wedding and you weren't there. Then you got married and didn't invite any of us.

"And now you are in the middle of this problem, this sensitive situation, and you want all of us to step up for you. We don't even know you."

At that point GP and Horace put in their two cents' worth. They told us we were hurting the team with our bickering back and forth in the papers.

Everyone was starting to calm down when I told Kobe, "If you ever say anything like what you said to Jim Gray ever again, I will kill you."

Kobe shrugged and said, "Whatever."

Karl said, "This has got to stop. It's petty and stupid and we're tired of it. I didn't come here for less money to deal with this bullshit."

They finally made us hug. It was a black bro hug. We tapped each other and agreed we'd have a truce.

But, from that day on, I was done dealing with Kobe. I was done dealing with Jim Gray, too. What goes around, comes around. When he got fired, he actually had the nerve to call me and ask me to help him out. What, did you lose Kobe's number?

In spite of all the fireworks, we started out that '03–'04 season winning twenty of our first twenty-five games. Kobe was dealing with the sexual assault charges every day, and even though the charges were eventually dropped, the stress was finally wearing on him. He was trying to fix it all on the basketball court by scoring as many points as humanly possible. Naturally I'm not happy about it.

By this point our relationship had really broken down, although we kept it out of the public eye.

Phil wasn't saying much, but he never did. He understood he was dealing with two alpha males. Two crazy dudes. Two crazy dudes, but we were winning and playing. People had this idea of what it was like on the outside, but it wasn't like that on the inside.

It was almost like a game. Kobe would use TJ Simers or Bill Plaschke to put the wood to me, then I'd come back and use JA Adande to get my message across.

Simers was the real joke. He liked to puff his chest out and say, "I talked to Kobe today." Good for fucking you. Nobody else wanted to talk to you anyway.

The back-and-forth stuff was uncomfortable for the other guys, but for Kobe and me there was a benefit to it, sort of an untelevised reality show. It kept us in the spotlight. We could handle it—until that final season.

Here's the funny thing about our so-called feud. All I ever said about Kobe is what everyone is saying now. I just had the balls to say it. I made sure I didn't belittle him too much because I knew we needed our one-two punch. I was putting up big numbers and he was putting up big numbers, so we weren't really all that worried about much. Phil knew what was going on, which was why he rarely stepped in. Phil knew what was driving me: Kobe. And he knew what was driving Kobe: me. In four years together I can remember Phil calling me and Kobe into his office only one time. He knew the tension was good for us, good for the team.

He also knew that sooner or later, two alpha males were going to tear each other limb from limb. Only one alpha male is usually left standing.

By February, our negotiations with the Lakers were at an impasse. They were offering two years at $21 million a season, and that wasn't going to work. After I won three championships and three Finals MVPs, they wanted me to take a $10 million pay cut—and they were willing to guarantee only two years.

Now, did I start acting crazy? I suppose I did. But their approach was a slap in the face. It was a sign of disrespect. Deep down, I knew I could get the money somewhere else. Perry told them if their offer didn't improve, I would be asking for a trade that summer.

Somehow Kobe and I made it through the rest of the year without any major issues. BShaw managed to get us back on track. It's kind of funny when you think about it. All these supposed Lakers leaders who care so much about the franchise, all these Lakers legends, none of them ever had the courage to say anything to Kobe and me. Not Kareem, not Magic, not Mitch Kupchak, none of them. Only Brian Shaw took us on. Yet when the Lakers job came up in 2011 they didn't give Brian Shaw a chance by looking right past him. Go figure.

Anyhow, Kobe and I put a lid on our little differences. Even if I don't like you, if you're open I'm going to get you the ball anyway.

Even though we backed off each other, we were still dealing with a divided team. You were either a Kobe guy or a Shaq guy. We even had two trainers. If Chip Schaefer taped me for practice, then Kobe wouldn't go to him. He'd use Gary Vitti instead. Childish stuff. Juvenile. We all got caught up in it.

Fun times with the Lakers. That gives you an idea of what my last season in Los Angeles was like.

Somehow we still won fourteen of our final seventeen games. Our championship chances took a big hit when Karl Malone injured his knee. He played in the postseason but he wasn't the same guy. We needed him more than we realized.

We still managed to beat the Spurs in the playoffs. We were tied 2–2 in games with San Antonio, and Duncan hit a tough fadeaway one-legged jump shot with ten seconds to go. We couldn't believe it.

So now it's our turn. We've got the ball out of bounds with 0.4 seconds to go, which leaves you barely any time to get a shot off. But we get the ball to a wide-open Derek Fisher and he drains the sucker. I saw the red light go on and ran as fast as I could before they could change the call. Lakers win. We go up 3–2 in the series and ended up closing them out. Everyone is asking me about DFish's miracle shot and I told the truth: "One lucky shot deserves another."

We're set to play Detroit in the Finals, and both Kobe and I felt we were the better team—we just forgot to play like it. Every time our offense bogged down, Kobe tried to take over. After the loss in Game 3, which put us behind 2–1 in the series, someone said to me, "They were going to you over and over again, and you were getting the ball down low and scoring every time, but then it seemed you guys went away from that."

"Yeah," I said. "Story of my life, buddy."

The Pistons beat us in five games. It was a little stunning. Nobody was very happy about it. Right away I could tell something was up. We had a dinner/reception at the hotel after the game, and my wife, Shaunie, and I were sitting there and who walks in but Jerry Buss.

He's never usually around, but there he is talking and laughing with Kobe and his wife, Vanessa. We're sitting just a few feet away but he doesn't come over, doesn't say a word to us all night, doesn't even look at us.

Nothing.

A couple of days later I'm at home, and I find out Phil Jackson isn't coming back. His contract was up and they didn't renew him. I turned to Shaunie and said, "It's over."

I was told by Mitch I was going to get an extension and be a Laker for life. The next thing I know I'm sitting in my kitchen eating my Frosted Flakes, and he's on television saying they'd consider trading me.

We had an agreement with the Lakers. The agreement was we would have no discussions with the media at all about my future from either side—them or us. If they were asked about whether they were going to extend me, they would say, "We'll leave that to ourselves."

Instead, there's Mitch telling everyone they definitely want to re-sign Kobe, but with me, they're looking at all their options.

That was it. That was the end of me in a Lakers uniform. Mitch broke our agreement. How could I trust him again? I called my agent, Perry, who was in London at Wimbledon. I told him what Mitch said.

Perry called Mitch right away. Mitch conceded he was trying to finesse his way through the press conference without lying to the media. He said since we didn't have an agreement he knew I would be asking for a trade. "I know what we agreed to," Mitch said.

"It doesn't matter," Perry told him. "We're done."

"What does that mean?" Mitch said.

"Well, Mitch, in ten minutes we'll be on the phone with the *LA Times*, and in fifteen minutes we'll be on the phone with the *Orange County Register*, and in twenty minutes it will be scrolling at the bottom of your screen on ESPN."

For months, I kept waiting for Mitch to come to me and say, "Shaq, you're getting older, we need some new players. Mr. Buss doesn't want to pay you and Kobe doesn't want you here." But that conversation never happened.

So that was when I demanded a trade. I couldn't trust Mitch anymore, and it was clear Kobe was now the one with all the power.

Right away my phone started ringing. Everyone had their own idea of what happened. A couple of my friends believed Buss never got over the "pay me" comments in Hawaii and the "hurt on company time" stuff after my surgery. Jerome figured it was economics. They didn't want to pay the money to keep me. Others were convinced Kobe wanted me and Phil out. Maybe Kobe had a hand in it, maybe he didn't. It doesn't really matter. If I wanted to fix it, I could have, but my ego and my pride were too strong, and my business style was even stronger. A big pay cut like that and a short contract after all I'd done for them? Nope. Not gonna work.

Deep down I knew they were making a choice between the old and the young, and in that case they always choose the young.

It was the same old lesson that I had already learned in Orlando—there is no loyalty in sports. None. They use you up, then they dump you.

Luckily for me I still had value. Luckily for me I was used to being a moving target. We had to quickly figure out where we wanted to go.

Larry Bird was running the show in Indiana, and he really wanted me to come there. He offered the Lakers anyone they wanted from his roster. Milwaukee and Atlanta were interested, too. LA could have their pick of their guys. Isiah Thomas was running the Knicks, and he offered up his whole roster, too, but he didn't have very much.

It came down to two teams—Miami and Dallas. Mark Cuban flew in and sat down with us, then he went back to the Lakers and said he'd trade anybody for me except for Dirk Nowitzki. Dirk was his guy.

Miami put together a great package that included Lamar Odom, Caron Butler, Brian Grant, and a first-round pick. Their owner, Mickey Arison, was very professional, very proactive. The idea of going back to Florida was very appealing to me. I thought I would be a Laker for life, but I was wrong.

So am I taking the blame for that? No way. I was the CEO. I was in charge. I had been there eight years, so it was my team. Was I being tit for tat with Kobe? Probably. Should I have handled that differently? Possibly. But every CEO has their own style. My style worked. We won three out of four championships in the Finals.

Do I regret how it ended? Not really. If Kobe doesn't ever want to talk to me again, I can live with that. But he knows and I know that won't erase the greatest one-two punch of our time.

Before the trade went down, Shaunie and I cleaned out the house in Los Angeles and packed our stuff and shipped it to the house at Isleworth in Orlando. The kids were kind of confused. They were like, "Dad, Dad, where are we going?" but we always ended up in Orlando for the summer, so we kept them from getting too upset. We put the LA house on the market and had it sold by the end of July. The Chinese Rod Stewart bought it.

He paid cash, too.

JULY 21, 2004

Miami, Florida

The 18-wheeler cab with the inscription "diesel power" snaked down Biscayne Boulevard to approving honks from passing cars and delighted squeals from the fans assembled along the sidewalks in the blazing sun.

Inside the cab, Shaquille O'Neal reviewed his mental checklist:

Edict Number One: display no bitterness. It was paramount that the newly minted Miami Heat savior concealed his crushing disappointment at the way he was dumped by the Lakers after delivering three titles to them.

Edict Number Two: embrace the Miami community, just as he'd done in Orlando and Los Angeles.

The big man's destination was his introductory press conference, with keys to the city and a red carpet awaiting, but not before Shaq leaned out of the cab and sprayed stunned but delighted onlookers with an oversized water cannon.

"I'm here for one reason only," Shaq declared. "When I was playing with the Lakers I was tired of hearing Coach Stan Van Gundy yelling, 'Three seconds, three seconds, get him out of the lane—three seconds!' So now I'll get to hear Coach Van Gundy yell, 'They are fouling him! They are fouling him!'"

Shaq seamlessly moved on to Edict Number Three: publicly embrace team president Pat Riley's rigid conditioning program, in spite of his own reservations.

"I just bought a house on the beach, and my wife likes me to walk around naked on the beach, so I'm going to be in very, very top physical shape," said O'Neal. He wondered aloud about potential nude photographs, then deadpanned, "Don't sell them to the *Enquirer* unless I get fifteen percent."

Edict Number Four: ingrain yourself into the fabric of the social scene.

"Get your tickets now. Buy cable now. Get your jerseys now. Pull your boats up to the docking stations now. Bring your Sea-Doos now," Shaq urged the fans. "If you can't afford a Sea-Doo, get a raft. If you can't afford a raft, go to Walmart and get a blow-up raft like I have at my house. You need to come, because it's going to be very, very exciting."

He guaranteed a championship and promised to breathe new life into a young, fledgling franchise.

"Sure I'm old," said O'Neal, "but like toilet paper, toothpaste, and other amenities, I'm proven to be good."

The Diesel grinned. The cameras clicked. The fans swooned.

And the Lakers were history.

I'VE LEARNED NOT TO LOOK BACK. I HAD TO. I DIDN'T WANT to ever be hurt again like I was by what happened in Orlando. I promised myself I would never look at my career again as anything other than a business.

So forget about LA. Forget about Kobe, Mitch Kupchak, all of it. Rearview mirror, baby.

That was why I wore an all-white suit to my Miami press conference. Their slogan was the "white-hot Heat." For me, it was a new, white, clean slate.

That was why when we played the Lakers for the first time since I was traded, and they asked me beforehand about Kobe, my answer was, "Who?"

When I got to town I told Pat Riley about my home in Orlando and my full-sized basketball court with the Lakers logo. I told him we could use it for shootarounds when we played the Magic. Pat said, "Okay, but you gotta change that logo." I said sure—as long as the Heat paid for it.

Which of course they did.

Pat wasn't the coach when I got there, but he was in charge. Everything that goes on in Miami even now, he's in charge.

I had always said I couldn't play for Pat Riley. I had heard stories about his style from Alonzo Mourning, from Tim Hardaway, all the guys who played for him. The three-hour practices, the four-hour practices, the yelling and the screaming and always feeling the need to show how tough you are. That works for some people, but after the résumé I built I felt I knew what it took to win.

After working with Phil Jackson—who would put us through forty-five tough, concentrated minutes, then look at me and say,

"Okay, Shaq, get on the treadmill"—it was obvious to me that Gestapo conditioning twenty-four hours a day wasn't the way to go. We responded so much better to Phil's way, which sometimes meant giving the older guys a day off.

So I had my doubts. But I figured since Riley wasn't the coach— that was Stan Van Gundy's job—he wouldn't be the dominating presence on the team.

My mistake.

Even when Pat wasn't coaching, it was definitely his team. He was there, all the time, probably drawing up plays in his office. His office overlooked the court.

He had cameras everywhere. Cameras on the practice court, cameras in the locker room, probably even cameras in the bathroom. He wanted to know everything.

No wonder DWade was so uptight when I got there. That was my first job. As soon as I arrived I thought, *I got to loosen this brother up.* DWade was just so afraid to do something wrong. I told him, "Hey, man, you've got to realize who you are and the power you have and stop tiptoeing around here so timidly all the time, because with your talent any team in the league would want you. So keep that in the back of your head."

I don't want to call Miami a jail, but everyone was walking around on eggshells. They were all scared of Pat. I went in there hoping to give them some life. I wasn't afraid of anybody—not even the great Pat Riley.

So why did I go there if I knew it was going to be like that? Because I needed another guy similar to Kobe to get me over the hump. I realized after I first got to LA, before Kobe turned out to be Kobe and I was putting up all those big numbers, the days of doing it myself were over. You need help.

Hell, I had already won three championships and I was looking to win three more. When I was thinking of moving on I looked at Vince Carter, wondering if he might be a guy that could work, but he was playing in Toronto and I didn't want to go there.

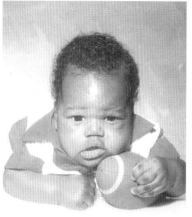

Me at three months, ready to play ball— but the wrong sport! *(Author's collection)*

At five years old, with my mom. *(Author's collection)*

My mom Lucille and me, at three months. *(Author's collection)*

Me as a senior talking to the media at Cole High School in 1989. *(Bob Daemmrich/Getty Images)*

My freshman year at LSU, 1989.
(Author's collection)

On the court at LSU
in 1992. *(Getty Images)*

LSU graduation in 2000.
(Bill Haber/AP Photo)

Pat Williams, Orlando GM, with the winning jersey of the NBA's No. 1 pick in 1992. *(Bill Kostroun/ AP Photo)*

With Commissioner David Stern when I was drafted in 1992. *(Nathaniel S. Butler/ NBAE via Getty Images)*

Facing off against Patrick Ewing in 1995. *(Fernando Medina/NBAE via Getty Images)*

A proud member of the 1996 US Olympic team. *(Michael Probs/AP Photo)*

Getting beat up by Zydrunas Ilgauskas. *(Lucy Nicholson/AP Photo)*

The Dunkman at work. *(Mark J. Terrill/AP Photo)*

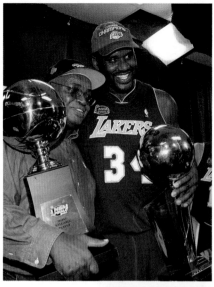

With my dad after a Lakers playoff game in 2001. *(Vince Bucci/AFP/Getty Images)*

With Phil Jackson in 2004. *(Andrew D. Bernstein/NBAE via Getty Images)*

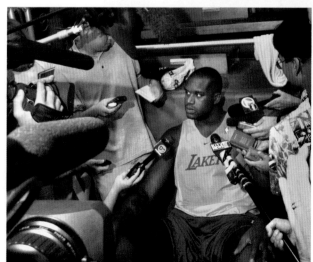

Talking to the media in LA. *(Lucy Pemoni/ Reuters/Corbis)*

Sports Illustrated, 1996. *(Peter Read Miller /Sports Illustrated/Getty Images)*

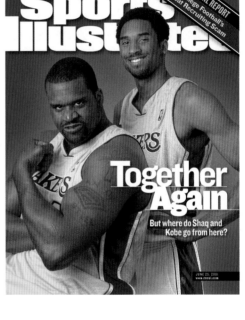

Sports Illustrated, 2001. *(Walter Iooss Jr./Sports Illustrated/Getty Images)*

Sports Illustrated, 2002. *(John W. McDonough/Sports Illustrated/Getty Images)*

With my dad, Sarge (Philip Harrison). *(Stan Honda/AFP/ Getty Images)*

Receiving the key to the city of Miami when I arrived there in 2004. *(J. Pat Carter/AP Photo)*

With Dwyane Wade in 2006. *(Rhona Wise/Corbis)*

Swearing in as a police
officer in Miami in 2005.
*(AP Photo/Miami Beach Police
Department)*

Happier days in
Miami with Pat
Riley in 2007.
*(David Zalubowski/
AP Photo)*

I always respected Dirk
Nowitzki's game. *(Vernon
Bryant/Dallas Morning
News/Corbis)*

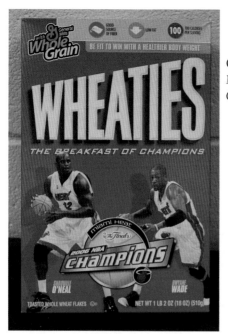

Gotta eat your Wheaties! *(Smiley N. Pool/Dallas Morning News/ Corbis)*

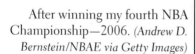

After winning my fourth NBA Championship—2006. *(Andrew D. Bernstein/NBAE via Getty Images)*

Me with President Bush in 2007. *(Jim Young/Reuters/ Corbis)*

Yao Ming: a flat-out terrific player
who had to retire much too young.
(Matt York/AP Photo)

LeBron and myself
in sync in 2010. *(Tony
Dejak/AP Photo)*

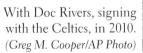

Dunkman in Boston in 2010.
*(Yoon S. Byun/*The Boston
Globe *via Getty Images)*

With Doc Rivers, signing
with the Celtics, in 2010.
(Greg M. Cooper/AP Photo)

Doc Rivers, Paul Pierce, and myself. *(Ron Turenne/NBAE via Getty Images)*

I only wish I had been healthier when I was playing for the Celtics. *(Charles Krupa/AP Photo)*

Kevin Garnett and yours truly. *(David Liam Kyle/NBAE via Getty Images)*

With Jay-Z. *(Andrew D. Bernstein/NBAE via Getty Images)*

Conducting the Boston Pops. *(Gretchen Ertl/AP Photo)*

With Peyton Manning. *(Kevin Mazur/WireImage)*

With my brother,
sisters, and Mom.
From left: Lateefah,
Ayesha, me, my
mother Lucille, Jamal.
(Author's collection)

My mom (Lucille O'Neal)
and my son, Shareef, holding
a Spider-Man doll in 2002.
(Mark J. Terrill/AP Photo)

My dad and myself with the first
President Bush. *(Bettmann/Corbis)*

Relaxing with my
mom. *(Neal Preston/
Corbis)*

At the MTV Video Music Awards in 2004. *(Chris Polk/FilmMagic)*

On *Shaq Vs.* with Albert Pujols. *(Tom Gannam/AP Photo)*

Showing new moves to Justin Bieber on *Shaq Vs.* *(Preston Mack/ABC via Getty Images)*

Hanging with Charles Barkley on *Shaq Vs.* *(Greg Zabilski/ABC via Getty Images)*

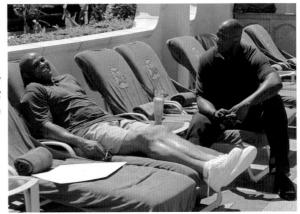

With Bill Russell. (*Andrew D. Bernstein/NBAE via Getty Images*)

With Magic Johnson. (*Fred Prouser/SIPA*)

With Dr. J—Julius Erving. (*Shareif Ziyadat/FilmMagic*)

On *Shaq Vs.* with Michael Phelps. (*ABC/Photofest*)

On the set of *Blue Chips* with Nick Nolte. *(Paramount Pictures/Photofest)*

President Obama trying to fill my shoes. *(Paul Connors/AP Photo)*

With Coach Dale Brown at my retirement press conference. *(Andrew D. Bernstein/NBAE via Getty Images)*

I was watching DWade on television one day and I said, "This kid could be special. He just needs somebody out there to give him some more room." So that's what I did—I gave him space on that court to operate, to do his thing.

Off the court I tried to teach him some flash—talked to him about swagger, about walking and talking like a star, doing the commercials.

The first thing DWade and I did when I got to Miami was go to lunch at a little place on South Beach. I told him everything that went wrong with Kobe and me, and then I said, "The reason I'm telling you this is because this can never happen to you and me."

I told him I was probably too hard on Kobe when he was younger and Kobe didn't know how to take it. He was going to be a great player anyway—we all knew that. I think my anger pushed him a little bit more, and Phil's anger pushed me a little bit more, and we got three rings out of it. My momma asked me once if I could do it over, would I do it differently? My answer is no.

Sometimes I do sit back and say, "Did I lose a friend by the way I treated Kobe?" Maybe, maybe not. We were never really that close. Kobe was always an introverted kid. Anyway, friendships don't matter much in professional basketball, because it's all about winning.

When you are a superstar and you get to a certain level in your career, it starts becoming all about how many championships you've won. Now, is that fair? Sometimes it isn't. You are going to tell me that Patrick Ewing, Karl Malone, Charles Barkley, and Dominique Wilkins aren't great players? That's just flat-out wrong.

Before I won my championships, people talked about me as one of the great centers in the game, but some reporter would always say, "You can't compare him to Bill Russell or Kareem Abdul-Jabbar because he hasn't won yet." I hated hearing that. Just hated it. But the more you hear it, the more you realize you are the CEO, and if you win you'll get all the credit and if you lose it's all your fault. So you want to know why I flexed my muscles during my time in the NBA? Because if it's going to be my fault when we lose, then we're doing things my way.

By the time I got to Miami, I wasn't the CEO anymore. DWade was going to have to be the CEO because he was young and hitting his stride. My job was to be his top advisor. But I realized pretty quickly I could not treat him the way I had treated Kobe. You couldn't be too hard on DWade. He wasn't as tough as Kobe, wasn't the type to fight back and challenge you.

I always tell people in terms of being tough on the young stars, I was a 10 with Kobe and a 4 with DWade and a 1 with LeBron. I didn't say anything to LeBron—didn't have to. He had it figured out at a very young age.

DWade was a good listener. I wasn't in his face like with Kobe. Instead of getting on him I'd say, "Hey, dawg, maybe you should try this."

I liked DWade. We always had a pretty good relationship, but I think toward the end Pat Riley probably put him in a bad position. He forced him to choose: Who are you loyal to, Shaq or me? I understood that. It was business. I didn't take it personally.

When I first got to Miami, Pat Riley was amazing. The two of us sat down and had a nice conversation. He told me all about the community in Miami, the team personnel, how great we were going to be, and how he had just fired all his marketing people. He fired them because he didn't need them anymore. The minute they announced I was coming the ticket sales went through the roof.

So Pat talked to me a little about DWade and how he saw the two of us working out and how he wanted me to take Wade under my wing. We were cool.

Of course, I already had my own plan about how I was going to turn Miami upside down business-wise. And we were going to win a championship while I was there—I made that guarantee to Pat Riley privately and to the city of Miami publicly.

Everything was looking great, except one thing: I didn't have time to do anything but work out all day long because Pat was all hung up on this body fat program. He was very serious about it. He expected all the guards to have 6 percent body fat, the forwards to have 7 to 8 percent body fat, and the centers to have 10 percent body fat.

It made no sense to me. I had been taking care of my body for twelve NBA seasons and we had won three championships, and I had never seen anyone from the Miami Heat even come close to winning anything. They may have been in the best shape, but I never saw any of them around when we were passing out rings.

I mean, look at Alonzo Mourning. He is a machine. Really. I wouldn't be surprised if we found out he was a robot. The guy was always in amazing shape. He always looked ten times better than me, but I used to kill him on the court, which tells you that body fat don't mean shit. It's all about what's in your heart and in your mind. Are you tough enough? Do you want it enough? You don't need to be at 10 percent body fat for that.

There's no question by trying to get my body fat down I became more injury prone. I never had any of the ticky-tacky injuries I got until I went to Miami. My massage therapist, Danny Garcia, who has been with me since I was with the Lakers, swears they made me too lean and my body couldn't absorb hits the way it used to. I had no cushion, no buffering. Pat forgot to take into account the pounding my body took, day in and day out, going for those rebounds he wanted me to get. I was too much of a power player to take that kind of abuse on that lean of a body. I had more injuries in my time with Miami than anywhere else in my career.

I didn't see how I could get down to 10 percent body fat, but I didn't want to hear the flack I'd get for not conforming. I was in a new place with a new team and a new coach, so I did it. I spent all day doing cardio and eating stuff I never eat. Salad, fucking salad— I hate the stuff. So I was eating salad, fish, and chicken. It was terrible. I drank water all day long. I've never had to make so many bathroom runs.

The summer before I was supposed to report to the Heat training camp I got this letter from Pat. He told me he was looking forward to having me there and the team had a body fat requirement of 10 percent for centers, but because I was bigger he was willing to let me come in at 13 percent. At the bottom, there was all this fine print that tells you, "If you don't make the body fat percentage, you will be fined $1,000. The next time you are fined again, and the third time you are suspended a game."

I'm reading all this and I'm groaning, because I know what my body needs. By the end of a long NBA season, my body is so tired, so sore, so *abused*, I don't do much basketball stuff in the summer at all. For the first two months, I do next to nothing, to give my body a chance to recover. Sometimes I gain weight, sometimes I don't.

Around August, I start doing cardio and some basketball drills. I also do a lot of swimming because it's easier on my joints. I rarely came into training camp in basketball shape. I need that recovery time. I'm lugging around a big body. I ain't no little guard flitting around the perimeter hoisting up three-pointers.

The way that worked best for me was to come in at 75 percent and work my way up. You can't come into basketball season in basketball shape unless you play every day, and I couldn't do that anymore without my body breaking down.

Clearly I wasn't going to be able to follow my regular routine and meet Pat's requirements. One of the first things I did was call up my business partners who helped me run these twenty-four-hour fitness clubs that I owned. I told them, "Hey, I've got to work out every night—we need a couple of gyms down here." So we opened up five of them in the Miami area right away.

I was my own best customer.

Even with all that work, I showed up to Miami in October 2004 with 16 percent body fat. Pat didn't fine me but he did call me into his office. I told him, "Hey, look, I'm trying. I'm on the damn treadmill all day long. I'm working at this, I'll do what it takes, but I've never been that low before."

I'm trying to also work into the conversation that I've been pretty successful at 18 percent body fat, but he's not listening. He's a dictator and he wants to do it his way, so I'm avoiding confrontation by yes-sing him to death. *Yes, okay, whatever you say.* The media asked me about Riley and I said, "He's the president. I'm the general. Unless I want to get impeached, I've got to do what he says."

We get checked once a week by Riley and his staff. My body fat is going down, and by midseason I'm at 13 percent, but I start having all these little injuries. I'm also as tired as hell. I'm practicing my ass off and my body is complaining. Loudly.

Of course, part of the reason I was tired was that Miami was such a lively town. I was out late, then up early eating horrible salads and having my waistline pinched. So some of that being tired, well, I guess that was on me.

Stan Van Gundy was the coach during all of this, although you'd never know it. Pat overshadowed him so much it was hard for Stan to put his stamp on the team. Stan was a damn worrywart. He was always worried about what Pat was going to say. He worried about everything. He worried too much. I'm sure he worried because he cared, but it drove me crazy.

There would be times we'd be up by 20 points with two minutes to go and a guy on the other team would hit a couple of three-pointers and Stan would call a time-out and start yelling at us.

He'd get all worked up and I'd look at him and say, "Calm your-self, man. We're fine."

Here's the other thing: I don't like to be jinxed. You know, the whole Spooky Wook thing. Stan would come in before the game and say, "You guys aren't focused, you aren't going to play well tonight." I'd hear that and go nuts. I'd tell him, "Stop saying that!" and he'd say, "I'm serious. You're not focused."

He didn't like all the silly stuff I did, like doing jumping jacks naked to get the guys to smile and relax. He didn't understand it was good for our team to be loose. He hated me and Damon Jones because we were always pulling a prank or getting the guys to bust up laughing.

Stan would come into the locker room with a hundred different things written on the board and we were all supposed to have our mean faces on, and I'm not like that. Every game was Armageddon and depended completely on this stat and that stat, and I'm sitting there thinking, *We're playing Milwaukee. I know Andrew Bogut is pretty good, but their record is something like 3-25. Why are we doubling this guy?* So we'd go out and double Bogut and the other players would hit open shots and we'd lose.

We all knew Stan was a dead man walking. I kind of felt sorry for the guy. He didn't deserve to get fired. My first year, in 2004–05, we went to the Conference Finals and lost to Detroit in Game 7. They let Stan go in December of the following season. I was injured at the time, but I was just about ready to come back. One of the things that ticked me off was people said I got Stan fired. They said I wouldn't play for him and I waited to come back until he was gone. I can tell you there wasn't an ounce of truth to that.

Are you crazy? Did you really think I wanted to play for Pat Riley instead?

Stan got fired because Pat wanted to take over, not because I wanted him out. I had no control over it—not a smidgen of control. We all kind of knew it was coming because Pat and Stan were always arguing. Pat would come down and tell Stan how to do something and Stan would want to do it his own way, and that was a fine game plan if you wanted to get yourself fired.

I will say when Riley finally did take over as head coach, he was tremendous. I had never seen him like that in my life. Guys who had been there before were commenting on it, too. He was the best that year. He even moved practices back to twelve o'clock. He said, "I know you guys like to do your thing, so let's start a little later." We were stunned. No one could believe it.

Pat was big on his motivating tactics. One of the first things he did when I got there was take us all to a private screening of *Glory Road*. He was involved with the movie somehow. He knew the producer and his name was in the credits. It was a team-building thing, and I have to say it was a very inspiring movie.

There were times when Pat did some nutty things, and some of them didn't make a whole lot of sense. One day he gave us a speech on how no team can truly succeed unless people are willing to sacrifice. He walked into the locker room with a freezing bucket of water. He put his head in the freezing water for something like two minutes. Everyone was trying not to laugh.

Riley also did some things that I was expecting, because his past players had tipped me off about them. He would storm in at halftime and break the chalkboard or trash the VCR or throw the remote across the room. He kicked more than a few trash pails while I was there. A lot of those outbursts, I'm sure, were premeditated.

It was all about intensity with Pat. He never let up and he wasn't going to let us ever let up, either.

For the first forty-five minutes of practice, we did this drill that I absolutely hated that was called the Indian drill. Here's how it works: Let's say three people are running. Pat blows the whistle, and DWade has to run full speed and come behind me with his hands up. Then the whistle blows and I run full speed behind him, hands up, then the whistle blows and it's Udonis Haslem's turn, running full speed with his hands up.

We'd be in a jog and he would blow the whistle and the last guy had to sprint all the way back around out in front of the guy.

We did all sorts of drills, very basic stuff, over and over and over again. My drills were jump hooks and rebounds, high school stuff. High school stuff I didn't need to do. We'd do that, get some water, then scrimmage full speed for an hour and a half. I was taking this terrific beating from Michael Doleac every day. He was the backup center trying to earn some playing time, so he was just killing me in practice, hacking me, bodying me, pounding me. By the time I got to game day I was all beat up.

I wanted to tell Pat, "This isn't going to work," but there was no way to reason with him. Coaches couldn't, the front office couldn't, the owner couldn't. No one could. So I wasn't going to rock the boat.

Pat gave a lot of motivational speeches. After a while, when he launched into one of them, my eyes kind of glazed over, to be honest. I can't tell you one speech he ever gave, because I knew it was all BS. I knew what I had to do as a player because I had already been given the blueprint by the great Phil Jackson.

Pat Riley was a big film guy, so after we lost we'd have an hour-long film session pointing out all our mistakes. He picked on DWade in those sessions. Pat always wanted us to fight over a screen, and DWade would always shoot the gap instead. Those sessions could get tough. We heard a lot of "See what happens when you don't rebound? You guys aren't in shape!" So then we'd go upstairs and practice for another three hours. Every time something went wrong, it was because we weren't in shape.

Even though the practices were hell, I really did love playing in Miami. I loved playing with DWade and I loved the guys on our team.

One of the best things was, we were able to get Gary Payton to come play with us. I felt I owed him a championship since things hadn't worked out in LA. You got to love GP. He's mean, he talked a lot of trash and he wasn't afraid of anybody. He was a fabulous player who was stuck going up against the great Michael Jordan, otherwise he would have had more rings.

Payton had a chance to come to Miami ten years earlier for more money than he ended up taking in Seattle, but he didn't want to play for Pat. GP figured he had a few years left, and he didn't want to get worn down by Riley's practices. By the time Gary came in 2005, he knew he was near the end. He just wanted the ring. "I'm coming because of you, Shaq," he told me.

James Posey was another one of my guys. I called him my designated hit man. If Dallas star Dirk Nowitzki was killing us I'd tell Pose, "Go touch him up a couple of times." Posey would foul him, put his foot on his ankle, whatever it took to make him uncomfortable.

I don't remember ever having a single bad conversation with Posey. He's one of those guys I owe everything to, and I've probably never told him how much I appreciated him. Robert Horry is a guy like that. Derek Fisher is another. Brian Shaw and Dennis Scott. Those players won't be in the Hall of Fame, but without them Hall of Famers like me wouldn't have been able to close the deal.

Alonzo Mourning wasn't in Miami when I first got there. We had a history and not a very good one, so when Toronto bought out his contract Pat called and said, "Do you mind if we bring him in?" I said sure.

I didn't know Zo at all but I didn't like him. He always thought he was better than me, or at least that's how it looked from where I was standing, so I felt like I had to show him who was the top dog. When I got drafted No. 1 he was No. 2. We both had great rookie seasons, but I was picked Rookie of the Year, and he thought he should have won or at least been a cowinner with me.

And, when he signed that $100 million contract, I made a comment in the press that if you paid a BMW this much money, how much is a Bentley worth? I was the Bentley. He was the BMW. That kind of fueled our feud a little more.

Of course once I met him I couldn't believe what a perfect gentleman he was. He was so generous and courteous and I thought, *Okay, I had this dawg all wrong.*

Antoine Walker came to us in a trade. He was a veteran who could score. 'Toine called me up before he got dealt to Miami and asked me if I would be willing to take a pay cut so they could fit him under the salary cap. He told me he really wanted to play with me, so, being a team player, I took an extension that was a five-year deal for $100 million with the money spread out instead of the three-year deal which would have paid me over $30 million a season.

We also had Jason Williams, who everyone called White Chocolate. I had always wanted to play with that dawg. He was a point guard, a tough little son of a bitch, and he could throw the perfect lob. I used to daydream about throwing down one of his passes.

Miami was a great city with a lot of potential. When we moved there I bought this big, beautiful house on Star Island. It was Rony

Seikaly's old house, and since Rony was a seven-footer I didn't have to do much of anything to it. The showers were already the right height; the ceilings were good. My wife loved the house, my kids were really happy. It was all good.

I used to host a party in every city while we were on the road. Basically I was showing DWade how it was done. I was also trying to get the team closer. The way it worked was, I had this guy named Money Mark who would deal with the clubs in cities when were out of town. They'd pay me to make an appearance and host a party. I got DWade to come with me, along with Damon Jones, Posey, GP, Antoine Walker, Udonis Haslem, and Dorrell Wright. Once in a while, if we were in Washington, D.C., or New York, Zo would show up wearing his little hat. Zo always had to wear a hat 'cuz he was bald.

We called the parties our "team meetings." We'd talk about having a "team meeting" right in front of the coaches. They thought we were sitting in a room talking basketball when we had those "meetings." We all knew what "team meeting at eleven meant." Be in the lobby ready to party.

Pat didn't like it because GP, Antoine, Posey, and those guys would go at it a little hard with the partying. Me? I'd be sitting in my little section drinking water. Damon Jones, who was only with us for one season, would grab the mic and we'd start rapping.

Damon Jones was the first one to call us the Heedles. Those dudes in Miami who call themselves the Heedles now stole that from us. We were six years ahead of them. C'mon, DWade, come clean. You know that's true.

We had a great time at those parties and it gave us a chance to do some bonding. It made it easy on my bodyguard, Jerome, too, because we'd all roll in the same limo and be in the same little section so he could keep track of all of us.

Miami was a young, fabulous city but they were a little short on young, fabulous people. I was just doing my Shaq thing, spreading the love.

We had some great parties at our house on Star Island. I used to take my kids to the zoo once a week and I got to be friendly with the owner. I convinced him to let me have a zoo party and he brought all the animals to the house.

When people drove up, there were the lions and tigers out in the front driveway in their cages so people could take pictures with them. We had camels and elephants wandering around the property. Monkeys, too. We had a big stage put up so people could dance and have fun.

Another time we had a Midsummer Night's Dream party. Guests had to dress like Egyptians. Everyone came—the actors, the politicians, the chief of police. We had superstars flying in from LA. Our guest list could have anyone from Donald Trump to Ludacris.

For one of my birthdays we had a Scarface party. Everyone had to come dressed in white mafia suits. We rented the house in Miami where the movie was shot and we passed out cigars. Every week, my wife Shaunie and I were in the papers. It didn't take long for me to take over the city. Zo called me "the Largest Human Wonder of the World."

But Pat didn't come to many of the parties. The only one he came to was when I helped the Heat out of a jam. They had some major season ticket gala they were planning and something went wrong and they were scrambling for a place, so I offered Pat my house. We put on an amazing party and Pat was really appreciative. All these boats pulled up to the island to hear Gladys Knight and the Pips put on a show for us.

Those were the memories of Miami that helped me get past how it ended in LA. Our team was stacking up Ws, the guys were gelling, I was in full Shaq mode, and we were going to win a championship. I could just feel it.

When the 2006 playoffs rolled around we had won fifty-two games and were peaking at the right time. Pat came into the locker room with this bowl. They were index cards all mixed up in there with everyone's name on it. His slogan was "15 strong." Each card had a little saying on it. Pat made it clear he wanted the contents of the bowl to be a secret. Each time we opened the locker room to the media the bowl was covered. He threatened us with a pretty hefty fine if we told anyone what was in that bowl.

One day he came in and said, "This is my championship ring, and I'm putting it in the bowl today." Sometimes he put inspirational DVDs in there. Other guys put pictures of their families in the bowl. I never actually put anything in, but I understood what Pat was doing.

Fifteen strong. It made sense to all of us. We bought into it, but I had to Home-Boy-ize it up to make it a little more interesting. The whole idea of it was kind of corny, so I made up a raunchy rap about the bowl so we could relate a little better.

Because I was the only one with a ring, the guys asked me all the time how to prepare. My advice was simple: do the same thing all season. If you started the year going to bed at 2:00 a.m., then end the year going to bed at 2:00 a.m. If you have been going out the night before a game all season, then keep doing that. I've found through the years that kind of consistency matters. Your body gets into a certain rhythm and you want to maintain that.

"I told the guys, 'Just go with it, dawgs. Let's ride this thing home. I can't wait for the playoffs. We're going all the way. I'm already thinking about what I'm going to wear for the parade.'"

We beat Chicago, New Jersey, and Detroit on our way to the Finals. None of those teams really gave us much of a scare.

So we got to the Finals feeling pretty good about our chances against the Dallas Mavericks. And that's when we got punched in the face. Jason Terry dropped 32 on us in Game 1, and the Mavericks won. Then, in Game 2, Dirk Nowitzki had 26 points and 16 rebounds, and suddenly we were down 2–0 in the series.

DWade reminded me a little bit of myself when I was in that first Finals against Hakeem. He was being too nice, too respectful of the opponent. I told him, "Get mean. Get hungry. You can take over this series." They were fronting me and backing me, so I couldn't do shit. DWade needed to step up and take over.

I told him, "All we've got to do is win one game and then we've got them. Trust me, I know those boys from Dallas. They're going to get tight. Jason Terry never did like pressure."

The Dallas owner, Mark Cuban, did us a huge favor. They were up 2–0 and he started talking about planning a parade. They actually published the route in the paper. Pat got ahold of it before I did.

He came into the locker room all pissed off. He was banging the table and throwing chairs and handing out body slams and shouting, "After all we've been through, fifteen strong, are we going to give up? This fucking guy is planning a goddamn parade."

A little bit of it was for show, but he got his point across. I got my boys GP and Antoine and Posey riled up, and DWade took care of the young guys, and we were good to go.

Yet somehow we still managed to fall behind by 13 points in Game 3. For a second I was wondering, *Hey, maybe we're not going to get this done.* But, just as I was thinking that, I looked at Posey and he had this "It ain't over" look on his face, and so did Antoine and GP and DWade. So we got in a huddle and I said, "Let's keep doing what we're doing."

Truth is, we were used to playing from behind. I loved that group of guys because they never panicked. We had our moments where we'd get mad at each other once in a while, but we believed in each other.

Udonis Haslem was a hardworking guy who would do anything you asked him. Anything at all. He *is* Miami. He was born and raised there, and he would do whatever it took to stay there. He had a couple of free-agent offers after the 2009–10 season that would have paid him more money, but he wanted to stay put. He loved Pat and Pat loved him. If Riles told him to run into a brick wall he'd say, "How fast?" His body fat was always right where it should have been. He never complained, whether he got a lot of shots or no shots at all. He's the kind of guy who helps you win championships.

Alonzo Mourning was the same way. He sacrificed a lot to be on that championship team. He could have gone somewhere else and played more minutes, but he was willing to play behind me for the good of the team.

In Games 1 and 2 I had missed 14 out of my 16 free throws. I was ticked off and embarrassed about that, so the night before Game 3, when we were back in Miami, I went to the gym to work on it. It was late—about nine or ten o'clock—and I heard music, and some noise.

There's DWade working on his fadeaways, his floaters. I was impressed. It was the first time since Kobe that I saw a young fella really working at it. I was just shooting free throws, but he was going full speed. He had a kid there throwing the ball off the backboard at half court so he could take off in transition.

Wade turned the series around for us. He was fantastic. He just took over. In Game 3 he scored 42 points and dominated. I chipped in with 16 points, 11 boards, and 5 assists. GP hit a monster shot to win it for us, and Dirk missed a free throw in the final seconds.

One thing about the Finals is, once you get some momentum, nothing can stop you. When Posey hit some threes, Antoine hit some big shots, and I finally knocked down some free throws, you could feel it all changing.

Our fans were awesome. Everybody in white, waving those towels, making noise. Once the crowd got into it, the look in Dirk Nowitzki's eyes changed.

In Game 4 it was our defense that won it for us. That, and another fabulous game from DWade. We held the Mavericks to 7 points in the fourth quarter, which was a new record.

During Game 4, Jerry Stackhouse was called for a flagrant foul on me. He was upset because in Game 1 he came to the hole and I just stood there, and he rammed into me and broke his nose. He probably wanted to get me back. The good thing about me is I'm groomed to take the punishment. Sarge made sure of that by the tactics he used on me growing up.

I was breaking to the basket in transition, and Stackhouse went up and put his elbow in the back of my head. I didn't even feel it.

When someone comes at you with everything they've got and you don't even make a facial response, you have them.

I learned that from Hakeem in my first Finals. I bowled him in the stomach and he said, "That was a good one." He never talked trash, never got mad. He came down on the next play, threw five moves at me, and hit a fadeaway. As we were running back down the floor he said, "You've got to hit me harder, big fella." I remember thinking, *Damn, so that's how it's done.*

When I went to the basket and Stackhouse tackled me, my first thought was to come up swinging, but *ding! ding! ding!* I can't do that now. The best thing I could do, especially being a terrible free-throw shooter, was just get up and knock down both free throws, which I did.

After the game they asked me about the play and I told them, "My daughters tackle me harder when I come home."

I've always known how to fight, but also how to take a punch. People ask me, "Who hit you the hardest? Who was the toughest?" I tell them, "It's my father. No one else is even close."

So we come back from being down 2–0 in the series to tie it 2–2, and Jerry Stackhouse gets suspended for Game 5 because of his attempted takedown on me.

Game 5 goes to overtime. At that point it seemed to me Dallas sort of panicked. DWade was destroying them and they had no answers, so they started blaming it on the refs. They claimed they weren't allowed to touch DWade and were getting nailed with "phantom fouls." DWade had 25 free-throw attempts in that game, which was as many as the entire Mavericks team, so maybe they had a beef, but they really lost their composure.

After DWade won the game for us on two free throws, Dirk kicked the ball in the stands, and Cuban was going after the referees and talking about conspiracy theories, and it was all falling apart.

The Mavericks started arguing on the court. Eyes never lie. That fierce look that Jason Terry had in Games 1 and 2? Gone. All that chest pumping—it stopped. In Games 3 and 4 the eyes of the Maverick players got bigger, and by Game 5 they were bug-eyed open. I actually heard one of them say, "The pressure's not on us."

Right. You're cooked.

What I always do during the national anthem is start with my head down, then I look up to see who is watching me. A couple of Dallas players were staring at me before Game 5, but as soon as I looked up and caught their eye, they looked down.

Same thing with Chris Webber when he was in Sacramento and Arvydas Sabonis in Portland. They'd look at me and I'd look back as if to say, *That's right. I'm coming for you.*

After we won three games in a row to go up 3–2, we had to fly back to Dallas to try and close it out in Game 6. Pat came in and said, "Everybody better pack only one suit. We're finishing this up in one game." He was serious. He told the guys, "If you pack two suits, then you might as well stay home. I'm not letting you on this bus." He actually checked our luggage as we got on.

I packed myself a black suit with a black shirt, because in my mind we were going to kick some ass and then have a funeral. Once we got to Dallas, Pat separated us from our families. He put them in one hotel and moved us somewhere else.

We beat the Mavericks 95–92 to win the championship. There was one guy I felt sorry for, and that was Dirk Nowitzki. Dirk was no front-runner. He's a great player. He's always done what he's supposed to do. He's a good guy, a hard worker. I'm one of those people who understands you can't do it alone. I knew what was about to happen to the poor bastard. It was going to be all his fault, even though he had played great.

After we won we had a fabulous party at the Crescent Court Hotel. We partied all night. Pat Riley was a dancing fool. I really enjoyed watching him let loose. A lot of guys got up on the mic and said what they loved about our team. I didn't say anything, though. It wasn't my show. It was DWade's night. I was so happy for him and Udonis and Zo. It was my fourth championship and they don't ever get old, but there's something about the first one that is always special. So I kind of hung back and watched the guys who had never gotten one before, like Antoine and GP and Posey.

Of course when we got back to Miami we were South Beach royalty. Everybody loved us. We ate free at every restaurant. We were offered free condos, free cars.

Everything I had promised the city of Miami had come true. We won a championship, we owned the city, and I had proven I could win anywhere—not just with some shot-happy guard in Los Angeles.

I wasn't the only one who had Laker baggage. On the night we won the championship, Pat Riley, who had won all of his championships in LA, grabbed me and hugged me and thanked me and then said, "We're back."

As I watched him dancing all around, this man who is all about being cool and staying cool and never letting his guard down, I remember thinking, *I guess Pat Riley isn't so bad after all.*

Like I said before, my mistake.

AUGUST 2006

Beijing, China

Shaquille O'Neal surveyed the thousands of Beijing citizens clamoring to get closer, craning their necks upward to steal a glimpse of his imposing seven-foot-one frame. The Chinese had dubbed him "the Big Shark" and consistently requested two things during his tour of their country: to touch him once, and to snap a photograph.

"It is almost like you are not real," confessed his translator.

Still basking in the glow of his championship with the Heat, O'Neal signed a deal with the Li Ning Company to sell his own brand of sports apparel.

Much like NBA Commissioner David Stern, Shaq had been looking to capitalize on the globalization of the game of basketball. Asia, Shaq determined, was a lucrative, untapped market. "As usual," noted one league official, "Shaq was one step ahead of his peers."

The Big Shark bowed respectfully to the swelling crowd in Beijing and announced, "Hello. I'm Shaquille O'Neal and I love China."

Clearly the feeling was mutual. Olympic gymnastics

legend Li Ning, for whom the apparel company was named,
chose O'Neal as his spokesman after studying data from
a poll that showed Shaq was not only one of the most
recognizable stars in China but also boasted one of the
highest favorability ratings.

This was true in spite of a major faux pas by O'Neal three
years earlier, when, in an attempt to be humorous in
answering a question about the beloved Chinese basketball
hero Yao Ming, he said, "Tell Yao ching-chong-yang-
wah-ah-so!"

Shaq's Chinese gibberish was immediately condemned as
disrespectful and racially insensitive. Yao graciously tried
to diffuse the controversy by joking, "Chinese is hard to
learn. I had trouble with it when I was little," yet the furor
persisted. Shaq had caused an international incident.

Within minutes of Shaq's blunder, his father, Philip
Harrison, called him in a rage.

"I thought I taught you better than that!" he thundered.
"That stuff isn't funny! Don't you do that to Yao Ming. He's
your brother. Show him the respect he deserves."

"Shaquille, shame on you," his mother scolded him. "You
owe that nice young man an apology."

The apology soon followed. Three years later Shaq also
extended his regrets personally to Yao's parents in a private
meeting.

Yet the people of China had clearly already forgiven him.
Li Ning announced he had commissioned a fifty-foot-tall
statue of O'Neal to be built just outside Chaoyoung Park to
enthusiastic roars of approval.

In subsequent years, Baron Davis and Evan Turner would
follow Shaq as spokesmen for Li Ning, which aimed to be the
Asian version of Nike.

Yet neither would have the same impact as the big man in the summer of 2006. Chinese journalists peppered him with questions, then posed for pictures afterward. One admiring reporter asked, "Can you win more rings with the Miami Heat?"

"I hope so," Shaq answered. "My body is a little beat up right now, but it's nothing a little rest can't cure."

More than 7,500 miles away in Miami, Florida, coach Pat Riley caught wind of the comments and grimaced.

WHILE I WAS ROLLING OUT MY NEW CLOTHING LINE IN CHINA, Pat Riley was busy sending us letters about our body fat. He had come up with some new and improved threats, but I didn't even open my letter. I knew I wasn't going to make my number.

Pat was concerned winning it all would make us too comfortable. And, to be honest, he was right. It did.

We celebrated a little too long and a little too hard. There were too many parties, too many commercials, too many celebrations. We lost our edge.

My trip to China was business, but it was also a chance for me to make things right. I felt so bad about what I had said about Yao. It was meant as a joke and it was wrong because the Chinese people are so honorable. It bothered me for a long time afterward. Yao was such a nice guy, and even though I was doing my usual thing by building up our rivalry in the media, I should have left it alone.

At the time I said it, my father was in charge of my fan club mail. He called me up and chewed me out, then he told me that Yao had been sending me Christmas cards for years. Every one said the same thing: "You are my favorite player."

Damn. I can be such a jerk sometimes.

When I met Yao's parents, they were so gracious. They brought me gifts, treated me like a king. I spent five hours with them. Before I left, I told them I thought their son was a warrior. They told me he was only trying to live up to his idol.

I felt even worse after that.

I showed up to training camp without any chance of making my target of 13 percent body fat. I wasn't the only one. Antoine and Posey both missed their target number and were suspended.

The body fat crusade was on overdrive and I was tired of it. Tired of walking around drinking water twenty-four hours a day. Tired of eating food for rabbits. I told the guys, "Do you honestly think Riley was doing this in LA? Do you really think he was pinching Magic Johnson's waistline every day?"

Pat was pissed that we didn't come back in top shape, so that meant he needed to crank things up.

The workouts were longer and more intense. After a hard practice we'd have to get on these exercise bikes around the court. They hooked us up to heart monitors and had these television sets with everyone's name on it so they could measure our heart rates. Each one of us had to keep it at a certain level depending on our age, weight, and height. Pat would pace back and forth checking the numbers, and if they weren't what he wanted, he'd yell, "Shaq, pick it up. Pose, pick it up." Each bike had a chip in it, and it recorded everything.

The idea was to embarrass you into keeping your heart rate at that level. It was demeaning, but we figured out to a way to rig it. Me and GP realized if you kept tapping and rubbing the monitor on your arm it would speed up the heart monitor even if you weren't pedaling that hard. DWade and Posey knew about it, too. Some days, we actually were smiling while we were on those bikes. I'm sure Pat was suspicious. He was probably wondering, *What the hell are they up to?*

Our team got off to a terrible start. On the night we raised our championship banner, Chicago crushed us by 42 points. We lost eight of our first twelve games.

Pat wasn't handling it well. He was big on suits and ties on the road, but after we won a title we got him to relax a little bit and go with jeans and sports coats. But once those losses starting piling up, we were back to suits again.

DWade had a bad wrist, so he wasn't 100 percent. Absolutely everyone was gunning for us because we had just won the title. On top of that, I hurt my knee against Houston just six games into the season. At first we thought I had hyperextended it but it turned out to be torn cartilage. I had arthroscopic surgery and missed thirty-five games.

I was only back for three and a half weeks when DWade dislocated his shoulder. Even Pat was hurt. He took a short leave of absence because of hip and knee problems.

Honestly? I think he really just needed a leave of absence from us. We were a mess.

The media was having fun writing "I told you so." We were too old, too "fat and happy," too spoiled. We betrayed the discipline that got us there in the first place. Blah blah blah blah. I had to tune it out so I didn't haul off and punch somebody.

I resorted to what I call my SHAM strategy. SHAM stands for Short Answer Method. That's when I start talking in very low, soft tones with one-word answers so the sound bite is practically useless. Note to media: when I do that, it means I'm sick of the same old questions. It means I don't want to talk to you anymore. It means I'm SHAMming you.

Even though I had been injured for a big chunk of the season, the fans still voted me as the starting center for the 2007 All-Star Game. Some reporters were squawking that I didn't belong there, but once again I will say it: give the people what they want. They wanted Shaq. They always have. I tried not to get mad about it. When someone asked me how I felt about making the team even though I missed so many games, I told them, "I'm like President Bush. You may not like me, you may not respect me, but you voted me in."

As usual, the NBA was counting on me to provide some All-Star entertainment, and I didn't let them down. We were having a "practice" at one of the All-Star jam sessions, and I started doing my break dancing at center court. I was spinning and turning on my head and doing my thing, and then I made my way over to LeBron and challenged him to a dance-off. Next thing you know the two of us are jamming together, wiggling and moving and shaking our booties.

Then I shimmied over to Dwight Howard and challenged him. He answered with a few lame moves of his own, but there was no doubt who the crowd was digging the most.

I may have been "old," but the Big Shark still had the moves.

Somehow, in spite of everything that went wrong, we still managed to win forty-four games during that 2006–07 season. When DWade went down I stepped up and tried to keep us above water. We won nine games in a row at one point but were swept by the Chicago Bulls in the first round of the playoffs. It's one thing when Michael Jordan and Scottie Pippen take you out in four games. It's something else when it's Luol Deng and Ben Gordon that do it to you.

DWade and I put up decent numbers, but we didn't get a whole lot of help. Antoine and Zo had a couple of big games here and there, but we were too beat up to pull it off.

It was the first time in fifty years the defending champion was swept in the opening round. Not the kind of stat you want on your résumé.

Gary Payton had somehow landed in Pat's doghouse, and he played in only two of our playoff games. He retired after the 2006–07 season, and I just felt he deserved a better send-off than that.

The whole feeling around the team had changed. Everything started to go sour. The "15 strong" had been replaced by "1 Mistake and You're Gone."

Like Posey. He was a big part of why we won our championship. Pat wasn't crazy about him, though, because he was a partier and he kept missing his body fat requirements.

So one night Posey was out and he parked his car in front of the club and he had too much to drink. He got into his car but he never actually started it up and drove it. They arrested him for something called driving under suspicion. He got to the police station and he called me because I'm friendly with a lot of the law enforcement people, but I got there too late. They had already fingerprinted him and booked him, so there was nothing I could do.

The next day Pat called us all in and gave us a lecture about drinking and driving. I knew what it meant. I knew Posey was on his way out. He finished the season with us but signed with Boston as a free agent in the summer of 2007.

I always suspected that Pat must have had some spies down on South Beach watching us. He always seemed to know what we were doing. I'd be out having fun, and the next day I'd show up for practice and he'd say, "Shaq, why were you at this club at two a.m.?"

I wasn't really that big of a club guy in Miami, but I liked to drive around the beach in my Crown Victoria with the police lights. Some nights I'd drive by and see Posey's or Antoine's car out front and I'd say, "Damn," because I had a feeling they would pay for it the next day.

They weren't the only ones being watched. We had a young fella on our team named Dorrell Wright. He had a ton of talent but he was your classic New Age player. A lot of guys come in, and you can tell right away they don't have the same focus as we did when we were eighteen years old. When I was eighteen, I was scared of coaches.

Not Dorrell. That guy came in and did what he wanted to do. He had about a hundred tattoos. My father would have absolutely killed me if I had that many. I got my first tattoo at twenty, in Hawaii. It was a little Superman tattoo. I didn't let Sarge see it for the longest time because I knew it would set him off. My mom hates them, too. Over the years I've collected a few more tattoos, but I keep telling my mother, "When I'm done you're going to see me in a suit and tie anyway, so don't worry."

Anyhow, Dorrell was very athletic. He could have been so much more effective if he just listened once in a while. But he was pretty sure he had it all figured out. Classic case of a young guy getting too much too soon without really earning it. But I'm not rooting against him. He had a really good season for Golden State in 2010–11, so maybe he's grown up a bit.

We liked Dorrell, so he came along sometimes for our "team meetings." He loved the nightlife and South Beach and the whole

Miami scene. However, I had a sense that Pat was keeping tabs on him, and that wasn't a good thing for Dorrell Wright.

So now when we played bad it was because we weren't in shape *and* because of the nightlife. Obviously since I don't drink, I can't say from experience if alcohol ruins your game. All I know is Jason Kapano didn't drink and always stayed home, and if you kicked it out to him, sometimes he made the shot and sometimes he didn't. And, if you kicked to Antoine, who was out partying all the time, same thing. Sometimes he'd make it, sometimes he wouldn't.

Antoine was supposed to be at 10 percent body fat. One day he weighed in at 10.6 percent and Pat fined him two thousand dollars. Antoine told me he was docked over fifteen thousand dollars his first year with Riley. He filed an appeal with the Players Association, and they agreed on a deal where he got half the money back and donated the other half to charity.

It wasn't hard to figure out that Antoine's days were numbered, too. The day before the 2007–08 season started, he was shipped off to Minnesota.

One by one, my boys were leaving. The white-hot Miami Heat had gone stone cold.

Things weren't so great for me at home, either. My wife Shaunie and I were having some problems. A lot of it was my fault. I was young when I got married. I'm not making any excuses, but because I was so focused on basketball all the time, I really wasn't putting enough time into being a good boyfriend/husband.

I went from this big kid who nobody wanted to a big man that everybody wanted. One day no girls would even look at me, and then all of sudden every girl wanted me. I never had to court a girl—they courted me.

It's hard to be married to a professional athlete. We're locked into this one thing—to win a championship—and when it doesn't work out, well, we're not all that fun to be around. We've also got people pulling at us all the time and sometimes we forget to push them away.

Besides, I was moody around the house. If I read a bad article that someone wrote about me, I'd take it out on my wife. I admit I was a male diva.

Eventually, Shaunie and I split up. These days she lives in LA with our five kids. I miss not seeing them every day. They have their own distinct personalities and they are changing so fast, and I hate to miss that. I always tell Taahirah (she's my daughter from a previous relationship), Amirah, Me'arah, Myles, Shaqir, and Shareef what my father told me: Be a leader. Not a follower.

The hardest part for me is opening the door to my house and not hearing six different voices when I walk in. Yeah, we have holidays and summers together in Orlando, but it's not what I planned for my children. It's not what I wanted for them. They will realize as they get older that relationships are hard. They take work. And even with all that work, sometimes it's best to move on.

When all of my kids were young, I loved to lie on the couch and let them fall asleep on my chest. I did such a good job of calming those little babies down that I'd be out at the gym working or doing some business and I'd get a phone call saying, "Come home, the baby won't fall asleep!"

My first child, Taahirah, is my original princess. Every macho guy will tell you they want their first baby to be a boy so they can name them "Jr." after themselves. All I can tell you is that when little Taarihah came out, I just wanted to hold her all day.

Taarihah is a very intelligent young lady. She has a lot of good ideas, and I'm very proud of her. She'll probably be working with me when she gets a little older.

My son Shareef is an athlete. I'm very jealous of him. He was doing things on the basketball court at the age of eight that I couldn't do until I was sixteen years old. I was his coach last summer and we were undefeated. He's very, very funny and very sensitive. Sound like anyone you know?

Then we have Amirah, my second princess. She's my protector. She gets very on guard when we are out and people start walking up to us. She doesn't like big crowds and she doesn't like to share me.

When she sees a mob of people coming she says, "C'mon, Daddy, let's go get some ice cream."

My youngest son, Shaqir, has many of the same athletic qualities as Shareef, but he's my mean, ferocious guy. He's got that fiery streak in him that both my father and I have. One day my mom came over and Shaqir did something crazy, and she put her fork down and said, "That's you right there, boy." So I tell Shaqir he's my twin.

Little Me'arah is just a sweet, sweet child. She likes to kiss, kiss, kiss her daddy on the cheek. She's the most affectionate one of all. She's very motherly, always herding everyone together. She's going to grow up and do something really special for people.

Myles is a teenager now. My ex-wife, Shaunie, already had Myles when I met her, but he's one of mine, as far as I'm concerned. He's a very smart kid, a reader, a real thinker. He's been the ultimate big brother to his younger siblings.

Both Shareef and Shaqir really love basketball. They are like little sponges. They want to know everything. They love the NBA, so I get some tape of Allen Iverson and we watch that, and then some of Tracy McGrady, and they can't believe how great TMac was before he got injured. They love seeing highlights of their uncle Kobe, too.

The other day Shareef was trying to get down Ray Allen's jump shot. Shaqir, he was working on Blake Griffin's spin move. I can't believe how sharp they are. I show them something once, and I come back to it a week or a month later and they've nailed it.

Someday they'll appreciate what their father did in his day, but right now the other players are more interesting. It's okay. I've got some Shaq highlight reels when they're ready to see 'em.

Our 2007–08 season in Miami was off to an even worse start than the year before. We were playing Utah on December 22 when I slid into the scorer's table chasing after a loose ball. I hurt my hip. Actually, my whole leg hurt—my ankle, my thigh, everything. I took a couple of days off, came back the day after Christmas, and reaggravated it. They took some X-rays, but nothing came up.

We tried rest, ice, anti-inflammatory medication, some stretching, but nothing really worked. My back was starting to get locked up, too, and the training staff didn't know what was wrong with me. I was getting really frustrated, but not nearly as frustrated as Pat. We were losing game after game and he needed me back.

The team was in the middle of a long road trip—and, as it turned out, a fifteen-game losing streak—when they told my bodyguard, Jerome, and me they had booked us on an early-morning flight to Los Angeles to see another doctor. We were in Minnesota at the time, so we threw some clothes in a bag, grabbed a cab, and got on this tiny little plane to LA.

By the time I got there after a few hours in that tin can, I was really hurting.

Pat set us up with this doctor that performed something called prolotherapy. The idea is they shoot sugar water into your ligaments and tendons to help increase the blood supply and stimulate the tissue. Up to that point I was getting shot up with cortisone. Once I started seeing blood coming out of the syringe, I signed off on the idea it might be time to try something else.

This woman that Pat sent me to stuck about fifteen needles in my leg, then shot me up with the sugar water. It was painful, but I didn't care as long as it worked. I stayed out there almost a week and got four treatments.

When I got back I was feeling pretty good for about two or three games but then everything went out of whack again, so I was back on a plane to California. I made that trip about three or four times. The problem was I'd come back to Miami and ask, "What's the follow-up treatment to this?" Nobody knew. There was none.

Our team was really slumping. I missed nine games and we lost all of them. Pat was angry with me, but I really don't know what he wanted me to do. I went to see the sugar-water lady in California like he asked me to, but it was only a temporary fix. I was worried. I thought my career was over.

In late January Pat had me undergo an MRI, which showed I had some soft tissue damage and some inflammation but nothing "structurally compromised." They started calling it bursitis, but I could tell Pat thought I was dogging it.

Pat tried to get me to talk to a psychologist. This guy came into our locker room and he was talking with a few players. I didn't like all the personal questions he was asking, so I was totally disrespecting the guy. He finally got around to me and was trying to get me to open up about my feelings and then he said, "You are angry. What are you angry about?" I told him, "I don't like people who don't have any idea what's going on and pretend like they do know. I know you're Pat's guy, so why should I talk to you?" That was the end of our conversation.

The injury was getting to me. One day I was standing at my locker and I was in a lot of pain and I kind of broke down. Zo tried to talk to me. He knew I was frustrated with the way Pat was handling me. He told me when he was the Heat's star and led the team in scoring, rebounding, and blocks, he was still Pat's whipping boy no matter how good his numbers were.

"Pat always gets on his stars," Zo said. "That's just his style."

Maybe Zo was all right with that style, but I wasn't. I had this injury that we couldn't figure out and Pat started telling people that he's faking it, he's getting a divorce, we've got a bad record, so he doesn't feel like playing anymore. When I got to Phoenix, the general manager there, Steve Kerr, told me Riley said I was "faking" the injury. I heard it other places, too.

I'm not going to lie. It stung me. If he had just pulled me aside and said, "Hey, this isn't working anymore. It's time for you to go," we could have talked business. We could have avoided all the ugly shit that's gone down since then. I'm not trying to embarrass the guy, but I don't like it when people lie about me. Don't tell your owner I'm faking after all I've done for your city, for your team, for you.

As soon as I got traded to Phoenix, the training staff there fixed me up. They recognized I had been getting the wrong treatment.

The Phoenix trainer—Aaron Nelson—was the one who solved it. He and his Phoenix staff have done amazing things to bring back injured athletes through the years like Grant Hill, Antonio McDyess, and Steve Nash, who has been dealing with a chronic back problem for years.

He also hooked me up with this dude named Michael Clark, who was the team physical therapist for the Suns, and explained to me that my body was breaking down due to a series of "misfires." My surgically repaired toe wasn't bending, which caused stress on my ankle and prevented it from rotating properly. That caused problems with my thigh, up to my hip, and even my butt muscles.

Everything was traced back to my stupid arthritic toe. Because the toe wouldn't bend, I was jumping off the ball of my foot. It changed my gait and the way I jumped, and it put a tremendous strain on the rest of my leg. It was kind of a chain reaction.

Nobody in Miami ever made that connection. Aaron Nelson and Michael Clark were the first to do that. They did a thorough examination of me and started having me work on my core strength, my flexibility, my balance. They got my butt muscles firing properly again. It took a couple of weeks, but by late February I was ready to play again.

As soon as I got back on the court Pat must have called up his boy Bill Walton, because the next thing you know Bill is on television saying, "Shaq's running around there looking fine. Why couldn't he do that in Miami?"

I took great offense to that. Here's Bill Walton, who was injured *most of his career*, who actually sued a team doctor because he thought they messed him up, talking about me and my injuries? No. Not a chance I'm going to sit there and listen to that bullshit.

Of course the media asked me about it. I told them, "I heard Mr. Walton's comments and I think Mr. Walton has broken the Big Man Pecking Order Code 225.7, which means his résumé isn't quite good enough to speak on what I've done."

Bill Walton won two championships—and one of them was from

hanging on tight to Larry Bird's ass. I had four rings at that point. He's going to tell me about winning? He scored something like 6,000 points in his career. I wound up with over 28,000. So I just didn't feel he was authorized to talk about me like that. The first couple of times he said stuff, I let it go. I had always shown him the respect all big men deserve. But when he kept doing it, I had enough.

I said, "I look at what Mr. Walton has said and the one thing I hate is a hypocrite. So if I'm 'faking' an injury, his entire playing career is a fake."

People like Bill Walton bother me. You know the kind—the guy who rides on your team plane and sucks up to you and all your teammates, then the minute he gets on television he goes off on the whole damn team and starts talking about you like you're some journeyman.

Show a little respect, Bill. Don't talk to me like I'm nothing. We're in the same Big Man Club, Top 50 Players Club, Championship Club.

There's an unwritten rule among big men. We understand the physical toll our bodies take and the criticism we have to listen to because everyone thinks the game is so easy when you are seven feet tall. It's not easy. You know that, and still you violated the code.

Pat told everybody I didn't get better because I refused to do the rehab they set up for me. I stopped doing their rehab because it simply didn't work. Miami trainer Ron Culp had me doing electrical stimulation, and it didn't help.

My ticket out of town was punched in mid-February. There was a lot of tension between Pat and the players. So we're about to start practice and Jason Williams comes in about ten seconds late.

Pat being Pat, he starts swearing at him and screaming, "Get the hell out of here!"

He and JWill start yelling at each other, and JWill turns to go and kicks over the training cart. He sends pieces of Wrigley gum flying all over the place. He's walking away and I say, "JWill. Come back. Don't go anywhere."

Pat hears me so he starts going ballistic on me. Now, JWill was my guy. I kind of brought him there, so I felt responsible for him.

I tell Pat we're a team and we need to stick together, not throw guys out of the gym. Pat is screaming at me and says if I don't like it, then I should get the hell out of practice, too.

That's when I said, "Why don't you make me?"

I start taking a couple of steps towards Pat. Udonis Haslem steps in and I shove him out of the way. Then Zo tries to grab me. I threw him aside like he was a rag doll.

Now it's me and Riley face-to-face, jaw to jaw. I'm poking him in the chest and he keeps slapping my finger away and it's getting nasty. Noisy, too. He's yelling "Fuck you!" and I'm yelling back, "No, fuck you!"

Zo is trying to calm us both down and he has this kind of singsong panic in his voice. He keeps saying, "Big fella, no big fella, big fella!" I finally turn around and tell him, "Don't worry. I'm not going to hit the man. Do you think I'm crazy?"

At that point Pat decides that practice is over. He walks out and goes to his downstairs office, and everyone just kind of stands there. Nobody is sure what to do. I think they were pretty shocked because it was the first time they ever saw anyone stand up to Pat like that.

Everybody was kind of backing away from me because I had that murderous "Shaq is about to go off" look on my face. They knew better than to mess with me at that point.

Obviously that was the end of me in Miami. Pat knew and I knew it. I called my uncle Mike and my agent, Perry Rogers, and told them, "Let's ask for a trade before he can control the story." I knew because Pat was such a control freak he'd want to spin it his way.

In the end, I was kind of sad about the whole thing because Miami was a city that was very nice to me, and I didn't want to be disrespectful to their fans. I also loved Miami's owner, Mickey Arison. He was the best owner I've ever been around. He was friendly, gentle, generous, and kind. He supported us but never interfered, which is what every owner should do.

I'm not a big schmoozer, but when I first got to Miami, Mr. Arison invited me on this beautiful yacht. He told me, "I'm glad you're here. Tickets sales are up, and I think we can win a championship. If you ever need anything, just call me."

That was really the extent of my relationship with him. I'm not the kind to hang with the owner, but whenever I saw him I always enjoyed it, even if all we did was say, "Hey, how are you doing? Shalom." I'm sure Pat complained to him about me. I'm sure he told him that I was faking my injury, and Mickey probably wasn't too happy to hear that.

Of everything that happened, that was what upset me the most. I still can't believe Pat questioned whether I could play. They wanted me to do all this rehab and then threw that in my face when I left because I didn't do what they wanted me to do, but I didn't trust them anymore. How many times was I going to fly to California to have somebody stick needles in my legs before someone said, "Hey, maybe this isn't working"?

Soon after my little incident with Pat, he called Perry and told him, "It's over. We're trading Shaq." Perry said: "Let me fly out there and talk this over with you." Pat said, "No, we're done."

He told Perry they had a deal to trade me to Phoenix. Perry called me and said, "What do you think?" I said immediately, "Let's go."

By the time I left Miami things weren't really all that good between me and DWade. It wasn't bad, but it just wasn't good, either. I'm sure someone got in his ear and said, "Stay away from Shaq, he's trouble." People ask me if I'm disappointed DWade didn't stand up for me, but I wasn't, because you can't stand up to Pat. If you do, you're gone, and DWade wants to stay in Miami for his entire career.

He's a bona fide star now. Very talented kid. Am I sorry we didn't stay friends? I don't know. It's not really about that. The job is to win championships. We got one championship together, so that's what I'll remember about Dwyane Wade.

When he traded me, Pat denied we were having any problems. He told the media, "I loved Shaq when I got him and I love him today."

He didn't mean it. He hated the way I called him out. He didn't like to be challenged. I'm sure he thought I was trying to destroy the culture he created. He was probably right. I thought his "culture" needed some tweaking.

The sad part is, a little communication could have fixed all of it. As long as I know what's going on, it's cool. Be straight with me and we'll be fine. Don't tell me, "We love you, we love you, you put our franchise on the map," then turn around and trade me a few days later. Just be honest with me. Talk to me like a man.

I can still hear Pat telling me, "I'm going to take down that 6th Man Michael Jordan jersey we have up in our rafters and put your number 32 uniform in its place. You have done so much for this franchise. Your jersey will be the first one up there, the first one ever retired by the Heat."

And then, just like that, I'm gone.

FEBRUARY 27, 2009

Phoenix, Arizona

Shaquille O'Neal positioned himself in the post and waited for the double team to come.

It never arrived.

"Coach," he said to the Suns' Alvin Gentry as he jogged by the bench, "single coverage."

Gentry grabbed point guard Steve Nash and instructed him, "Give the big fella the ball."

He was one week shy of his thirty-seventh birthday, but Shaq had jumped into his time machine. As a series of Toronto players, Chris Bosh among them, tried to stop him, the Big Cactus kept sticking them with dunks, jump hooks, and putbacks. When he was finished, he'd scored 45 points in 20-of-25 shooting, his most prolific output in six years.

"I think I'm the only player who looks at each and every center and says, 'That's barbecued chicken down there,'" Shaq said afterward.

The Suns won 133–113 on a day Toronto coach Jay Triano conceded his team had "no match for Shaq."

It was evidence, Shaq would later say, that although he was old, he could still get it done given the proper touches.

Bosh begged to differ. He sniffed O'Neal was "camping" in the lane all night.

"I mean, if they're not calling three seconds—I thought it was a rule, but I guess not," Bosh groused.

"That's a big statement coming from the RuPaul of the NBA," Shaq shot back. "Chris Bosh? How would he know about three seconds? He's afraid to go inside."

With the Big Shaqtus waiting for him in the lane, it was hard to blame him.

I WENT TO PHOENIX IN PEACE, ARMS UP IN SURRENDER. I WENT from punking Penny to fighting with Kobe all the time to chilling out with DWade and banging heads with Pat Riley. I was burned out. I didn't want to fight with anybody. My motor was shot. So I wasn't about to punk Steve Nash. It was "Okay Steve, do whatever you want, let me know what you need from me."

But it never really worked out for us. Of course in my line of business that falls on me. My fault again. They said I slowed Phoenix down. I don't really think that was true, but people are certainly entitled to their opinion.

You won't hear anything negative from me about Phoenix. I loved it there. The guys were great, and Mike D'Antoni was excellent. The training staff was phenomenal. They saved my career and they helped me understand my body, and I will always have their backs for that. Athletes are spoiled. They do amazing things, and then when their body breaks down, they go to the medical people and say, "Fix me." We don't care how or why, just do it. I learned a lot from Aaron Nelson and Michael Clark on how to take care of myself while I was playing, but also techniques I could use after I'm done playing to keep myself healthy.

Phoenix was a good fit for me at that point of my career because they were an up-tempo team that ran all the time. Mike D'Antoni was careful not to burn us out in practice. Our practices lasted something like twenty minutes.

We'd go out there, play a game to 7, and then we were done. We'd watch some film, talk about what we should have done, and go home.

That was why they were able to run all the time. Mike was smart enough not to overdo it. He could do that because he respected his leaders, Steve Nash and Grant Hill. He knew they would always come into camp in shape.

Those guys were true pros. I have never met a single person who doesn't like and respect Grant Hill. He's a great guy. He's also one of the hardest workers I've ever seen. If he didn't have the *if* next to his name, he would have been one of the greatest ever. He was stuck with the *if* because he had a foot injury that got all messed up and misdiagnosed, and it cost him a huge chunk of his career—the prime of his career, really.

So he gets tagged with the *if*, the same way Alonzo Mourning did. If Zo didn't have his serious kidney issues and the surgeries and if he didn't miss all those years, he'd be another "greatest ever."

Grant was able to reinvent himself as the ultimate role player after his injuries. He'd stand back and watch and absorb what was going on in the game and then adjust to it. His basketball IQ was off the charts.

Steve Nash was a guy who liked to do things perfectly. I wasn't used to his Amare Stoudemire one-step bounce pass. It took me a few games to catch on to that. I also wasn't used to the way he ran a pick-and-roll. We never clicked on the court the way we should have. There wasn't any negative vibes—we just didn't have the time to develop any chemistry. We were both old-timers used to playing a certain way.

Amare was a hardworking kid, very friendly. He had a lot of offensive weapons. He was young and wealthy and successful and just starting out on his own fabulous journey.

I ended up selling him my Lamborghini. It was a car I bought while I was in Miami. Whenever I have a lot on my mind, the first thing I do is jump in my car, crank the music, and go for a long, long ride. I can think better that way. So I'm in Miami and Pat and I have a blowup, or me and my ex-wife have a fight, so I take a drive from Miami to Ft. Lauderdale. I sit there and watch the water, listen to the waves, calm myself down, and start to head home.

I was driving fast—way too fast—probably around 190 miles per hour. So I'm flying down the road and this car cuts me off and I've got to make a quick turn. I cut away from this other car and I go into about five different spins. My first thought was, *I'm going into the wall and flipping over into the water. This is it. This is how I'm going to die.* But I'm a lucky guy, and the car just misses that wall and keeps spinning, and when it finally stops I'm facing the opposite direction. I put the car in reverse and get out and try to stop my knees from buckling.

Right then and there I decided, "I'm never driving this car again." And I didn't.

When I got traded to the Suns I brought it out to Arizona so Amare could look at it. He offered me $120,000 for it. I was trolling the *Robb Report* and found what would eventually be the Shaq-Liner for $110,000. I figured I'll sell the Lamborghini to Amare for $120,000, buy the Shaq-Liner for $110,000, and put another $10,000 into it and I'll be even.

That's being a Shaq-a-matician, except for one small little detail. The Lamborghini cost me $600,000 originally. So I lost a lot of money on it. The reason it cost so much was I bought a brand-new Lamborghini and then I bought an old, beat-up Lamborghini, and in order for me to fit into it, they had to chop them both in half and then superglue it together. It was a beautiful car, hardtop, platinum silver.

I have to say, when I was driving that car around, it made me think about those rich drug dealers from my neighborhood in Newark. I can still remember one guy cruising around in his muddy-green Benz and the other one, tooling around in his souped-up Volvo. I wanted so badly to be driving around in a cool car, so I closed my eyes, whipped up some happy thoughts, and put myself into some of the finest automobiles in the world. That's the great thing about being a dreamer. It always works out exactly the way you planned.

That's not always true in real life, but by the grace of God and some damn hard work, many of the things I wished for as a little warrior named Shaun have happened.

By the time I sold my Lamborghini to Amare Stoudemire, I was done with it. The thrill was gone.

Amare had a certain flair about him that I could relate to. He wasn't a big personality like I was, but he could pull off the Lamborghini thing. While I was there, he was having all sorts of problems with the media and the owner, Robert Sarver. Every week it was the same thing: "Is he getting traded? Is he signing an extension?" There's no question it got to him. You could see it on Amare's face. It wore him down, and it affected the way he played. He's only human. It would have bothered anyone.

He would ask me all the time, "What should I do?" I told him, "Do what's best for your family." Truthfully, I didn't want to get involved. I didn't want to hop on anyone's emotional roller coaster. I had too many rides of my own like that.

I played hard and did what I had to do in Phoenix, but I wasn't as invested as I have been in other places. I knew they brought me in as hired help, as a last-ditch chance to win it all. I wasn't expecting to be there a lot of years.

So why was it that Phoenix never won with all that talent and experience? We had no alpha dogs on the team. You need dogs to win a championship. Steve Nash is an alpha but not a mean dog.

He's a great leader and a great player, but you need a mean dog who will bite your head off, and Steve just isn't that kind of pooch. Mike Jordan was an alpha dog in Chicago. Bird in Boston. I was one, too.

If Steve got really mad, he'd come down and shoot a three, or come down and dish out five straight assists, which was cool—team ball—but it wasn't enough. Face it. He was caught in this loop where he had three great teams that were always in front of him.

Maybe he could get past Dirk and the Mavericks, but then you've got Duncan and the Spurs and Kobe and the Lakers. It had to be frustrating. When you work as hard as Steve Nash and Grant Hill do, there should be some rewards on the other end. But that's not how life works, and it sure as hell isn't how sports works. Don't you dare tell me that Nash and Grant Hill aren't winners. Please. If they don't end up with a championship that will be a shame, but don't judge them on that.

When I played for the Suns, Steve was the first option, Amare was the second option, and I was the third option. Amare was all about score, score, score. I didn't blame him. I was the same way when I was young.

They were always messing with Amare about his defense but I was never clear on why they singled him out. It didn't look to me like there were many other guys on the Suns worrying about defense.

When I joined the Suns I tried to keep it light, but it seemed like there was always something going on while I was there, and for once it didn't have anything to do with me. The Phoenix politics were in full swing during my time there.

My first season, Mike D'Antoni and Robert Sarver were fighting. The next year Mike left, and Terry Porter came in and wanted to play slow-down, so that got Amare ticked off and he wanted to be traded. Terry lasted fifty-one games before they fired him and promoted Alvin Gentry. After that, I was the one traded. Everybody was moving around so much it was hard to ever settle in, get something done.

I was excited to play for Mike D'Antoni. Mike was the one who pushed to bring me there. He told me, "I know you can still play. I want you to be a part of the offense." I told him, "I don't need much. Maybe a couple of shots here and there."

Mike loved Phoenix and he loved the players, but I sensed he just couldn't deal with Sarver, so he left. I think if you talked to him now, he'd do it differently, given the chance. He didn't realize how good he had it with so many professionals in his locker room. He had a great situation in Phoenix.

His successor, Terry Porter, got a raw deal, in my opinion. He knew the game. He wanted to put the brakes on a little, move the ball around, get it inside now and again, but Steve and Grant couldn't really do that. They were used to one way. Every day they'd ask the same thing: "Can we run? Can we run?" Terry would hold two-hour practices and everyone hated it because they were used to something else. I felt bad for Terry Porter. He got all tangled up in the system. He never really had a chance.

The general manager, Steve Kerr, was trying to manage it all but he had his own issues with the owner. Steve is one of the most honest GMs I've ever been around. When I got there, he told me D'Antoni was very excited to have me. Then he told me point-blank he was taking a huge gamble by bringing me in and he wasn't 100 percent sure it would work. I told him I'd do everything I could to help him.

I did a pretty good job of putting the Miami Heat in my rearview mirror even though everyone wanted to talk about them all the time. My first trip back to Miami wasn't until March 4, 2009, so I had been gone more than a year.

I wasn't expecting a parade or another key to the city. They booed the crap out of me, which was what I figured would happen. At one point in the game DWade drove to the hole, so naturally I knocked him on his back and stood over him. I didn't help him up and that got the crowd really fired up, so they started chanting, "Shaq, you suck!"

Hmmm. Does that mean you want to vacate that 2006 championship? Get back to me on that.

The pace in Phoenix was much more laid-back, low-key. They treated you like adults in that organization. Your time was your own. They left it up to you to make good decisions. They were pretty community oriented, which I liked.

So I'm hanging in the Valley of the Sun, and I get a phone call one day from Oprah Winfrey. She says, "Shaq, I need your help with something." Obviously, when Bill Gates calls, you listen. The president calls, you listen. Same with Oprah. Whatever she wants, you do it.

Turns out there was a twelve-year-old boy named Brendan who suffered from a genetic abnormality that forced him to keep growing.

He was seven foot two when I first met him, and he was struggling. Kids made fun of him, his health wasn't good, and he couldn't find any clothes to fit him. Oprah said I was his favorite player and she asked if I could help, so the first thing we did was load up a bunch of my sweat suits and sneakers and jackets and shipped them to him.

We flew him out to the 2009 All-Star Game in Phoenix as my guest and we gave him a brand-new pair of my Dunkman sneakers, which weren't even on the market yet. I took him out to eat in my Shaq-Liner, and he got to enjoy a longtime Shaq custom: dessert before dinner.

Then I took him to my personal tailor and we got him a custom wardrobe.

I really felt for the kid. He was so sweet, really intelligent, very sensitive. I told him, "I've been through it all, Brendan. The bad days, the aches and pains, the kids picking on me. I know how you feel."

He's a teenager now, still growing. It's tough, and his outlook isn't all that good. I still send him clothes all the time. I gave him one of my mink coats. He's kinda cool now because he's friends with Shaq, but my heart goes out to him. No kid should have to suffer like that.

For the most part I kept a fairly low profile when I was in Phoenix. I had a few reality TV projects on the back burner but nothing concrete. So one night I'm watching Michael Phelps swim and I said, "Damn, that dude is fast." I'm talking to my boys and I said, "Do you think if Michael Phelps went down and back for one lap and all I had to do was just go down for half a lap, could I beat him? I think I could." We started laughing, and I said, "That's it. That's my show. *Shaq Vs.*"

The show *Shaq Vs.* turned out to be a lot of fun. The general idea was for me to compete against professional athletes in their sports, with me getting some kind of handicap to make it fair. So I played football against Ben Roethlisberger and baseball against Albert Pujols. The Michael Phelps show was definitely my favorite. He was a real clown, an absolutely terrific guy. My only regret was I didn't think of the show when I was a little younger. I might have had a shot at beating some of those guys if I was still at the top of my game.

You should see the way Michael Phelps eats. Incredible. At the time we were filming I was on a diet because the season was coming up, so I'm eating salads and this kid is eating pizza, burgers, cookies, Twinkies. The reason he eats so much is his warm-up is fifty laps and he swims every day and he's burning calories all the time, so he can eat whatever he wants.

He invited me to his place, and it's a house of horrors for me because there's cookies, ice cream, and cake everywhere. I told him, "Mike, you're killing me!" He was such a sweet guy, a big star who doesn't even know he's a star. He kind of reminds me of Blake Griffin in that way.

When I lost my race to him, I dressed up in this badass pink bikini and walked down the beach in it. A bet is a bet, so I had to do it. People were pulling out their camera phones right and left.

Every show we did was enjoyable because the people we picked to compete against were the masters of their craft. I had a great time with the two women volleyball players, Misty May-Treanor and Kerri Walsh. I got a little competitive and I was trying to spike it like they were, and when I got up the next morning I couldn't move.

The hardest was my race car show. I was terrified driving against Dale Earnhardt Jr. They had to build a special car for me that I could fit into. I squeezed myself into this race car, and when I was getting ready to go out there I'm thinking about the ratings and I thought, *If you want to get good numbers for the show, you should really crash into the wall.*

So that was my plan, but just before I rev up my engine the guy in the pit tells me, "Listen, you have a fireproof suit on, and if you hit the wall and catch fire it should take us about two minutes and then we'll come out and get you." Two minutes! So now I'm absolutely terrified. I'm driving 70 miles per hour around the track, which is slower than when I'm driving to work, and Dale Earnhardt Jr. is going 130 miles per hour, and I look like I'm driving a go-kart. They are in my ear shouting, "You gotta go faster" and I'm thinking, *The hell with you. I'm not going to die!* So then I hear Dale in my ear saying, "Okay now, keep it steady, keep it steady, I'm going to pass you on the right," so I grip the wheel and he goes flying by me.

When I lost to Dale Earnhardt Jr., I had to pull out that pink bikini again and run around the track in it. When I lost to Roethlisberger, I had to send him my championship ring so he could wear it for a week.

Even though I was the "elder statesman" on the Phoenix Suns, it didn't stop teams from trying to take me out of the game. The Spurs coach, Gregg Popovich, went to the Hack-a-Shaq strategy a little bit, which disappointed me. Pop is a great coach. One of the best. I never had a problem with him, but I hate that Hack-a-Shaq thing.

Don Nelson started it. The first three minutes of the game, he fouled me. Shawn Bradley and Sean Rooks would come in the game and start fouling, because Nelson's thing was if I shot 50 percent from the line he'd take those odds. We'd be up by 15 and he'd start in, and it really pissed me off. That's when I called him a clown. The next game we played him he showed up wearing a clown nose.

The free-throw shooting is always what humbled me. It kept me grounded. I used to joke with people that if I shot 80 percent from the line it wouldn't be fair. I'm already too dominant at everything else.

I told reporters, "Once the Hack-a-Shaq works once, you know I'm going to see it again. The only thing worse for basketball than that defense is the Lack-A-Shaq offense, where I have to go to the bench because of foul trouble. There's no fun in that."

Even though I thought a lot of Pop and Duncan, I said some crap about the Spurs through the years. But the truth is, I didn't mean it. Those two guys knew that. They understood how I rolled.

But you know at some point Pop is going to get me back. So they foul the shit out of me in the '08 playoffs and I'm a little irritated.

We play them in the season opener the following year, and the first time I touch the ball—I'm talking like five seconds into the game—they hack me. I look over at their bench like, *Are you kid-ding me?* and there's Pop, laughing his ass off, giving me the two thumbs-up. You gotta love a guy who has a sense of humor like that.

Pop understood that even though I respected him I had to market myself and sometimes that meant saying stuff to amp up the game. It was never personal. So he played along. Sometimes the people involved take it the wrong way unless you fill them in on the plan.

For instance, take the Maloof family in Sacramento. I loved those guys. They take care of me every time I go to Vegas, but that doesn't mean I'm not going to go at their team. So the time I called them the "Sacramento Queens." Joe Maloof calls me up and says, "C'mon now, Shaq." I told him, "Hey, I'm just playing, baby. Do you know how many people are going to be at that game now? I just put your team on the map." He said, "You're right, you're right. Tell your mother I love her and I said hello." I said, "All right, talk to you later, and by the way, I'm coming to Vegas, I need a room."

After the Spurs eliminated us from the playoffs, they got knocked out by the Lakers. Check this out. It was the first time in ten years neither Tim Duncan or Shaquille O'Neal was playing in the NBA Finals.

I was in New York doing a number of promotional things while the Celtics were beating the Lakers to win the 2008 NBA Championship.

Anyhow, I went to a club and I started doing some freestyle rap, and of course I've got to mention Kobe in there somewhere. I'm rapping "Kobe can't win without me" and "Tell me how my ass tastes." I went a little overboard with the language, but other than that, it was good fun. The crowd was eating it up.

If some wise guy hadn't recorded it and posted it on YouTube, then nobody but the people there would have even known about it. But, instead, some guy sells it for $1,500 and everybody makes a big deal out of it.

Why? We've been rapping for years, breaking each other down.

It's called freestyling. It's done all the time, and everyone knows that. But now this rap has caused a big stink so I've got to call Kobe and say, "My bad." He told me, "Don't worry about it, dawg. I'm cool."

But people kept on playing it, so eventually Kobe got annoyed with it. I don't think it was wrong to do it, it was wrong it got out to the public. My mother made me apologize, so I did. I tried to explain to her I'd done the same thing hundreds of times before, grabbed a mic and made fun of friends and teammates. If I rapped the same thing about Derek Fisher no one would have cared.

But because it's Kobe and Shaq, it's another chapter in our long running, unscripted reality show.

Don't think for a minute we didn't manipulate y'all from time to time. Remember in 2006 when the Heat played the Lakers on Martin Luther King Day? I went up and shook Kobe's hand before the game and it was breaking news. World headlines, because before that our relationship was kind of frosty.

Everyone asked me why I did it and I told them, "I had orders from the great Bill Russell. Me and him were talking in Seattle the other day, and he was telling me how rivalries should be. I asked him if he ever disliked anybody he played against and he said, 'No, never,' and he told me I should shake Kobe's hand and let bygones be bygones and bury the hatchet."

Naturally everyone lapped that up. The Great Bill Russell! Detente with Kobe and Shaq! It was a great story, but that's just what it was—a story.

I can tell you this now: I made it up. I was just trying to add to the mystique of the great Bill Russell. I did talk to Bill Russell in Seattle and we discussed many things, but we never even mentioned Kobe. We talked about Red Auerbach and all the racism Bill endured in Boston and how he learned to become a leader.

I was so impressed with him I wanted to elevate his status a little bit. People seemed to have kind of forgotten him a little bit, so I figured if I made him peace broker between Kobe and me that would amp his credibility. He is one of the greatest players of all times and deserves respect.

By the time I had been in Phoenix a couple of seasons the whole Kobe thing was irrelevant. We had both moved on. We played together on the West team in the 2009 All-Star Game and they voted us co-MVPs.

I'm there with my son, and we've got this one trophy, so I said, "Here, Kobe, you take it." He said, "No, give it to your son. I'll get mine later. Give it to your little guy."

My kids absolutely love Kobe Bryant. They call him Uncle Kobe, and his girls call me Uncle Shaq. If you look at our relationship from the eyes of a kid, it's pretty simple. We played together, we won together, and everyone thinks we were the best together. They don't need to know the other stuff.

So here's my son Shareef coming home with this big trophy and he tells all his friends, "Kobe gave me his MVP trophy." I don't think he even realized I got the MVP trophy, too. It was all about Kobe. It almost brought a tear to my eye.

Seriously. I mean it.

Right after that was the game when I went off on Toronto and Chris Bosh and scored 45. I was in a bad mood that night, but I started off with a couple of good looks, and they were trying to guard me with just Bosh in single coverage, so I took that as a sign of disrespect and just went off.

My teammates were laughing and high-fiving me and slapping my hand. I guess it was funny to them to see me go off, but I wasn't laughing, because I knew even at thirty-six years old I could do that if they gave me the ball.

People thought my game was falling off, but to me "falling off" is consistently going 2 for 13, and I've never done that. I've shot 60 percent before in a season, and 58.2 percent for my career. My numbers might be down, but that's because the shot attempts are down. Give me ten to twelve shots a night and you'll be satisfied with the results.

My final season in Phoenix we won forty-six games but we didn't make the playoffs. I knew what that meant: time for me to go.

Steve Kerr called me and said, "Cleveland has been asking around about you. Mr. Sarver wants to save some money, so I wanted to give you the courtesy of knowing we might make a move."

I was impressed. That's all any player wants—to be treated fairly and honestly. I told him, "I appreciate it. Go ahead and do what you have to do." He didn't have to call me. It was his right to do whatever he wanted, but he made the effort and I appreciated it. He was like that the whole time I was there. He'd say, "Hey, I need you to do this" or "We're going to sit you and rest you this game." I'd say, "Are you sure?" and he'd say, "Yes, we think it would be good for you." I would have done anything for Steve Kerr. All he had to do was ask.

When they pulled the trigger Steve called me again and said, "Hey, I'm sure you are watching the news. I understand this might be hard." I told him there were no bad feelings. I understood Sarver was a businessman and he wanted to be under the cap and I had a big salary and I was thirty-six years old. Made sense to me.

I was going to Cleveland to win a ring for the King, LeBron James. That was what I told them when I arrived, and that was what I aimed to do.

LeBron was a huge star. He was as big as I was in 2000 in LA when I was dominating the league. My kids are too young to remember any of that. My sons love LeBron more than they love me. I'm a little jealous about that.

You get around LeBron and you realize he's everything he appears to be. He's a strong kid with a ton of confidence who works his ass off. He doesn't quite have Kobe's range yet, but I bet he will. He's not going to stop until he wins multiple rings.

He's also a great team player. I give him the edge over Kobe on that. He's going to do what it takes to win, knowing that he can take over the game whenever he wants, but understanding you've got to keep your teammates involved.

LeBron takes losses a little differently than most superstars I've been around. He's not the kind to blow up after a bad game. He's not going to be in your face, spitting at you. I heard him say more than once, "There's eighty-two games in a season. Let's be real with ourselves." He got it. At a very young age, he was already acting like a veteran.

Once in a while if the guys weren't responding, he'd come, curse a few people out, and say, "You can work harder than that. I know you can."

LeBron is also a pretty good X and O guy. He used to talk to Mo Williams and Boobie Gibson all the time about how he was going to get them open. He'd say, "Fellas, these guys are disrespecting you. You gotta make them pay. I'm going to have three guys hanging on me and I'm going to kick it out to you, and you make sure you have the right angle so you can make the shot. Got that? Hit a damn shot. Loosen it up now, fellas. C'mon now. I'm counting on you."

There was talk Mo Williams and I had words while I was with the Cavs. Mo was fine. He just took too many shots. He thought the team should be a one-two punch of him and LeBron, and as a result guys like Boobie were underutilized.

Doc Rivers said he heard I turned the team against Mo. How was I going to turn everybody against Mo, anyway? He was LeBron's boy. They were tight. And it was LeBron's team. Everyone was afraid to rock the boat when it came to the King, so he got to do things his way. I don't blame him. All the pressure was on him. It was LeBron and everyone else. I was in the "everyone else" category, and that was fine with me.

LeBron was a leader, clearly the top dog, but he was likable. In all the time I was with him, I only saw him get really mad once. I remember during the playoffs after one of our losses he smacked the bathroom stall, but that was it. He wasn't crazy like me.

Maybe he was different before I got there. It's kind of pointless to snap or go nuts when you are in first place all year. We won sixty-one games. We were at the top of the league. It wasn't like we were staring in the face of adversity every night.

Our coach, Mike Brown, was a nice guy, but he had to live on the edge because nobody was supposed to be confrontational with LeBron. Nobody wanted him to leave Cleveland, so he was allowed to do whatever he wanted to do.

He didn't really abuse it much because he was a team player, and if you were open LeBron was going to throw the ball to you. It wasn't like he was out there being a prima donna or anything, but Mike Brown kind of tiptoed around him, and sometimes that was a problem.

I remember one day in a film session LeBron didn't get back on defense after a missed shot. Mike Brown didn't say anything about it. He went to the next clip and there was Mo Williams not getting back and Mike was saying, "Yo, Mo, we can't have that. You've got to hustle a little more." So Delonte West is sitting there and he's seen enough and he stands up and says, "Hold up, now. You can't be pussyfooting around like that. Everyone has to be accountable for what they do, not just some of us."

Mike Brown said, "I know, Delonte. I know."

Mike knew Delonte was right. Delonte was fearless. He and Mike Brown used to go at it all the time. Delonte would storm out of practice and sit in the locker room, and they'd have to bring a therapist in there to straighten him out.

It was a respect thing with Delonte. He just felt Mike Brown didn't treat him the way he should have been treated. Delonte never went at Doc Rivers like that, though, when he was with the Celtics. When Delonte and Von Wafer got into a fight when we were in Boston, Doc's attitude was "Get him the hell out of here. We don't need that for our team." But both KG and I stuck up for Delonte. KG said, "I'll talk to him. Let me handle it." And Doc said, "You better tell him if it happens again, he's gone."

Delonte has had his share of problems, but I really like him. He

was a good teammate, both in Cleveland and in Boston. He played
the game the right way. The year we played together with the Cavaliers, I really believed we were going to win the championship. I
thought we were good enough.

The Celtics were just smarter. They knocked us out of the 2010
Eastern Conference Finals and they did it by doing a great job of
loading up. I was trying to tell LeBron, "Hey, if you get the ball do
something fast, so they can't get into position." But when he got the
ball and did the Jordan stare, now Kendrick Perkins can come over
and meet him at the baseline. Then Paul Pierce has time to rotate.
If we had moved the ball a little more, we would have had more success. You'll never beat any team that's standing there waiting on you.

I know everybody wants to know what really happened in those
2010 playoffs. There's been all sorts of crazy stories about what went
on in our Cleveland locker room during that time. There were a lot
of rumors after LeBron left Cleveland that he and Delonte had some
personal beef. Trust me, I lived thirty minutes outside of Cleveland
in Richfield, Ohio, so if something went down, I missed it—and I
didn't miss much.

There's no question in Game 5 LeBron was kind of out of it. He
didn't even score a basket until late in the third quarter and was
something like 1 for 11 from the perimeter. But that's not as unusual
as people think. I've seen plenty of superstars have a bad shooting
game and get into a funk. I can remember that happening to Dominique and even Larry Bird. Shooters get rattled sometimes when
they don't shoot well. Scorers get frustrated when they don't score.

Now some of my teammates told me later they were trying to talk
to LeBron on the bench and he wasn't responding. He was, said one
of the guys, almost catatonic.

I never approached LeBron that night. We were in first place all
year. The kid was in total control and, to be honest, he didn't really
seem to need anything from me, so I took his lead and stayed in the
background. It was his team. It didn't feel right to me after all season

of leaving him alone to start getting in his face in Game 5 of the Eastern Conference Finals.

Only LeBron knows what was bugging him. Maybe it was personal problems, maybe it was his sore elbow, maybe it was all that pressure and expectations. Hard to say. He kind of checked out for part of the 2011 NBA Finals against Dallas, too.

I always believed he could turn it on at any moment, but for some reason he didn't. Not against the Celtics in 2010 and not against the Mavericks in 2011.

It was weird. It's one thing to be a passer, but you are supposed to be the One. I'm watching him play against Dallas, and they're swinging the ball and they get him a perfect open look—and he's kicking it to Mario Chalmers. Makes no sense. I told people, "It's like Michael Jordan told me. Before you succeed, you must first fail."

Those Heat guys put a ton of pressure on themselves. They got up there with their little coronation and their little concert and they're saying, "Not one, not two, not three, not four" rings.

I've done stuff like that a few times in my career. When I went to Miami and that huge crowd was there to greet me I wanted to connect with them, so I gave them my word we'd win a championship. My word is my bond, so that was going to motivate me. In LA, after we'd already won a title, I stood up there at the parade and said, "Can you dig it?" and told them I'd see them again next year.

I like the pressure. I feed off it. But if you are going to put pressure on yourself like that, you can't have a bad game when it's on the line. That's what really puzzles me about LeBron. I've never seen a guy with that kind of ability come up that short. He looked completely out of sync to me against the Mavericks.

Still, I wouldn't bet against him.

When I left Cleveland in 2010 I wished LeBron luck in free agency, but I had no idea where he'd land. I never heard from him again once I left town.

I wished I had more of a chance to help the Cavaliers win. I feel like I could have made a difference, but not everyone in Cleveland was on board with that theory. I kept my mouth shut and packed my things and went home.

I even seriously thought about retiring.

In June 2010, the Lakers beat the Celtics for the championship, and they asked Kobe Bryant what it meant to him. "Just one more than Shaq," he said. "And you can take that to the bank."

Hey, I couldn't blame the guy. He was holding the trophy, so he had bragging rights. I sent Kobe my congratulations via Twitter and said, "Enjoy it, man. Enjoy it. I know what u r saying, 'Shaq how my ass taste.'"

I didn't know it at the time, but the owner of the Celtics, Wyc Grousbeck, listened to Kobe say he had one more ring than me and told Danny Ainge, "Let's get Shaq."

Hmmm. The Big Shamrock. Guess those retirement plans were on hold again.

DECEMBER 2010

Boston Garden

Boston, Massachusetts

Shaquille O'Neal fidgeted while Doc Rivers reviewed the game plan on the chalkboard. The big man was trying to concentrate, but he was having difficulty getting his oversized frame loose. His hips had been locking up, and the training staff instructed him to keep moving, keep stretching, keep engaging his muscles before each game.

Shaq glanced around the locker room for some free weights to warm up his biceps. There were none. He looked around once more and spotted Mike Longabardi, the diminutive Celtics assistant coach.

"Hey Mike," he whispered. "C'mon here."

"Huh?" said Longabardi.

"Let me pick you up. Right here in my arms, brother," said O'Neal.

Without another word, Shaq scooped up the startled assistant, then refocused his attention on Rivers as he lifted then lowered Longabardi in a fluid, curling motion.

Kevin Garnett, who had come to represent the very

essence of Celtics intensity, lowered his head to stifle a giggle.

"I was doing my best not to bust out laughing," said KG, "but it's not every day you see a guy bench-pressing your assistant coach."

Rivers valiantly tried to press on, but as Shaq sat expressionless, using a grown man as a free weight, his teammates collapsed in convulsions of laughter.

"Aw, Shaq," protested Rivers, before grinning in spite of himself. "Okay, guys, let's play."

"Don't worry, Coach," the big man said, patting Rivers's shoulder on his way to the parquet. "I'm nice and loose now."

So were his teammates.

PLAYING FOR THE BOSTON CELTICS WAS ONE OF THE GREAT honors of my career. I only wish I could have finished what I went there to do—help them win a championship.

I don't care what anyone says. If I could have stayed healthy, I really believe we could have done it.

In the beginning, I wasn't sure if it was going to work out with Boston. We were talking to a bunch of teams, including Atlanta, and I wanted to get the midlevel exception. The Celtics chose to give that to Jermaine O'Neal. That kind of bothered me. Danny said they gave it to Jermaine because he was thirty-one years old, a lot younger than me, and he was coming off a great year—except for the playoffs. Danny said JO had an injury in the postseason and that was why he'd played bad. He said Kendrick Perkins told him to go out and get Jermaine O'Neal.

When Perk suggested it, Danny said, "But he played so bad against us in the playoffs."

"Don't hold that against him," Perk answered. "Everybody plays bad against me."

What it came down to was, if I wanted to play for the Boston Celtics, I was going to have to take the minimum, which was about $1.5 million.

I was going to be thirty-nine years old, and it was obvious to me I needed to go somewhere that wouldn't ask me to do too much by myself. I had already done it my way, I already had four rings, so where could I go to further my legacy?

I looked at all the contending teams, and Boston stood out for a number of reasons. For one thing, Perk was out after knee surgery, so they needed help in the middle. The other thing was, I already knew their Big Three very well. KG and I had been friends for years. Paul Pierce was a big-time scorer, and I was the one who gave him the nickname "The Truth." Ray Allen's mom and my mom have been real tight for a long time, so I knew what I was dealing with in terms of those guys.

What attracted me most to Boston was they played like a team. They shared the ball, and you never heard about any personality conflicts on the team. My one year in Cleveland when they beat us in the playoffs, Rajon Rondo killed us in Game 1, then Paul Pierce killed us in Game 2, and then in Game 3 they decided to put me on KG, and then he killed us. I'm watching them, thinking, *Nobody cares who scores the points. That's pretty cool.*

There was some talk about me going back to the Lakers. Jeanie Buss was pushing her dad to consider it, and Phil Jackson would have signed off on it, but Dr. Buss wasn't gonna go for that.

Danny Ainge called me just after midnight on July 1. He told me he wanted to sign me for the minimum. Perry, my agent, said we'd take the midlevel exception, but Danny was worried about my age and how much I had left in the tank. He said with Perk out he needed to make sure he had someone that could go every night. We decided to hold off until we looked into some other options. In the meantime, the Celtics and the Cavaliers talked about some sign-and-trade deals, including one that involved Anthony Parker, but they couldn't agree on the Boston player.

The summer went along after the Celtics signed JO, and I thought, *Well, maybe not Boston.* But I never really got them out of my mind. Paul Pierce was talking to me saying, "Come, big fella. We need you." Ray was really pushing for me, too. The fans in that city had always been so fantastic to me and those veterans were really appealing, so I told Perry, "Go back at them."

It was early August, and Danny was fishing with two of his sons on the Colorado River. There was no cell phone service on the river, but he had a satellite phone with him and that's how Perry reached him.

They talked about the minimum, and Danny told Perry that Doc

Rivers wasn't sure about having me come on board. He'd heard some stuff out of Cleveland that Mo Williams and I had some issues, and he wasn't too happy about it. He was a big fan of Pat Riley's, too, so I'm guessing he got an earful from Pat about me.

I called Doc on his cell phone. He had just landed in Orlando, where he lived during the off-season. My house was about twenty minutes from his place. I asked him, "Can we talk?"

He agreed, so I went to his house and we sat down. He had this list of things he wanted to go over with me. The first thing he said was, "Shaq, for the first time in your life you are going to have to be a role player. I'm not sure you can deal with that." He told me he wouldn't guarantee me any playing time. It could be twenty minutes some nights, fifteen minutes other nights. He wouldn't guarantee me a starting job.

"And no perks," Doc told me. "No bodyguards, no entourage. If you want those people, you will have to pay for them yourself. No superstar treatment here. That's not how we do it."

I'm listening, and so far I can live with all of it. I told him, "Doc, I just want to win one more title. That's all I care about. I want to help the Celtics get another ring."

He said, "C'mon, Shaq," and I looked him dead in the eye and said, "I'm serious. You won't have any trouble with me. I'm here to win."

I told him, "Look, the breakups I had in LA and Miami, was I a bit of an ass? Yes, because they were putting all sorts of pressure on me, so it had to be done my way. My philosophy in those situations was if you don't like me, move me. But with this team, I don't have to be like that. I see how you guys play, how you move the ball. It would be idiotic of me to come in here and mess it up. I want to get five rings. I'm on my way out either way. Whether I get one million, two million, ten million, it's still coming down to the finish for me."

I could see he was coming around to it. I had been working out all summer and I looked pretty good, and he made a comment about that.

Then he said to me, "I will cut you on the spot if I think you are messing up my locker room."

"It won't happen," I told him. "I promise."

Next thing you know, I'm signing with the Celtics, and KG is calling me and he's all juiced up, and I pick out number 36, and I'm ready to take over Paul Revere's city by land and by sea.

Doc told me, "Jermaine O'Neal will probably start while Perk is out, and you'll come off the bench."

I said, "That's cool."

Now on the inside I'm thinking, *We'll see about that,* because I'm competitive and I knew I was going to come into Boston in great shape and they would realize pretty quickly they would want me in that starting lineup over JO. But I promised Doc I wouldn't make any waves, so I kept all those thoughts to myself.

When I showed up at training camp, I could tell they were impressed. The training staff looked me over and gave me two thumbs-up. The coaching staff went over some stuff with me and I picked it up pretty quickly, so now they are thinking, *Shaq's a fast learner.* Right away the guys understood having me on the floor would open up all sorts of things for them offensively, so they were happy, too. JO had some problems with his knee, so I ended up in the starting lineup after all.

That was a good decision. Turns out when I started and played twenty minutes or more, our team was 21-4. Not bad for a thirty-nine-year-old guy making the minimum.

The Celtics were a crazy bunch. I fit right in. They were loose, a little nutty. I've always said KG is one of the funniest guys in the NBA—he just doesn't want to let the public in on that. I used to see it when we played in All-Star Games together. He does great imitations, all in that rat-a-tat voice of his. He does a very good Shaquille O'Neal, actually. He's got my mumble down.

One day we were hanging out and me, KG, Nate Robinson, and Glen Davis did a video in the locker room. We put on some Halloween masks, and I wore a wig with a ponytail, and we started dancing to "Hard in Da Paint" by Waka Flocka Flame. KG was wearing some kind of evil duck mask and a towel, and I'm telling y'all, that boy has rhythm. Everyone agreed it was vintage until Nate Robinson tweeted it, and Danny Ainge turned up the volume and started listening to the lyrics. They were kind of raunchy and they had a lot of words you shouldn't say around kids, so Nate got fined.

That might have been my fault. When we were in training camp I heard Danny talking to Nate and Glen Davis about tweeting. He was trying to tell them to be careful and to remember they were representing the Celtics, and the team had certain guidelines they were going to expect them to follow.

I'm listening to all this and after he's done I go up to Danny and say, "You know, everything you said is right, but you're not speaking their language." Danny is looking at me kind of funny and I said, "If you really want them to get the message you say this: 'If you are irresponsible about tweeting, I'm going to fine you twenty thousand dollars.' They'll understand that."

The next day we have a "social media" session where this expert comes in and talks to us about tweeting and YouTube and all that stuff. We have a pretty interesting debate about freedom of speech. The expert starts giving us examples of athletes who have tweeted something and gotten themselves in a bunch of trouble. You can tell Nate and Big Baby aren't even listening. The next thing you know, Danny stands up and says, "Okay, let me make this clear. It will cost you twenty thousand bucks if there is profanity, nudity, or bad language. Use the F word and it's going to cost you."

I swear, it must have been four or five days later that we did the video. That was a private thing, something between the guys. We had a blast doing it, but it was never intended to leave our locker room. If it hadn't, it would have been no harm, no foul. But once Nate tweeted it, that was on him. When Danny hit him with the fine, KG was saying, "Twenty thousand dollars! Hell! That's the last video I'm doing."

That kind of stuff is one of the reasons Doc never really warmed up to Nate. I wasn't surprised at all when he got traded.

Nate was always trying to get noticed by the public. He was always tweeting videos of himself punking his teammates. You've probably seen clips of him putting salt in my water or dunking on my head when I had my back to him in practice. He and Paul started throwing popcorn in my mouth when I fell asleep in the theater. In training camp Nate put on my size 23 shoes and tried to do a wind sprint in under thirty seconds.

Let me let you in on a little secret. Most of those "punks" were staged. I came up with most of them for Nate. Some people are a little too focused on Twitter, and Nate was one of them. He was too worried about how many followers he had. He kept saying, "Shaq, I need more people. Help me out."

I made sure I didn't go around telling any of the Celtics how to play or what to do. When you think about it, the star power we had in that room was incredible. Between KG, Paul, Ray, and myself, we had racked up almost 96,000 points, forty-four All-Star appearances, and seven championship rings.

What I did try to do with some of the younger fellas was talk to them about marketing themselves and promoting their own brand. Just like Magic Johnson had done with me, I tried to explain to a kid like Rajon Rondo that he shouldn't be satisfied with just endorsements. He should go beyond that. He should create his own Rondo portfolio.

I loved the guys. Almost all of them. They were a terrific group, very professional, but they loved to laugh and sing and dance and keep it light.

They had their moments, like any team. Rondo was always a topic of conversation. I've been in a lot of leadership positions. I'm getting my PhD, so I've been reading all sorts of leadership books. The one thing you can't do is this—a millionaire can't change a millionaire.

People want to change Rondo. It ain't happening. He's a talented kid, but he's a stubborn kid. I love him. He has a great future ahead of him, but he probably needs to meet his teammates halfway once in a while.

The good thing about me is I speak everyone's language. Always have. I can get gutter with Delonte West or I can raise it up and talk Harvard talk with Ray Allen.

The first couple of months with Rondo, I didn't say anything to him. I just watched him. I was trying to learn what made him tick, because the other guys had told me how important he was but how frustrating he was at the same time.

After a while, I felt like I had a sense of how he rolled. Most guys his age think about scoring. He only thinks about passing. So I went up to him one day and I said, "Hey, man, throw me a lob, I'll make you look good." So he did. And I made him look good.

So now we start talking. Rajon is a great player, he's got great instincts, he knows what to do, so I never told him what he should do. The minute you do that, you lose him.

He's looking to connect with me and throw me that lob, so when he threw it and I missed it I'd tell him, "Hey dawg, that's on me. I screwed up our highlight. My bad."

I spent a lot of time trying to lift him up, make him feel good. He had ticked off so many of the veterans over the years that they kind of liked it when he got put in his place, so I was trying to counter that.

What I liked about him was he gained the respect of Paul, KG, and Ray the old-fashioned way, by playing defense and dishing the ball instead of that home-boy between-the-leg nonsense. Rondo knows all the other team's plays. We'd be out there and the other team would call something and he'd start yelling, "Paul, shade over that way" and "Shaq, they're coming with a screen." Very intelligent.

He and Doc used to get into what I call "respectful beefs." They'd argue about a play or a call or a decision Rondo made. It was good dialogue. Sometimes it got a little heated, but that was healthy. It was a classic relationship between a point guard and his former point guard coach.

My goal was to make Rondo feel like he was a Hall of Famer because I knew he was very, very delicate, much more than people realize.

Most stars in the NBA are—me included.

Let me give you an example of what I mean. Remember that stretch right after Perk got traded and Rondo was struggling so badly? He definitely was nicked up and fighting some injuries, but something else happened that I think affected him.

In early March some of the guys went to the Museum of Fine Arts for a fund-raiser and got to hang with President Barack Obama. Everyone was a little bit in awe. The president turns to Ray, points at Rondo, and says, "Hey Ray, why don't you teach this kid how to shoot?" Everyone starts laughing, and Ray says, "Nah, that's why he's got to give the ball to me. I'll take care of the shooting."

KG told me he saw the look on Rondo's face and the kid was devastated, embarrassed. Dissed by the president, even though I'm sure Obama didn't mean any harm. Rondo smiled and went along with all of it, but KG told me he could see it in his eyes. It bothered Rondo. It killed him.

The next day Rondo shot the ball horribly. He stopped taking shots after that. He's so sensitive. I think it was a real jolt to hear the outside perception of a basketball fan who happens to be the president of the United States. It messed with his mind. I'm sure of it.

I kept telling him how great he was, trying to boost his confidence, bring him back up to speed, because without Rondo we were screwed. And that was what I kept telling him. He knew it, too. Most of the time he had enough confidence for all of us. But once in a while, he would fall into these stretches where he had serious doubts. When that happens to you, it's the veterans' job to prop you back up.

When I was with the Lakers, I was playing with Derek Fisher, who is a hard, hard worker, but he's not a natural talent. He was an okay player, but I made sure he was always involved in what we were doing. When teams disrespected him by laying off him, I'd always tell him, "Shoot it, Fish." He'd say, "No man, I'm missing all the time," and I'd say, "You're going to hit this next one." So he keeps shooting and his confidence gets up and he hits some big, big shots for us. He thinks I trust him, so his confidence starts peaking. Same with Rick Fox. My thing was, let me establish myself as a pure scorer. I'll hit a few jump hooks and a free throw, and then let me kick it out to Fox to get him involved.

I would have done more of that with the Celtics, but I just wasn't in a position to have the ball all that much. Believe me, I understood. When you've got Paul and KG and Ray, they should get the majority of the shots.

It didn't take me long to settle into the Boston area. I rented a house in the great town of Sudbury and felt immediately at home. The fans loved to interact with me, but they were also respectful. When I rode the subway (or the T, as they call it) on Halloween dressed as Shaquita, a big, busty, sassy lady, people laughed and took pictures, but gave me my space.

Same thing when I came up with my brainstorm to sit in Harvard Square in Cambridge and become a statue. I sat there for almost one hour without moving. People would try to tell me jokes, or get me to laugh, but I stayed completely still, for the most part. The only guy that got me was the one who said, "Do you have any tickets to the Miami game?" I didn't answer him, but I turned my head and shook it no.

After it was over I told reporters, "Now I can always tell my friends I went to Harvard. I went to Harvard, I stood at Harvard, and I graduated from Harvard. So now I'm smart."

Here's why I did the Harvard thing. For one thing, I was bored. Second of all, I wanted to connect with the fans. Third of all, I knew the media would eat it up. It took very little of my time, and everyone was tweeting about it, and it was a nice little thing for me and the Celtics.

At that point I was feeling good and playing well. Once I started having injury problems, I stopped doing things like that. You don't want to be seen all over the place when you are hurt and can't help the team—unless it's for charity. I don't care what anyone says about my charity work. I'll never stop doing that, even if I'm on one leg. One of the best nights I had in Boston was going to an old folks' home and watching television with them. Sweethearts. Every one of them.

Before I got injured I got to conduct the Boston Pops at Christmastime. I was waving that wand while we played "Sleigh Ride," "Can You Feel It" by the Jackson Five, and "We Are the Champions" by Queen. It was a fabulous experience and led to yet another nickname: The Big Conductor.

Of course we did our annual Shaq-a-Claus trips to help the underprivileged kids have a nice Christmas and Shaq-a-Bunny during Easter. We did a Marine Toys for Tots promotion, and I called out my teammates to join me. I told everyone, "My goal is to get one big-time person in each state. I'm doing this here in Boston, in New Jersey, in Florida, and California, so there goes four states. So I say we get Paul to take care of California, and KG to take care of Minnesota, and Ray to take care of Connecticut."

Just like everywhere else I've ever been, people were asking, "Is Shaq doing too much?" Danny Ainge handled that perfectly for me. He understood I was away from my family and my children, and that was hard for me. He knew I had time on my hands. As he explained it, "Doing fun things at Harvard Square and helping the community? Why not? The other guys are playing video games. Ray is playing golf. As long as Shaq puts in the time in practice and gets treatment for his body, I'm good with it."

We opened our season against the Miami Heat, which was supposed to be the next dominant team. Honestly, I thought with that lineup they would win it all. Do you think our guys were a little pumped up for that game? We played great. Everything clicked. It was so cool to be out there with Ray and Paul and KG. After we won 88–80, Doc told us, "That was the most dominant half of basketball we've played since I've been in Boston."

I tried to adjust to my new position as a role player. Some days went smoother than others.

In January, I played thirty-five minutes against Charlotte and dropped 23 points on them. I missed only two shots and hit all three of my free throws. I also had five blocks. After the game, I ran into Danny Ainge in the hallway and said, "Not bad for a guy who's making the minimum."

There were other games when I just didn't touch the ball. The way the offense was running that night didn't include me. I remember after a home game against Sacramento in January, I took only three shots in the game. It was frustrating for me because I felt so good and I wanted to contribute more, but you kind of just have to roll with it.

That's not really my strong suit. When I got back to my house in Sudbury I was so frustrated I punched a hole through my glass window. Smart, huh?

The Celtics were a very tight team, but I didn't hang around with them all that much. I was a loner at that point of my career. When we went to most of the major cities, I had business appointments. In Miami, I was hanging out with my police buddies. If I didn't have something going on in a particular city, I usually just sat in my room and did a video chat and laid low. I didn't have my bodyguard, Jerome, with me anymore, because he had stayed in Phoenix with the Suns as their security guy. When I had him, it was different. When I had Jerome, I didn't have to worry about going out and giving someone a chance to be famous. I could move about freely. Without him, why chance it?

All in all, I was a model Celtics citizen. There was only one little stretch where things got a little hairy, when we flew to the West Coast and played the Lakers on January 30.

I wanted to get off against LA. I won't lie to you. I knew I wasn't going to get a ton of shots, but I was running the court and getting open and I know I'm not the focal point but how about throwing me the ball when I'm four feet from the basket? I was ducking in, getting great position, and Doc made it clear when I was doing that to give it to me.

"Big Baby" Davis kept looking me off and taking it himself. Doc is shouting at him to go inside, but he won't. So Doc calls time-out and draws up a play for me.

I go out there, and I back Andrew Bynum way under the rim. I'm loose, I'm ready. I've got Bynum under the basket and again, Baby won't give me the ball. So I go up to him and say, "If you ever miss me again I'm going to punch you in the face." I was hot.

Two nights later we're playing in Sacramento, and here we go again. I take three shots the entire game, and again I've got my man isolated underneath the basket, and Baby ignores me and takes a jump shot. So the next time we're in the huddle I let Baby have it.

I tell him, "Pass the fucking ball inside." He comes back at me a little bit, and now I'm really heated. All hell is breaking loose. We're going back and forth. Doc is standing there and he's not saying a word. The message was pretty clear: work this out yourselves. I tell Baby, "You are a selfish player. Everyone on this team knows it." Hey, all the fans knew it. He takes shots when he shouldn't.

I really am ticked off and I want to go off on him 100 percent, but I can only go off on him 15 percent because my mother is sitting behind the bench. I start cursing Baby out, and I look up and there's my mother wagging her finger at me so I have to stop. Baby looks stunned.

Because of the way I am, I wouldn't let it go. I was going off all week. I was mad, really mad. I worried a little bit that no one was willing to put Baby in his place. Doc did, because that kid drove him crazy, but he was the only one.

Here's what really ticked me off about Big Baby: he didn't realize how much I helped him when we were on the floor together. I was such a presence on that block that whoever was guarding me didn't dare go help, because if he did I was catching it and dunking it on his head. When my guy stays with me, that opens up the lane for everyone else, including Glen "Big Baby" Davis.

Baby should have remembered the game against Orlando when he was posting up Ryan Anderson. Normally Dwight Howard would come over from the weak side to help, but when Baby made his move and got past Anderson, Dwight didn't dare leave me. So what happens? Glen Davis gets a layup.

You're welcome, Baby.

Doc never confronted Baby on it, but a few days later, we're having a film session and there it is, on the screen, me, wide open. Doc didn't single Baby out, he just said, "When Shaq is ducking in deep like this, we've got to get him the ball. He's almost unguardable in that situation."

Thanks, Coach.

I actually talked to KG about Baby. I said, "Hey, you should do something about that." He said, "Why don't you just talk to him?" I said, "Hey, KG, this is our last go-around. We don't have time for crap like that. I don't mean to interfere in how the Big Three runs things, but you got to keep that stuff in check or it will come back to bite you."

Kevin has mellowed a lot now that he's older. Me? I wouldn't let that shit ride. Of course, later on Paul reminded me that KG yelled at Baby so hard once that he sat on the bench and cried.

Both Paul and Kevin are dawgs, and Ray is just Ray. Paul will say, "C'mon, we're playing like crap. Let's go," but he won't really jump on guys.

The only one who will do that is Rondo. He'll even get on the Big Three if he thinks they deserve it. The kid has guts.

One thing I quickly realized about the Celtics is they weren't about drills. Doc knew it. We were too competitive. Put us in a scrimmage and keep score and you are going to see some serious shit. The veterans were as competitive as any group I've ever been around. They were dinged up a lot, but when we were in those scrimmages and it was tied 5–5 and the game was to 6, the elbows were flying, brother. At one point during the season it got out that Delonte and Von Wafer had come to blows in a practice. Let me tell you: that wasn't the only skirmish. That's what makes a basketball team edgy, tight.

Everything was going as planned until we played my old team, the Orlando Magic, on Christmas Day. I didn't even take a shot. Not one damn shot. I never saw the ball. I was running down the floor and I tried to accelerate and I felt something kind of pop. It was the back of my heel. The next night we played in Indy and I told our trainer, Ed Lacerte, to tape it real tight. I played pretty well that night. I had 9 points and 4 rebounds in sixteen minutes of time, but the next day I got up and I couldn't move. My heel was killing me.

Both Ed and Doc were so great about it, so gracious. They said, "Take some time off, big guy. Take your time. We've got Perk back, we're okay, get better." They were so fabulous about it. They made me feel so at ease about everything. I hung in there a little longer before I finally sat down in mid-January for three games. After those three games I came back, but it was a mistake. Something was wrong with my Achilles. I had to take a seat.

So basketball is out for a little while, but I'm still going to the Thoreau Club in Concord every night and I'm swimming. I'm riding the treadmill, I'm working out, I'm coming back home, I'm getting massages, and I'm watching the games. The next day I'm going to practice, riding the exercise bike, coming home and taking a nap, then going for treatment, then back to the pool.

I had a key to the Lincoln-Sudbury High School gym, which was right across the street from my house, and they had a little weight room in there. So I'd go there to lift some weights and take some free throws. I usually went around eleven o'clock at night when no one was around. I ate right, stayed active. I lost fifteen pounds, but that damn Achilles just wasn't responding.

Just before the All-Star break I got a call that the Lakers were unveiling a statue of Jerry West outside the Staples Center. The All-Star Game was in Los Angeles, and I was invited to come to the ceremony. I told my assistant, "No, I'm a Celtic now. I'm not going." But a couple of weeks before the event we got another call telling me that Jerry would really appreciate it if I showed up.

I was surprised it meant that much to him, but once I heard that I made sure that I was there. I knew I was Jerry West's guy once, but I guess I thought he'd moved on. It was pretty damn gratifying to get to that event and be sitting in the audience while Magic and Kareem and Elgin Baylor and Pat Riley and Jerry Buss were sitting on the stage, and to have Jerry West find me in the crowd, point to me, and say, "I love you."

It blew me away. I went up and talked to him after it was over, and he was crying and telling me I was his favorite. It's funny. He never really said stuff like that when I was playing for his team. Usually when we had a conversation it was because he was chewing me out for something I'd done wrong.

I want to thank Jerry West for remaining true to me. I want to thank him for remembering what I remember—that together we brought a championship to the Lakers, along with Kobe and all the other guys. That together we were a pretty good team and created some pretty cool memories for a lot of people in Los Angeles.

Just before the trade deadline in February, Danny called me up and told me they were thinking of trading Perk. There's been a lot of talk about that trade and why they did it, but let's keep it real: they traded Perk because he wanted a big extension and they weren't going to pay him. Simple as that.

It was business, baby.

Danny admitted that was the reason, along with the idea they had to get younger, and Jeff Green would do that for them. He wanted me to know that Doc believed when I got healthy I'd be a great fit with the Big Four and that we could probably win it all.

I felt I had to be honest with Danny, so I told him, "Listen, win or lose, there's a better than 60 percent chance I won't be back next season. My heel isn't getting better. I don't think you should trade Perk."

The reason I said that was because I had already been out awhile, and even with all the work I was doing to get my heel right it wasn't improving. To be honest, at that point I was getting kind of nervous and scared, because I didn't want the whole thing to hinge on me and then have it all fall apart because I couldn't get out there and play.

I had been blamed so many times in so many places when

things went wrong, I didn't want that to happen again. Not there. Not in Boston. I didn't want it to be my fault if the Celtics lost. In fact, because I've turned into one of those conspiracy guys, I actually put my call with Danny on speakerphone so everyone who was there with me, including Danny Garcia, my massage therapist, and Nikki, my girlfriend, could hear me say, "I don't know if I'm coming back, bro."

They traded Perk anyway. The locker room was pretty quiet for a few days. Perk was a popular guy, a hard worker, a sweet kid. His opinion of himself might have been a little inflated, but hey, join the club. You could probably say that about all of us.

It took a while for us to adjust to all the new faces. The Boston Celtics scene is kind of intense, and Jeff Green and Nenad Krstic looked a little shell-shocked the first few weeks. For one thing, no one had ever asked them to play defense like that before.

The season was winding down and I still hadn't played, and I was getting really uneasy about that. We had five games to go, and I told them I wanted to try and play against the Pistons on April 3.

I knew they'd have to give me a cortisone shot or I'd have no chance. They didn't want to give me the shot. They didn't want me to play, but I hadn't touched a ball and I felt like we were running out of time. I told them, "Just let me get in, let's see if I still got it."

The adrenaline rush of being out there and playing after so long was amazing. When I went into the game the crowd just exploded. They gave me a standing ovation. That got me pumped. I was flying. I was flying and feeling good. I hit my first three shots, including a little up-and-under move that no one was expecting.

And then just like that, I felt another pop. They called it my calf, but it was really the area around the Achilles again. It felt like somebody had shot me with a gun. I was running along and I felt it and I was like, *What the hell was that?*

So now I'm worried. Really worried. I'm calling everybody I know. I'm getting stim machines flown in, I'm having double massages. I call my boys from Phoenix, who helped me so much when I was there.

They fly in and help me loosen up my hips and I'm starting to feel a little better. Doc was great. He wasn't putting any pressure on me. He was telling me, "We don't need you in the first round of the play-offs." I still had some pain back there behind the heel so our trainer Eddie Lacerte was saying, "Give it one more week. One more week."

We knock out the Knicks in the first round of the playoffs, and we get to the Miami series and I'm not ready, but we're out of time. I understand that. So I tell them, "Shoot me up. Let's go."

Dr. Brian McKeon, the Celtics team physician, was really against that. We had a couple of pretty big blowouts over it. But I told them, "If you don't shoot me up, I'll find someone else who will." I ended up getting about fifteen shots before we were done.

Dr. McKeon kept telling me, "Shaq, this is no good. I don't want that thing to rip." I said, "You've been so nice to me, so hospitable. I need to do this. If it rips, it rips."

I played in Game 3 against Miami and I couldn't move. I played eight minutes and got my two fouls in, but I was having trouble. It upset me because I had worked hard to get in great condition, but that heel really limited my mobility. And there's Magic Johnson on television telling people I'm not in shape. Wrong, Magic. It's called an injury.

They shot me up again and we gave it one more try in Game 4, but I lasted only three minutes. Doc came to me afterward and said, "Shaq, we want you to stop. We appreciate all that you've done, but it's over. I won't play you."

He could tell I was completely bummed out. I could barely look at the guy. The next day he told the media I was done and said, "The guy is devastated. None of you have any idea how hard he's worked to get back."

It was brutal to sit there and watch Miami beat our team. I was crushed. I hated it. The Celtics were the best. People don't realize how physically screwed up Kevin Garnett was all season. His legs and his knees were all messed up. He was in pain all year. If you ask him, I bet he'll tell you he thought about retiring, too.

I'm watching that series and Miami has no inside presence, and it's just killing me. In the game I did play, the Miami players thought about driving the lane, but when I touched them up they never really came back in. LeBron, DWade, Chris Bosh, they were all thinking twice about going in there because they knew I had every intention of using all six of my fouls.

I felt bad for Paul Pierce in that series. He struggled. It all started when he got tossed in Game 1. I didn't understand where the referee, Ed Malloy, was coming from on that. The referee kind of panicked and was moving too fast. Paul had picked up a technical earlier in the game, and then a few minutes later DWade nailed him with a moving screen, so Paul said something to the official but he wasn't real demonstrative when he said it. It wasn't like he was showing the guy up. Everybody talks. We all do. Ed Malloy should know that. But he's new and young, and he panicked and he tossed Paul Pierce. Even though we all sympathized with him, he still got an earful from Doc. "You've got to be smarter than that," he told Paul.

Miami went on to beat us in that series. LeBron was a beast. I've never seen him play like that before. He sure as hell didn't play like that against Dallas in the Finals.

I'm just really upset and disappointed because I believe this was the Celtics' year. This was the first time in my nineteen-year history that all the powerhouses were gone. They brought me in to bang Dwight Howard, and he was gone. They wanted me to rebound against the Lakers. They were gone, too. I thought it would be us and the Spurs, me and Tim Duncan, two guys with four rings going at it—but they were gone, too.

I did everything I could to get back on the court. I have the holes in the back of my heel to prove it.

What a great organization Boston was. What a great town. I had no idea the people there were so fantastic, so knowledgeable of the game, so appreciative of their stars. Everybody was so nice, so hospitable, especially in Sudbury. They let me be Shaq. I wish I had something left in the tank to reward them for how graciously they treated me.

I had a meeting with Dr. McKeon before I left. The only way we could have gotten that Achilles right again was to go in and clean up the area all around it. If we did that, I'd be out nine months and then we'd be back where we started again, people waiting and wondering when and if I was ever coming back. I didn't want to hold Boston up like that again. That city deserved better.

Now, if it had been a two-month recovery, maybe that would have changed my mind.

The tendon is actually in decent shape, but all the muscles around it are almost ripped in half. They are shredded. So, I can chill and let it heal with a ton of scar tissue, or I could have Doc McKeon go in and clean it up for me. Either way, it isn't good.

I feel like I let Boston down. I didn't want to hold Boston hostage. That was why I announced my retirement. They want to go out and try to get younger. I would have loved to come back, but they say once your Achilles is damaged it's never the same.

Doc Rivers is right up there with Phil Jackson as one of the great coaches in the game. He commands respect because he is so consistent in how he approaches things. He also speaks our language. Phil spoke some kind of foreign zen "cousin of weed" language, but because of his great track record everyone listened.

Doc was able to get down to our level. He'd say, "Hey, you've got the Big Three out there, so why the hell are you pulling up and trying for a three-pointer, Big Baby?" He knew our lingo, knew how we think.

He never stopped preaching team. Ever. He expected us to act like professionals, and if we didn't we heard about it.

Let's say Ray hit four or five shots in a row and then Doc called a different play. Ray would say, "Yo, Doc, I'm feeling it," and Doc would say, "But it ain't about you. It's about the team." He never stopped stressing that. He didn't care how many points you had, how many rebounds, how many assists. As long as the team was playing well, as long as we were winning, that's what it was about.

Doc never believed in embarrassing or humiliating anyone. Take our film sessions. If Paul got into one of his stretches where he was taking the ball one-on-one too much, Doc could have put together a nice little film package of that and called out The Truth in front of his teammates. That's not his style. Instead, he put together a tape of plays where guys were making selfish decisions and just ran it. No commentary, just the proof, right there on film.

Sometimes the pictures speak for themselves.

Paul was the leader of the Big Three, no question about that. He was the guy who was going to do things the way he thought they should be done, and you'll never hear any criticism from me on that, because I was the same way. I respect Paul's position. For years, it was all on him. If they lost, everyone was pointing the finger at him. So Doc would have to call Paul out every now and then, but Paul always handled it like a pro.

Ray had his moments, too, because he had to have everything a certain way, and you knew with a bunch of knuckleheads like us that wasn't going to be possible. Paul liked to mess with him a little bit. I left it alone. Ray's an interesting guy. I would tell him, "When I'm posting and your guy's head is turned, just get to your spot and I'll find you." That was how I used to roll with DScott and Glen Rice. But some guys are stubborn in how they want to get the ball.

I think Ray is more like Dirk Nowitzki, an off-balance type of shooter. He likes to come off the fly, catch it, and go up. He's a hell of a shooter and an extremely nice guy. He and Derek Fisher are going to be general managers somewhere, because those guys are inside the system. They know the game, and they hang with the front office guys. Ray and Danny played golf together all season. Doc, too. Ray is almost like a front office guy already.

By now you know I always root for storybook endings. I'm not a fake dreamer anymore. I deal in real dreams. My dream of winning a championship with Boston came up short. I feel terrible about it. I probably won't get over it for a while.

But the Boston Celtics will move on, and so will the NBA. That's how it works.

Here today, gone tomorrow.

Except for me: I'm not going anywhere.

JUNE 2, 2011

Windermere, Florida

When the big dreamer fantasized how it would end, the scenario was always the same. Shaquille O'Neal danced at the victory parade, celebrating another NBA title in yet another city. The crowd was electric and squealed with pleasure at Shaq's championship antics.

When the moment was right, he grabbed the microphone and thanked them all, declared his latest zip code "Title Town," then dropped the bomb:

It's over.

I'm done.

He thought this would happen in Boston. In June 2011, he expected to be rolling down Boylston Street on a championship duck boat with KG and Paul and Ray.

Instead, he was in his Isleworth home with Michael Downing, the CEO of Tout, a new social video service Shaq planned to use to announce he was finally stepping away from the game of basketball. Tout was virtually unknown when it came to him looking for a boost that only Superman could provide. Shaq committed to breaking his big news via Tout in return for a spot on their advisory board and a small equity stake in the company. But, more importantly, it was a new way for Shaq to connect with his fans.

The retirement announcement was devoid of confetti, duck boats, and championship rings, but not without fanfare.

When he sent his fifteen-second video message, it drew half a million viewers to Tout over the next three hours.

"We did it. Nineteen years, baby. I want to thank you very much, that's why I'm telling you first, I'm about to retire. Love you, talk to you soon," Shaq touted.

With that, 28,596 career points, 13,099 rebounds, 3,026 assists, 2,732 blocks, 4,146 fouls, and 15 All-Star selections were frozen in time, a final stat line of a career that spanned six teams and four championships.

O'Neal approached his subsequent interviews that day with his trademark merriment, yet when the sun set on his lakefront home and he put the finishing touches on the finality of his career, he was sideswiped by a wave of melancholy that followed him into bed and into his dreams.

"I was sad," Shaq admitted. "I hate it when I don't get to write my own ending."

WHEN I RETIRED USING TOUT, I DECLARED MYSELF "THE emperor of the social media network." It's a new world out there and you've got to keep up. I remember my first few years with the Lakers, my advisors came to me and said, "There's this new thing happening on the Internet. It's a search engine, and you can type in almost anything you want and it will call up all the information about it." That sounded really interesting to me, so I invested in this new company called Google.

To be honest with you, I kind of forgot about it, but one day we're at practice and our trainer, Gary Vitti, has a newspaper and he's reading an article about Google and all the investors who made big profits from it, and he says, "Damn you, Shaq! You're into everything!"

That is correct.

You have to be careful how you use the social network. I get really turned off by people who tweet every detail about their lives, even if they are superstars. "I ate a chicken sandwich. It was soggy." Who the hell cares?

If you handle it properly, the social network is a very valuable tool. You can use it to get your message out. You can use it to sell things. You can use it to communicate with people. If I have three million followers, I'm not going to jam it down their throats how cool I am, how rich I am, how fabulous I am. You're not going to see me touting, "I'm in my $500,000 car right now," or "I'm backstage with Beyoncé right now." Some of the athletes who are out there tweeting are so self-centered it's a major turnoff.

Tout is a cool medium because now you can add video to your tweeting. And you know how I can light it up for the camera when I feel like it.

As soon as I announced my retirement, both ESPN and TNT called. They wanted to hire me as part of their basketball coverage. I ended up going with TNT. Me and Charles Barkley, talking hoops together. Can't wait. Because Turner also owns the Cartoon Network, we got to work talking about an animated show starring yours truly.

I held my retirement press conference at my house in Isleworth. My mom lives nearby, and my dad is still in Orlando and his health isn't the best, so I wanted to make sure they could both make it.

We had all sorts of people at the house beforehand, and I was a little jittery. My man Dennis Scott showed up, and we did a little interview for NBA TV before the press conference, and then I put on my suit and went out there and did my thing, kept it together, thanked all the right people, stayed away from tears and went for laughs instead.

We opened it up for questions, and the first one was from my mother. She said, "It's been a while since I've heard you talk that fast."

"I was nervous, Mommy, sorry," I said.

The reporters asked me a lot of questions, and one of them was if my retirement was permanent. So many superstars, even MJ and Magic, retired but came back again a few years later.

I told them, "I won't be back and let me tell you the reason why. Toward the end of my career I started getting a bit selfish. I've always heard the two most dominant players were Shaquille O'Neal and Wilt Chamberlain. Wilt is at 31,000 points and I'm at 28,000. If I had a hundred points fewer than him, I would come back to pass him up and that would put me as the most dominant player in the world.

"Me and my father were talking the other day. He said, 'How many points you got?' I said, 'Twenty-eight thousand.' He said, 'You dummy. If you hit them free throws like I taught you to, you would have had thirty thousand points.' I said, 'You're right.'"

Basketball has been such a huge part of my life, but I've got plenty of other ventures to keep me busy. I've got fitness centers in

Fort Lauderdale, Boca Raton, Coconut Grove, and Orlando. I have twenty car washes in Houston, Baton Rouge, Atlanta, and Orlando. We also have eighteen self-serve outfits where you put the quarters in and wash the cars yourself.

There's my Dunkman shoe brand, which we created for low-income families who couldn't spend a hundred dollars on a pair of sneakers for their kids. I've got a new watch bearing my name and a line of sunglasses. I've also invested in some Five Guys Burgers franchises. I have a wonderful relationship with the Kraft company, which makes those delicious Oreo cookies you see me eating on television.

I have what you call FRA—Facial Recognition Advantage. Because of who I am and what I've done, I can have a conversation with anybody. I recently had a meeting with the CEO of Dunkin' Donuts about owning a couple of franchises. Now, if I wasn't Shaq, I probably wouldn't have those opportunities. But I am Shaq. Bigger than life, brother. Bigger than life.

So what kind of opportunities are out there for professional athletes? It's up to them, how they market themselves. I can tell you what's out there if you are Dwight Howard or Magic Johnson. There's potential for a guy like Rajon Rondo—if he wants it. His personality is a little different, so he might not like being out front all the time.

Now you take a guy like Big Baby. He wants it yesterday. But he's not high enough on the FRA scale to get what he wants.

When I looked to expand my portfolio, the first thing I did was buy my little self-serve car washes. The second thing I did was invest in Google. The third thing I did was invest in Vitamin Water. The fourth thing was the twenty-four-hour fitness centers. Then I invested in a jet company. So I'm an owner of all these things, but if you don't have FRA it's going to be hard.

I own a piece of Muscle Milk. When the economy went in the tank I invested in a few real estate deals. Most of my investments have been very sound, very successful.

But, like anyone, I had some that got away.

One of my biggest regrets has to do with my dealings with the great Howard Schultz, the CEO of Starbucks. He was looking to bring Starbucks into the inner-city communities. He was talking to Magic Johnson about being his front man, but Lester Knispel, my moneyman, had a tight relationship with Howard, so he said, "Give Shaq a crack at it." Howard said, "I'm pretty far along with Magic," but Lester helped him get started with Starbucks, so Howard agreed to meet me.

We went to his house in Seattle and had dinner. His wife was lovely and his kids were really cute. We had a wonderful time. At one point I excused myself from the table and took his kids upstairs to play video games.

While I was gone Howard said, "Lester, you are right. He's charming, engaging, and intelligent." In other words, we had a deal.

They called me down and Howard had a whole table set up with different coffees and espressos. He was smiling and Lester was smiling, so I knew things were going well. He started serving everyone and he said, "Shaquille, what can I get you?"

I answered, "Nothing, thanks. I don't drink coffee."

Lester looked like I'd punched him in the gut. Howard looked kind of flustered, so I explained, "I'm sorry, I just don't like the taste of it."

The truth was, I'd never seen black people drink coffee. I thought it was a white person's drink.

So we get in the car and Lester says, "You know this deal is off, right?"

It will probably go down as one of my worst business decisions ever, but what can I tell you? I just don't like coffee. Can't fake that one, brother.

There was one other potential business deal I'd like to have back. When I first moved to Isleworth, someone approached me about buying the orange groves across the street. All I could think of was

Kareem and his bad investment in the soybean fields, so I said, "I'm going to pass." Now I drive by there every night in the summer, past the multimillion-dollar houses they built there.

Even though I left LSU after three years of college, I promised my mother I would graduate, and I did. Honestly, furthering your education is important if you want to keep building your brand. I graduated from LSU while I was with the Lakers. I said a few words and told the good people of Baton Rouge that from now on LSU stood for Love Shaq University.

In 2005 I earned my MBA from the University of Phoenix. Now I'm working on my PhD at Barry University in Miami in Leadership and Education with a specialization in Human Resource Development. The topic of my dissertation is "The Duality of Humor and Aggression in Leadership Styles."

What that means is my alter ego, Shaq, is now on life support. In fact, by the time you read this, he'll probably be dead. I'm killing him off. It will be Dr. O'Neal from now on.

That doesn't mean I won't have some silly moments. I'm still going to do jumping jacks naked if I feel like it. I'm still going to have dessert before dinner. I'm still going to paint my toenails.

They've already got some things cooking in Hollywood for me. Adam Sandler called me in June 2011 and said, "I want you to be in some of my movies."

I have a lot of opportunities. It makes me want to go back to LSU and find the marketing professor that told me "Big guys don't sell" and ask him to revise his syllabus. I don't remember the guy's name, but one day I was goofing around in class and he told me, "I hope you make a lot of money playing basketball, because big guys aren't good spokesmen."

Oh, really?

I've stayed fairly low-key about what I own. For instance, out of the fifteen twenty-four-hour fitness places I own, only three have my name on it. None of the Five Guys I own have my name on it. None of the clubs I own in Vegas, either. I own Pure and Chateau and the biggest candy store in the Paris hotel in Vegas, but you won't see Shaquille O'Neal plastered all over the Strip.

That's just business. Now, even though I'm a businessman I'm still going to act like a kid, especially when I'm with my own kids.

I built my house in Isleworth so my children would have everything they need for the summer without having to leave their house. We've got the gym, the movie theater, the video games, the swimming pool with the rock wall to jump off. They've got their own rooms and a big kitchen.

Now they are getting older they think it's cool to leave the house, so I let them go to the YMCA to hang out with their friends. I love that! Here we've got this amazing house and they're asking to go to the Y. Makes me proud of them.

My kids have no idea what it's like to be poor. They can't possibly understand what it was like to walk through the streets of Newark ducking bullets and drug dealers. That's a blessing.

But they will understand how important it is to give back to those who don't have as much as you do. I'll make sure of it.

One of the things I'd like to tackle is how to solve the problem we have in this country with homeless people. There are too many of them in too many cities across the United States.

Every time I see a homeless person it bothers me. Once I was in LA and I gave a guy some money, and then I saw him go into the liquor store and buy booze with the money I'd just given him. I couldn't be angry. It was my fault, really. Another time some homeless guy asked me to help him out because he was hungry, so I give him a wad of bills. Then I'm driving around and he and some other guy are making an exchange, so clearly now I'm paying for this guy's drugs.

At that point I decided, *You know what? I don't want homeless people to go hungry, so next time they want money I'm gonna buy them food instead.*

Now when I see a homeless person and he looks down and out and smells kind of bad, I take him into a restaurant, put him in the corner away from the other customers, and tell the manager, "Here's a hundred bucks. Let the guy eat whatever he wants—but no booze."

The first time I did that the homeless guy was so excited. He says, "I'll take a burger." I tell the waitress, "Bring him three burgers and some 'to-go' bags of food."

Sometimes I take the homeless guys into a grocery store and we fill a carriage. I make sure they have some of those wipes and a lot of bread and some stuff that can keep for a few days, and they walk out of there happy as hell. Of course, I drive away wondering what's going to happen to them tomorrow. There's got to be a better way.

People keep asking me what I want my legacy to be. I don't know. How about this: I was generous, I was dominant, I was unique. That would work.

One thing I'll tell you about the NBA: you are witnessing the death of the true big man. The game has changed. I can remember watching games when guys used to get down there and fight for position. Big men using their bodies, pounding each other. No more. Even power forwards are dead. There won't be another Charles Oakley or Charles Barkley. Being a power forward now is all about stepping out, shooting jumpers, picking and popping. There's no banging in there.

Dwight Howard is by himself. If he doesn't get four rings I'll be disappointed in him. There's no one for him to go up against. When I was playing I had Ewing in his prime, I had Rik Smits, Arvydas Sabonis, Alonzo Mourning, Dikembe Mutombo. I had Vlade Divac, Kevin Duckworth. I caught some of David Robinson. Ostertag. Guys with size. Now, I couldn't name five centers.

Dwight Howard and I don't really have a relationship. I don't like people who lack originality. The whole Superman thing doesn't work for me. The first time I heard Howard being called Superman I was watching the dunk contest with my kids.

He lays down a marvelous dunk and Reggie Miller and Kenny Smith start saying, "Superman is in the building."

So I'm thinking, *Hmm, I believe that name is already taken.* But I'm not getting into it. Hey, my little kids are running around with a little cape on and I'm not going to burst their bubble. The dunk Howard did was fabulous.

I didn't really blame Dwight. I took it as a sign of disrespect from Reggie Miller and Kenny Smith. I'm not sure why they decided to give him my nickname.

There wasn't much to be done about it, though. It's not like Dwight is twenty-seven and I'm twenty-nine. He came along a little too late for me to make a statement about it. If I was the same age I would have killed him like I killed all those other guys.

Look, he's a talented player. Very talented. I envy his jumping ability. He probably jumps four inches higher than I did at his age. His body is something. Genetics. And he works at it—I know that.

It's kind of weird how he's handled his career. He wants to be Superman. They're talking about him going to LA when his contract is up. When I go back to the Orlando area on the off-season they are doing all the same things for him they did for me.

But that's a mistake. He's Dwight Howard. He's not Shaq. Be your own man. Create your own brand.

I do feel for him sometimes. It's all on his shoulders, just like it was all on mine, and when he doesn't get it done he's the one standing there trying to explain, even though he put up huge numbers. Nothing changes in the NBA. It's not always fun being Dwight Howard, but if you call yourself The Man, well, you gotta deal with it. When I complained about people dogging me in Orlando, Sarge would tell me, "Shut up. They're paying you forty million dollars. You gotta take it."

A couple of years ago I had a little fun at Dwight Howard's expense. He's a little thin-skinned, so I tweaked him. In 2008 I didn't make the All-Star team and I was a little disappointed. We played Orlando right before the All-Star break, and they were fronting me and backing me. So I decided to stir up a little controversy. I started saying, "Superman, my ass. When I was a young fella I played all the great centers straight up—by myself. If you want respect, play me straight up." So Dwight takes the bait, and now all through All-Star weekend everyone is talking about Shaq and my comments about Dwight Howard, even though I'm not playing in the game.

Dwight Howard said he could use more help around him. But if he wants to be a leader, he's got to make a guy like Ryan Anderson feel important. Ryan Anderson isn't a great player, but he can shoot. So when you get the ball, kick it to him once in a while for a three. Make him feel like he can play. Tell him, "Great job, man. You are the best shooter I've ever played with."

When I watched Orlando against Atlanta in the 2011 playoffs, Dwight kept trying to do it himself. He wasn't keeping the other guys involved, and they didn't have any rhythm. So finally, in the fourth quarter when he tried to kick it out to them, it was too late.

It was interesting to watch the Miami Heat after they signed LeBron and Bosh. When I saw their "Big Three" I thought of two things: (1) they could be like the 72-10 team that Michael Jordan had in Chicago; and (2) "Get ready, boys. You are going to feel pressure like you've never known in your life." LeBron, I think, was ready for it. The other two guys? I'm not sure. DWade is a clutch player, but he doesn't like all the chatter. He wants good press. Anything negative gets him thinking about the wrong things.

Some guys come into the league without a ton of props, so there's not a whole lot of pressure on them. Then they sign a big deal and all of a sudden they are thrown into the spotlight. Chris Bosh is like that. He's getting all this attention, so he starts believing he's really that good. C'mon now. We know better. He's a player who can put up some numbers, but he's not an elite player. He was in Toronto eight years and they were never a factor, never a playoff team. Don't get with those other two guys and start pounding your chest. I ain't buying it, and I'm not the only one.

People ask me all the time: If you had to choose between DWade and LeBron, which one would you take? Which one would you make the CEO?

It's just a really tough question. LeBron is a better decision maker. DWade will hit more last-second shots. Lots of superstars in their position want and need to take that last shot. LeBron is more of an "opportunity" CEO. He's not afraid to take the last shot, but he won't hesitate to pass it to an open Mike Miller, either.

So where do those two guys measure up against Kobe? Kobe is a scientific dawg. He works out every day, practices every day. Most of the other stars are just dawgs, not scientific dawgs. Me, I'm a freak-of-nature dawg because of my size. LeBron could be a scientific dawg like Kobe, but he's got a lot going on like I did, so that's preventing him from being one.

Kobe will always have the edge because of his range and his killer instinct. LeBron has the killer instinct, but he can't shoot like Kobe can.

I'll be interested to see how DWade and LeBron do going forward. It was all about winning in 2011. There was so much pressure on them, they didn't have time to worry about how many shots each of them were getting, or who was the number one dog, but that could change as they keep going.

When it was me and Kobe, I was the Top Dog. Point-blank. No discussion. But, as soon as Kobe got as good as me, I had to go. It wouldn't have worked any other way. As I mentioned earlier, two alpha dogs means trouble.

I'm not sure if Kobe is going to listen to Mike Brown. LeBron never really did. Here's what we do know: Kobe will definitely be in charge. He's had so much success he's going to do it his way. That's a fact. And, at some point it's going to come up that all that success was with Phil Jackson, so that's a tough situation for Mike Brown to be in.

Mike Brown knows the game, there's no question about that. But there was one thing I didn't think was right when we were in Cleveland. We were a great defensive team and we had excellent schemes, and so Mike Brown developed this reputation as a sharp defensive coach. That's fine, but the mastermind behind our defense was our assistant, Michael Malone. It was him. That dude was clever. His father, Brendan Malone, was a longtime assistant coach for Detroit and the coach of the Toronto Raptors, so he learned it from the womb. He's got the knowledge. He went to New Orleans after Cleveland, and I bet he turns them into a great defensive team, too.

Of all the new players in the league, the one who raises my eyebrow is Blake Griffin. He plays hard, he's a natural, and he came in from the word *jump* doing it. I saw him at the All-Star Game in 2011 and gave him some props. He deserves them. He's the next great one in my mind. He's athletic, he's powerful. One night I was home watching him, and one of his guys threw him an off-balance lob and he still corralled it, brought it around, and threw it down for a reverse dunk. Yeah, that's what I'm talking about.

Kevin Love is putting up Moses Malone numbers and that certainly catches your eye, but his team is in last place. I don't understand that. I don't know Kevin Love, but what's missing?

I love Kevin Durant. I love the way he plays. He's aggressive. He's fearless. He's a quiet leader, seems to have a lot of poise. Russell Westbrook is a good sidekick with a lot of talent and a lot of confidence. He should probably pass the rock a little more to the big fella, though. (Hey, you know I'm going to say that.)

Derrick Rose is a great player, but, to be honest, I don't know how he got the MVP over LeBron in 2011. I've seen a ton of great players, and in order for me to give you MVP props, I've got to see something different. I may be biased, but I've seen Mike, Dominique, Magic, Bird, David Robinson, Ewing. They brought something unique. Derrick Rose? Great player, but lay something on me I'm not expecting.

Yao Ming was something I had never seen before. I was so disappointed when I heard he was forced to retire. His career ended much too soon. He's such a good guy, such a big, strong player. I respect his game. When he first came in I went right at him. I tried a few oopsy-doodles under the rim, and he blocked all three of them. So I had to turn my wrist on him. I had to start dunking, because my usual stuff didn't work. All Yao's strength came from his lower body. He was as strong as anyone I played. I couldn't move him.

I think I've made it pretty clear how I feel about Tim Duncan. One of the best ever. The Spurs have changed their offense to protect Timmy a little. He's always been a team player, so you'll never hear him complain. I ran into Gregg Popovich in the bathroom in the spring of the 2010–11 season, and I asked how Timmy was doing, and Pop said, "His knee is bone on bone." He's probably got only one or two years left.

It's strange to see us all get to that point. They always warn you it's coming, but you never really see it until it's staring you in the face. Father Time is the only guy who ever stopped me on the basketball court.

I was lucky to have people in my life looking out for me and also calling me out when I needed it. There are five controllers of me: my mother, my father, my uncle Mike, my bodyguard, Jerome, and Dale Brown. If I do something and one of those five people call me and chew me out, then I know it's wrong. My momma calls me every once in a while when I say something stupid in the media and she'll say, "That wasn't funny, boy," so I have to say, "Sorry, Momma."

Most of the time Dale Brown and I communicated through e-mail, but if he saw something during a game that ticked him off he wouldn't wait. He'd call me up after he saw Tim Duncan do a couple of pick-and-pops, and he'd say, "Shaquille, why didn't you go right back at Duncan?" I'd tell him, "Coach, that ain't my role anymore. It's a different situation." He'd get all worked up and say, "Well, then, why the hell did they bring you there?" and I'd say, "Now, Coach, it's all about winning, remember?" Then he'd calm down and we'd have a nice conversation, and that would be it— until the next time I didn't get enough touches for his liking.

My uncle Mike is one of my top advisors, a calmer, cooler version of my father. He's not afraid to tell me if I messed up. He and Jerome were both New Jersey detectives, so they've done it all, seen it all.

They are family. I know I can trust them, and when I have people around me I can trust it alleviates the pressure on my brain.

My father is still a force. That's the best way to put it. Even now, when he's battling some health issues, the fire is still there. He's having a harder time with my retirement than I am. I told him that the Lakers said they are going to hang my jersey up there with Kareem and Magic and Jerry West. I thought it would cheer him up.

I can tell you it thrilled me. My time with the Lakers were the best basketball years of my life. Thanks, Dr. Buss, for putting our differences behind us.

I won't be playing basketball anymore, but I've got to keep working out, keep my body from locking up. I have these exercises that Michael Clark gave me that I'll have to do for the rest of my life.

First thing in the morning when I wake up, I put my leg on the wall and do lifts. Then I've got to stand with straight legs and reach back and engage my muscles in my rear end. If I don't get those ass muscles to fire, then they shut off, and the hips shut off and my whole body goes to hell. That's what happened in Miami.

When I met Aaron Nelson and Michael Clark in Phoenix they solved that problem. Pat Riley got mad at me for dissing his training staff, but I wasn't dissing them. They were just old-school trainers who did things their way. The guys in Phoenix were new-school trainers with new ideas, who used technology and other techniques to figure out what makes the body work.

My body told me it was time to retire. My mom wanted me to stop three years ago. Same with Dale Brown. The only one who wants me to keep going is Sarge. He keeps telling me, "You've got unfinished business. Let them fix your leg, come back one more year, then retire."

Sorry, Pops. I can't.

The question I've been asked the most these past few months is how I think I will be remembered. I just hope people can respect what I've accomplished.

Seems to me players are forgotten five minutes after they are gone. I was fortunate once to meet the legendary George Mikan. It was about three years before he died. We were in Minnesota, and he was in a wheelchair. When I came in he had the biggest smile on his face. He had a pen and paper in his hand and he said, "Would you please sign this autograph for me?" I was blown away. I said, "Are you serious?" He said, "Yes, my kids love you."

It is a shame that George Mikan isn't remembered the same way as some of the other more recent stars. He was the first dominant big man. Let's get real: he has a *drill* named after him. When he passed away, I helped pay for his funeral. I was honored to help out.

When I look back on nineteen years in the game, I'm grateful for the opportunities I had. I played with some of the best of all time: Kobe Bryant, LeBron James, Dwyane Wade, Kevin Garnett, Paul Pierce, Ray Allen, Steve Nash, Amare Stoudemire, Grant Hill, Alonzo Mourning, Penny Hardaway. That's a helluva list.

But teammates come and go. It's the other people in your life who stay with you no matter how many points you score. People like Danny Garcia, my massage guy. People like Joe Cavallero, my high school teammate. People like Poonie, my "second mother" at LSU.

I met Poonie when I used to go with my teammate Harold Boudreaux to a little town in Louisiana called Cecilia. Whenever we had time off, all the other guys were going to New Orleans to raise hell, but me and Harold would go to his little hometown. There was a girl named Catice that I had my eye on, so we'd go down there and wind up at Poonie's house. Her real name is Evelyn Huval. She has a son, Dane, and he played high school ball with Harold.

I might have gone down there chasing a girl, but the ones I ended up falling in love with were Poonie and Dane. Poonie was so sweet. She'd wash all my dirty clothes, and we'd hang out or go to the mall, and then on Sundays I'd sleep all day. I'd do my homework, and she'd make me these little chicken sandwiches, then send me back to LSU.

It was a very simple existence, but that's what I like. The Shaq you see on television, at the clubs, that's a different person than Shaquille, who was never happier than when he was at Poonie's house, hanging with Dane and the fine people of Cecilia.

When I started playing pro ball and got some extra money, I bought Poonie a new house. I've been going to visit her in the summers for the past twenty years.

That's why I don't really care if I ever have another conversation with Kobe or DWade. It's not a personal thing. We played together, won championships, we're in the history books, it's all cool. But are you asking me whether I'd rather hang with Kobe and DWade or Poonie? It's not even close, brother.

I won't lie to you. My relationships with women haven't always been the best. It started all the way back at LSU, when I fell in love with a girl who was dogging me behind my back. She was with me, but when I wasn't looking she was with a few other fellas, too. I was so blinded by love I never saw it coming. Looking back, I think she was more in love with the glamour of my life than just caring about me.

Sometimes you see that coming, sometimes you don't. I look at it as simplifying things. I'm a car. Everybody likes me. I look good, I'm a nice car. Now that you've bought me, I've got to get you to like me for just being me. Not because I have power doors or a leather interior.

I realize I get to meet a lot of people because I'm Shaq. A lot of doors open that way. But once you say hello, shake my hand, I've got to make you like me for me. I learned that at an early age.

What I never learned was how to have courting skills. I never had to. Regular guys learn how to date, talk to the parents. Not me. I never really mastered that. Now all of a sudden I get to LSU, and *bam!* I've got everyone's attention with my silliness.

You know as well as I do relationships are about maintaining. For ten years I never had to take anyone out to dinner. It wasn't the big stuff, it was the small stuff, and that's my fault.

I had things to do. I was trying to win, trying to make some money. I admit I wasn't the best partner. I just didn't know how. I'm learning now.

I'm lucky to have met Nicole Alexander. Nikki is fun, she's outgoing, and she has a wild side. We're two wild people who truly respect each other, two wild people who have been hurt too many times, and we're ready to settle down.

At one time my ex-wife Shaunie and I were happy, but I admit it—I was a guy. I was a guy with too many options. Choosing to be with some of those women, well, that's on me. In my mind, I never did it disrespectfully, but obviously I shouldn't have done it all.

With Nikki, I don't. We've been together a year now, and I'm trying hard to keep myself on the straight and narrow. I'd like to think I've learned my lesson, and become a better man. Nikki and I have a contract. I talk about all the bad stuff that's happened to me, and she talks about all the bad stuff that's happened to her, and we've promised each other it won't happen to us.

It's different with Nikki. We do stuff on the fly. One day we rented a tandem bike just for the hell of it. I need that. I used to be all over the place. She was the same way. Now we're two wildflowers that have finally bloomed in the same garden.

I bought an RV and we're going to see the world. Maybe we'll go on a Shaqfari. Maybe we'll do a reality show together.

By the time you read this, they will have unveiled a statue of me at LSU. I don't get excited by very much, but I certainly was honored my school wanted to do that for me. It's nice they want to have me be part of their permanent history.

My connection to LSU is very strong. I've very quietly donated millions of dollars to them over the years. There are so many people there I care about, from secretaries in the athletic department to some of the janitors who still work there. I still stop by the same restaurants, say hello to the same people, and I love that. It feels like my second home. I guarantee if I ran for sheriff in Baton Rouge, I'd win by a landslide.

I hold a golf tournament at LSU every year. Each time I go back, I make sure I go to a football game. When I'm sitting there, it takes me back to that night when they turned out all the lights and shone that spotlight on me. It was my first taste of being a star, and I still get jitters when I think about it.

I'm ready to be done with basketball. I have some regrets, of course. I regret missing all those free throws. I wish I could have found a way to win one more ring.

When I look back on it, I did things my way. Not everyone agreed with the way I went about it. My critics are welcome to say what they like.

But I've got four rings—and a lifetime of memories I wouldn't trade for anything.

INDEX

ABOUT THE AUTHORS

SHAQUILLE O'NEAL was the No. 1 overall pick in the 1992 NBA draft, out of Louisiana State University. During his illustrious nineteen-year professional career, O'Neal won four league championships. Overall, he scored 28,596 points, grabbed 13,099 rebounds, had 3,026 assists, and had 2,732 blocks. He was named to the NBA All-Star team fifteen times. In 1993, he was named Rookie of the Year while playing for the Orlando Magic. In 2000, when playing for the Los Angeles Lakers, he won the NBA MVP, was the All-Star Game MVP, and was also the NBA Finals MVP.

Off the court, O'Neal is known as a true Renaissance man. He has released four rap albums, conducted the Boston Pops, appeared in several films, and starred in two television reality shows. He's also trained as a police officer, is well-versed on new developments in social media, and is in the process of finishing his doctorate. O'Neal retired as an active player from the Boston Celtics in 2011.

JACKIE MACMULLAN is considered the nation's leading basketball writer. A former top player at the University of New Hampshire, MacMullan was a longtime columnist for the *Boston Globe* and *Sports Illustrated*, and she now serves as a constant on-air presence on ESPN. She has written several best-selling books, and in 2010 she received the Curt Gowdy Media Award from the Naismith Memorial Basketball Hall of Fame for her contributions to the game—the first woman ever to have received this honor.